Technology and Offshore Outsourcing Strategies

Technology and Offshore Outsourcing Strategies

Edited by Peter Brudenall

First published 2005 by
PALGRAVE MACMILLAN
Houndmills, Basingstoke, Hampshire RG21 6XS and
175 Fifth Avenue, New York, N. Y. 10010
Companies and representatives throughout the world

PALGRAVE MACMILLAN is the global academic imprint of the Palgrave Macmillan division of St. Martin's Press, LLC and of Palgrave Macmillan Ltd. Macmillan® is a registered trademark in the United States, United Kingdom and other countries. Palgrave is a registered trademark in the European Union and other countries.

ISBN-13: 978–1–4039–4619–5   hardback
ISBN-10: 1–4039–4619–1   hardback

This book is printed on paper suitable for recycling and made from fully managed and sustained forest sources.

A catalogue record for this book is available from the British Library.

Library of Congress Cataloging-in-Publication Data
Technology and offshore outsourcing strategies / edited by Peter Brudenall.
    p. cm.
    Includes bibliographical references and index.
    ISBN 1–4039–4619–1 (cloth)
    1. Information technology–Management. 2. Contracting out.
3. Contracting out–Law and legislation. I. Brudenall, Peter, 1968–

HD30.2.T427 2005
004'.068'4–dc22
                                                    2004065059

10   9   8   7   6   5   4   3   2   1
14   13   12   11   10   09   08   07   06   05

Printed and bound in Great Britain by
Antony Rowe Ltd, Chippenham and Eastbourne

Contents

List of Tables

List of Figures

Foreword
Michael F. Corbett

Outsourcing: Just the end of the beginning

Over the past decade or so, outsourcing has gone from a newly-embraced management idea to one of the most talked about and hotly debated topics of our times.

However, the current visibility and debate surrounding outsourcing should not be confused with a deeper level of understanding and knowledge. While this newfound attention may have turned outsourcing into a household word, it has done far less to substantially advance it as a fully-realised and powerfully-executed management practice. As a result, the current wave of interest in outsourcing actually creates the need for great books on the topic, of which this is one, that much more important.

As a manager, I think the first thing you'll be struck by in reading this book is how far outsourcing is moving beyond the simplistic, popular notion of achieving cost savings by substituting 'cheap labour' to do some of a company's work. In a survey we conduct among global executives who attend our Outsourcing World Summit annually, less than half tell us that cost savings is the primary goal of outsourcing.[1] What they do tell us is that focusing the organisation on the core of its business, creating a more variable cost structure, gaining access to better skills, improving quality, conserving capital, and tapping the brainpower of others for new innovations are just as, if not more, important goals. The simple truth they've uncovered is that in today's hyper-competitive, global economy it's hard to imagine any organisation being fully successful if it sets out to meet the needs of its customers using only its own internal knowledge, capabilities, and resources. Or, as James Brian Quinn of Dartmouth so aptly puts it, 'No one company acting alone can hope to out-innovate every competitor, supplier, and external knowledge source around the world.'[2]

But, for outsourcing to truly achieve its larger goals – that is, to move past the end of its beginning – the leaders tasked with creating and managing these highly complex and interdependent relationships are going to have to push the boundaries of their own management approaches and do so in some very real, very tangible ways.

We may not yet know the end point of their journey, but there are certainly some principles emerging that are likely to form the basis of the future of outsourcing. A few of them are introduced here. These and many others are echoed and expanded upon throughout the chapters that follow.

Principle #1: A repeatable management process for decision making and execution

Outsourcing began, and is still thought of by most, as an intervention – something done to the organisation to fix a problem. But, to reach its full potential, outsourcing has to become part of the organisation's central nervous system – that is, the part how it thinks about itself and acts. This means weaving outsourcing into the most basic planning and operational systems of the company; just as technology, human capital management, budgeting, and quality improvement are today.

A repeatable management process better enables outsourcing opportunities to go from ideas to operations in a disciplined way. Decision makers, from the most strategic to the most tactical, can then be engaged in the right decisions, at the right times, based on the right criteria. Just as importantly, the organisation can develop a common framework for looking at its operations and accurately predicting those areas that will be right for continued in-house investment and those that are becoming ripe for outsourcing. This kind of 'outsourcing mindset', if you will, needs to eventually become part of the very culture of the business.

Principle #2: A focus on results not resources

Successful outsourcing has everything to do with customers defining the results they seek and far less to do with dictating the resources they think are needed to do the job.

In fact, some of the most important work of successful outsourcing takes place during the upfront effort to define the results being sought. It's hard work. It's hard because few organisations really understand the results they need from each of their discrete business processes. These results have seldom been captured in clear, complete, measurable terms that can be objectively communicated to potential partners. Outsourcing elevates the importance of defining results precisely because so much of the execution shifts to outside partners. With outsourcing, defining results increasingly becomes both the art and science of the new management.

This changes the business of companies providing outsourcing services just as much as it changes their customers' businesses. Traditionally, services have been about the work to be done and the promised level for their performance. Service providers too often sell themselves to customers based on their resources, not on their proven ability to deliver results. However, outsourcing can only continue to flourish if providers learn how to go from service level agreements to balanced scorecards that truly reflect and connect the provider's focus and success to their customers' intended results.

Principle #3: A hiring mindset, not a buying mindset

Until now, outsourcing has been dominated by a procurement mindset. In the future, however, companies are only going to be successful if they learn how to approach outsourcing more like the way they recruit, select, and hire a key executive. After all, in many ways, that is exactly what happens with outsourcing. The organisation is bringing in a lead executive, supported by an entire team of people, using their processes, enabled by their technologies, and supported by their supply chains. You're essentially hiring this team, not buying a service.

The difference between the two is profound. Just a couple of examples will make it clear. First, when hiring, your primary goal is seldom to find the cheapest possible employee to do the work. Instead, you seek the right person, with the right background and experiences. The organisation understands that to attract and retain that person takes a fair and market-based compensation package. They certainly don't say, 'Let me find the lowest salaried person willing to take on the job.' This, however, is still what happens in far too many outsourcing engagements.

A second example of the difference is that when a company evaluates an executive candidate it isn't done at arm's length. Instead, a lot of effort goes into spending time with the candidates to find the one with the right 'fit' – to evaluate their personality, work style, experience, and proven performance – in an effort to improve the odds that the person brought in will be successful.

Outsourcing success would take an order-of-magnitude leap forward if organisations moved away from the classic procurement model and toward the executive recruitment model.

Principle #4: An outsourcing relationship is an asset

Outsourcing relationships replace many of an organisation's traditional assets – people, technologies, facilities, methods, and methodologies. Simple logic suggests, then, that an outsourcing relationship is itself an asset. The new relationship is just as important to the organisation's long-term success as were the assets replaced.

Once this is adopted as a basic principle, the need for an ongoing investment in the management of this new asset becomes obvious. As a result, the organisation begins to put its energy and resources into ensuring the ongoing success of the relationship – by strengthening the management systems, investing in new technologies to improve overall information sharing, jointly developing risk management approaches, including the provider's organisation in its ongoing operational and strategic planning, making sure that both organisations' long-term interests are considered, and more. It's an approach to managing outside relationships that few organisations have fully reached.

Principle #5: Embracing the new organisational realities

Once created, the new 'outsourced enterprise' is fundamentally a different kind of organisation.

Its employees' jobs fundamentally change. In the future, only the most specialised of skilled employees – those directly involved in the company's core business – will operate much as they do today. Everyone else will increasingly find themselves needing to work effortlessly across both old-fashioned department boundaries as well as fast-changing company boundaries. Doing this well will take the right skills and the right attitude. Employees will have to be confident that all the organisations they depend upon have a shared commitment to providing superb customer service.

Not only do new skills need to be developed in people, but new management tools and operational approaches need to be developed for the organisation as a whole. Management tools, such as real-time dashboards that use technologies like XTML to integrate data from across the organisation's network of partners, are needed. Project management offices have to be reinvigorated at a new level of sophistication. After all, every single thing the organisation of the future does will require both intra-company and inter-company coordination. Even strategic business planning will no longer be something the company does on its own. After all, many of its best ideas will now be found in the partners' experiences and people.

In reading this book, keep in mind that we are not just using an outsourcing transaction to achieve a specific, near-term business goal. Outsourcing is changing the very nature of organisations: how they plan and operate, how their leaders lead and how their employees work. It's unleashing a powerful wave of innovation that can make what was once impossible quite doable. But, while it's doing that for your company, it's doing the same thing for your current and future competitors.

Before too long, success in business will be indistinguishable from success in outsourcing.

Notes

1. Audience Survey, The 2004 Outsourcing World Summit, February 23–25, 2004, Lake Buena Vista, Florida.
2. James Brian Quinn, 'Outsourcing Innovation: The New Engine of Growth,' Sloan Management Review, Summer 2000, 13–27.

Notes on Contributors

Graham Beck is a partner with PA Consulting. His career has seen him hold executive appointments in the sale, marketing and delivery of outsourcing solutions. This, together with his substantial client consulting and advisory experience, has led to him being recognised as one of the leading exponents of outsourcing. He regularly advises on the design, procurement and implementation of sourcing arrangements for both the public and private sectors. Graham has extensive experience in IT and business change, which positions him as an authority on the acknowledged void between business operations and its supporting technology suppliers.

Dr Dan (B.D.) Bhide, PhD, MBA is Founder & CEO, Outsourcing Consulting & Management, Corp. San Diego. Dr Dan (B.D.) Bhide, a Sourcing and Supply Chain Advisor, helps clients in the US, Canada and Europe reengineer their business processes and IT functions to rationalise their product and process procurement lifecycles in global sourcing networks. He has managed delivery of several outsourced initiatives for business processes, IT functions, and manufacturing from the consulting as well as client sides of the table since 1994. He has held senior engineering and management positions with Fortune 500, multi-national, small as well as start-up companies. Dr Bhide has over 18 years of engineering, development, operations, management, and consulting experience in leading high profile business process reengineering, transformation, integration, and optimisation initiatives. Dr Bhide holds a PhD in Chemical Engineering (Process Reengineering and Optimisation) from Syracuse University and an MBA in Finance from Dowling College, New York.

Peter Brudenall, the editor of this book, is a partner in the leading IT & Telecoms group at the law firm Simmons & Simmons in London. Peter graduated with Honours in Law from the Australian National University in 1994, and obtained a Masters in Law from the University of New South Wales in 1997, specialising in Media, Communications and Information Technology. Peter advises on all areas of Information Technology Law including IT and Business Process Outsourcing, Systems Integration, IT Security, Intellectual Property, Software Development Projects, data protection, Internet and e-commerce issues. He has advised on some of the UK Government's most significant outsourcing deals in recent years and has been widely published in legal journals in the UK and Australia, and is a regular speaker at outsourcing conferences around the world. He can be contacted at peter.brudenall@simmons-simmons.com.

Jonathan Chevallier, BPO Market Development Director for Xansa, has over 15 years of experience in business and IT services including consulting, marketing, project management and outsourcing and specialises in the development of strategy, new services and propositions for Xansa.

Mike Chiasson is currently an Assistant Professor of Management Information Systems in the Haskayne School of Business at the University of Calgary. His research examines traditional IS topics in health care and entrepreneurial, professional, and legal settings. Dr Chiasson's aim is to uncover assumptions about IS theory, practice, and public policy in these settings. His IS research interests include systems development, knowledge management, interpersonal conflict, project management, e-commerce, IT outsourcing, information privacy and security, e-medicine, history of electronic technology in business, and qualitative and critical research methods.

Michael F. Corbett is one of the world's best-known experts on outsourcing and the author of *The Outsourcing Revolution: Why It Makes Sense and How to Do It Right*. He is the Executive Director and Founder of the International Association of Outsourcing Professionals and his company produces.... His company produces 'The Outsourcing World Summit', a global conference series that brings top executives and practitioners together, and publishes the highly-respected Web portal Firmbuilder.com.

Sara Cullen is Managing Director of Sara Cullen and Associates. Sara is a former national partner at Deloitte Touche Tohmatsu. She has a leading profile in Australia and is one of the nation's most experienced practitioners. She has consulted up to 85 private and public sector clients in 107 projects with contract values up of to $1.5 billion per annum. The 50 functions she has helped improve include call centres, claims management, construction, facilities management, finance, food services, HR, logistics, IT, maintenance, property, recreational services, sales, and security. She has designed innovative partnering arrangements, franchise-type agreements, shared risk/reward structures and incentive programmes in addition to traditional arrangements.

She is a widely published, internationally recognised author, having written 19 publications, conducted seven reviews for the government, featured in 40+ articles and presented in 100+ major conferences. Her publications include *Intelligent IT Outsourcing*, *Outsourcing: Exploding the Myths*, *Contract Management Better Practice Guide*, *Best Practices in ITO*, *Lessons Learnt in Outsourcing*, *Management of IT Outsourcing*, *Outsourcing Guidelines* and *Outsourcing: What Auditors Need to Know*, in addition to research with Oxford, Warwick and Melbourne Universities since 1994.

Dr Darren Dalcher is a Chair Professor of Software Project Management at Middlesex University and Visiting Professor of Computer Science at the University of Iceland. He leads the Software Forensics Centre, a specialised unit that focuses on systems failures, software pathology and project failures. He was recently appointed Director of the newly launched National Centre for Project Management in the UK.

Dr Dalcher is active in a number of international committees, steering groups and editorial boards. He is heavily involved in organising international conferences, and has delivered numerous keynote addresses and tutorials. He has written over 100 papers and book chapters on project management and software engineering. He is Editor-in-Chief of *Software Process Improvement and Practice*, and the *International Journal of Project Organisation and Management* and Reviews Editor of *Technology Analysis and Strategic Management*. He has recently edited a special issue of the journal *Technology Analysis and Strategic Management* focusing on systems failures and is currently organising a major international survey to establish and compare the success and failure rates of IT projects.

Paul Davies is the Managing Director of Onshore Offshore Ltd, a consultancy which provides services from initial advice through to implementation and delivery of offshore IT and BPO projects, advice on how to enter western markets for offshore companies, as well as providing international executive search for both interim and permanent positions. After a career in IT, that included marketing, sales and senior management roles in the UK, Europe and the US, he was responsible for business development in Africa, the Middle East and India, latterly the Managing Director of Unisys India. Prior to that he taught and has a PhD on the novels of George Eliot. He can be contacted at paul.davies@onshore-offshore.biz. He is also the author of *What's this India business?*

Ashok C. Devata is a marketing analyst with academic and business experience in India and the US. His areas of interest are marketing and international business management especially in the technology industry. Ashok holds an Engineering degree from Andhra University, India and has an MBA, Beta Gamma Sigma, from the Whittemore School of Business and Economics at the University of New Hampshire.

Al Dexter is Professor Emeritus of the Sauder School of Business, The University of British Columbia. He has published well over a hundred articles in a career spanning four decades. While his main area of work is in Information Technology, his publications have appeared in a wide variety of other fields, e.g. Accounting, Finance, General Management, Law, Management Sciences and Marketing. He has been an expert witness in the Supreme Court of British Columbia on several occasions, providing testimony on issues relating to intellectual property which have included reverse engineering, systems design and development, and software copyright infringement.

David Feeny holds an MA from Oxford University and an MBA from Harvard Business School. Before returning to Oxford in 1984 he was for many years a senior marketing manager with IBM. In addition to teaching and conducting research, he is a consultant to a number of leading industrial and commercial organisations, and was formerly Vice-President of Templeton.

Mike Friend is Research Manager at IDC, a leading global market intelligence and advisory firm in the information technology and telecommunications industries. He has over 10 years experience in the IT sector, working for both suppliers and for research agencies. Prior to joining IDC, Mike held several business development and account management positions for Input, DATAPRO and Intuition Publishing, a leading provider of Web-based training services for the Investment Banking market. Mike is based at IDC's UK office in London, where he is responsible for managing IDC's European Business Process Outsourcing (BPO) programme. He provides analysis of customer spending patterns and insights on competitor trends and service delivery models in the BPO market to executives and service providers in the rapidly evolving Human Resources, Customer Care, Finance and Accounting, Procurement, and Industry-specific BPO markets. In addition to his commentary on the European BPO market, Mike is also responsible for IDC's research and analysis on the European Human Resource Management Services and Recruitment markets, which includes coverage of the HR consulting, payroll, learning, benefits and employee administration outsourcing markets. Mike Friend is a frequently quoted analyst and speaker at BPO and HR services events as well as a contributor to various trade magazines and journals. He has a European Business BA (Hons) degree from Nottingham Trent University.

Jeff Kaplan is the founder and Managing Director of THINKstrategies, a strategic consulting firm that helps IT enterprise decision-makers with their sourcing strategies, solution providers with their marketing strategies, and venture firms with their investment strategies. Prior to forming THINKstrategies, Jeff served as Vice President of Marketing and Business Development at InterOPS Management Solutions – an Internet Operations Management Services Provider. Prior to joining InterOPS, Jeff was Director of Strategic Marketing at Lucent Technologies Worldwide Services, as a result of its acquisition of International Network Services (INS) in October 1999, where he was responsible for strategic positioning and branding programmes, analyst/press relations, and service programme planning and development. Prior to INS, Jeff spent 13 years as a leading industry analyst and market research consultant. Jeff began his career in the market research and consulting industry as the Senior Analyst and Programme Director of Communications Industry Research at IDC. Jeff serves as the Site Guide for ITworld's Utility Computing web portal [www.utilitycomputing.itworld.com] and is the Outsourcing Expert for TechTarget's SearchCIO [www.searchcio.techtarget.com] and SearchSmall-BizIT [www.searchbizit.com] web portals. He is also a member of AMR Research Board of Directors, has served on the Board of Advisors of CeBIT America, ComNet Expositions, and is a member of the IT Services Marketing Association (ITSMA).

Mark Kobayashi-Hillary is an Executive Director of Commonwealth Business Council Technologies Ltd and Trading Process Director of FX Auctions PLC. He is the author of *Outsourcing to India: The Offshore Advantage* and is presently researching a new book – with co-author Mahesh Ramachandran of Ford – on the future of business process outsourcing (BPO). Mark has previously worked at a senior level managing investment bank equity trading IT in the UK, Singapore and India.

Rachna Kumar is Professor of Information Systems at the USI College of Business in Alliant International University. She has a doctorate from New York University in the area of measuring and monitoring software development enterprises. She has published extensively in journals, books, and conferences on the topics of information technology effectiveness, software productivity, offshoring and internet strategies. Her current research projects include designing effective programmes for transferring information systems skills to developing countries, studying coordination strategies for offshore outsourcing, and testing the role of technology in organisational performance. She has consulted for firms in New York, Philadelphia, San Diego, Bay area, Mexico and India.

Dr Mary Lacity is a Professor of Information Systems at the University of Missouri-St. Louis, Research Affiliate at Templeton College, Oxford University, and Doctoral Faculty Advisor at Washington University. Her research interests focus on IT management practices in the areas of sourcing, IT privatisation, relationship management, and project management. She was the recipient of the 2000 World Outsourcing Achievement Award sponsored by PricewaterhouseCoopers and Michael Corbett and Associates. She has written five books: *Netsourcing Business Applications* (co-authors Thomas Kern and Leslie Willcocks); *Global IT Outsourcing: Search for Business Advantage* (co-author Leslie Willcocks); *Strategic Sourcing of Information Systems* (co-author Leslie Willcocks); *Beyond the Information Systems Outsourcing Bandwagon: The Insourcing Response* (co-author Rudy

Hirschheim) and *Information Systems Outsourcing: Myths, Metaphors, and Realities* (co-author Rudy Hirschheim).

Paul Morrison is Managing Consultant and offshore expert at ALS Consulting, specialist adviser on BPO and shared service centre strategy. Paul was formerly head of Offshore Advisory Services at Percept Risk and Strategy. He has written on a range of globalisation issues and also co-organised the Percept-Foreign Policy Centre Roundtable 'Beyond the Headlines: The Real Impact of Offshoring'.

Hilary Robertson is responsible for the strategy and market development of Xansa's Indian offshore propositions. She has worked to develop Xansa's BPO business since its foundation in 2001, having created its overall strategic positioning as well as specific hands-on client BPO solutions.

Theophanis Stratopoulos is an Assistant Professor of Management Information Systems at the University of New Hampshire with several years of teaching experience at undergraduate and graduate level. In 2001, he received the outstanding teaching award by the graduating Executive MBA class. Professor Stratopoulos' current research interests focus on strategic management of information technology investments and its implications on a company's performance and competitive advantage. His research has been published in numerous journals. He has presented his research, and reviewed and discussed research papers in national and international conferences. Professor Stratopoulos has consulted with various companies and non-profit organisations.

Dr Leslie P. Willcocks has an international reputation for his work on e-business, information management, IT evaluation and information systems outsourcing. He is Professor of Information Management and E-business at Warwick Business School. He is also Associate Fellow at Templeton College, Oxford, Visiting Professor in Information Systems at Erasmus University, Rotterdam, Professorial Associate at the University of Melbourne, and Distinguished Visitor at the Australian Graduate School of Management. He holds a doctorate in information systems from the University of Cambridge, and has been for the last 12 years Editor-in-Chief of the *Journal of Information Technology*. He is co-author of 23 books, including *Global IT Outsourcing: In Search of Business Advantage*, *Moving To E-Business*, *Building the E-Business Infrastructure*, *Managing IT as a Strategic Resource*, *Strategic Sourcing of Information Systems*, *Delivering IT and E-Business Value*, and *The Relationship Advantage: Information Technologies, Sourcing and Management*. He has published over 140 papers in journals such as Harvard Business Review, Sloan Management Review, California Management Review, MIS Quarterly, MISQ Executive, Journal of Management Studies, Communications Of The ACM, and Journal of Strategic Information

Systems. Recent co-authored books are: *Second Wave ERP: Implementing for Effectiveness* and *Intelligent IT Outsourcing.*

David Wotherspoon is a partner in the Vancouver office of Fasken Martineau DuMoulin LLP and a member of its Litigation and Dispute Resolution Department. With a background in corporate and commercial litigation, most of David's practice now relates to resolving technology and intellectual property disputes.

Introduction
Peter Brudenall

According to Meta Group, almost all global companies will have outsourced some of their information technology requirements by 2006. While this appears to be an amazing statistic, it is perhaps not surprising that outsourcing – both of IT and business processes – is becoming so prevalent given the apparent benefits. From the customer's perspective, a service provider agrees to take over part of their business and perform those services to the same or a higher standard for a lower cost. As more companies start doing this, it is simply not cost effective for a business to maintain specialist, non-core services in-house when the market can deliver such services to a level and for a price that cannot be matched internally.

However it is fair to say that customer expectations have often not been realised, and the rate of outsourcing 'failure' – where an outsourcing deal is either terminated or re-negotiated – has been consistently high. While this is due to reasons such as bad planning, bad advice, lack of a coherent strategy or simply choosing the wrong partner, there is no doubt that customers today (particularly those who have already had some experience of outsourcing) expect far more from their service providers.

Essentially, customers expect their outsourcing partners to do more than simply offer a service that meets the pre-contract standard for a slightly reduced cost. Customers are now looking to tap into the additional benefits they hear so much about: the increased agility to respond to short-term changes in the market, greater adaptability and flexibility to meet challenges from technology, variable pricing structures and alignment between the services being provided and the overall business objectives. There is often a disconnect between the service provider's sales pitch and the team providing and managing the services. The issue remains: how can customers start to fully realise the value of outsourcing, understand how outsourcing can be used to transform their business, and avoid costly renegotiations or deal failures?

This book is intended to answer these questions.

As a response to the more strategic and sophisticated outsourcing deals that customers are now seeking to develop, and the need for customers to see their way through the hype associated with 'offshore outsourcing', 'business process outsourcing', 'utility computing' and so on, there was in my view a need to collect the views of some of outsourcing's thought-leaders – the individuals who are dealing with outsourcing every day and understand the dynamics of what works, and what doesn't, when embarking on an outsourcing partnership. The authors involved in this book collectively represent decades of experience, and many hundreds of outsourcing deals, and come from academia, suppliers, advisors and analysts. Offering practical and constructive advice and insights, anyone considering embarking on an outsourcing relationship, or currently in the middle of one, will be able to apply the best practice principles set out in the book and, at the same time, minimise the chances of failure.

The book focuses on seven key outsourcing themes:

- what is the framework for successful outsourcing?
- reviewing current thinking and strategies with respect to offshore outsourcing;
- examining the dynamics of business process outsourcing;
- understanding how outsourcing – particularly business process outsourcing – can 'transform' a business;
- how to successfully manage the relationship with the supplier;
- understanding and applying the legal aspects of the outsourcing relationship; and
- examining what outsourcing might look like in the future.

However, if there is one overarching theme that governs this book it is that anyone considering an outsourcing relationship must develop and then apply a clearly-thought out strategy. It is simply not enough to enter into an outsourcing deal because 'everyone else is doing it'. If you do that, without careful planning, good advice, and structured management, there is no doubt you will find yourself in a costly mess that will be difficult to unravel.

A framework for successful outsourcing

Part I, and the chapter from Professor Dalcher, is very much an overview of many of the ideas touched on in this book. In explaining the benefits, opportunities and risks in outsourcing, Dalcher also uses a case study of a disastrous IT failure to highlight some of the risks in outsourcing which is followed by a set of recommendations and lessons for improved practice.

Strategies for offshore outsourcing

Part II is devoted to offshore outsourcing. Clearly, the difference between outsourcing today and outsourcing of 10 to 20 years ago is the ability of companies to take advantage of offshore services. By using the vast pools of highly skilled, educated labour in Asia, Africa, Eastern Europe and parts of South America, companies are dramatically reducing their costs for outsourcing by up to 60 per cent. In this context, Dan Bhide's chapter highlights the important decision analysis process for evaluating offshore options, and the best practices for risk mitigation and value maximisation. However, in the current political climate, offshore outsourcing has a distinct political dimension with fears about job losses dominating discussions on the topic. This may lead to regulating authorities seeking to adjust laws to either make offshore outsourcing more difficult, or subject to a greater level of scrutiny. Paul Morrison's chapter aims to provide the political dimension to any best practice of global sourcing strategy. Finally, this section is completed with an examination by Paul Davies of the hidden benefits and costs associated with offshore outsourcing. If not thought through carefully, the benefits of offshoring will be reduced significantly once these costs are taken into account – often too late.

Issues in business process outsourcing

Part III looks at the huge increase in business process outsourcing. The chapter from Devata, Kumar and Stratopoulos reviews the factors driving and enabling the business process outsourcing market, the companies providing outsourcing services and what constitutes best practice when considering outsourcing business processes.

Secondly, the chapter from Chevallier and Robertson of leading outsourcing service provider Xansa highlights some major, but often hidden, hazards and issues to be addressed when developing a strategy for an offshore business process outsourcing.

Achieving business transformation through outsourcing

Part IV of the book examines how outsourcing can be used to transform a business. The chapter from Willcocks, Lacity and Feeny describes, by way of a case study involving BAE Systems and business process outsourcing supplier Xchanging, an innovative and strategic approach to outsourcing involving risk-reward contracting and the enterprise partnership model. Secondly, the chapter from Mike Friend of analysts IDC looks at how service providers are engaging with their customers to achieve sustainable transformation through BPO and how they are measuring these cost and service delivery gains.

Managing the relationship

Part V deals directly with the one of the key reasons for outsourcing failure – the inability of both suppliers and customers to successfully *manage* the outsourcing relationship. This is consistently recognised as being an area of outsourcing practice that needs improvement if success rates are to increase. Sara Cullen's chapter addresses the nature of outsourcing relationships and highlights select practices that have been applied to design successful relationships. Graeme Beck from PA Consulting describes in his chapter the need for customers, as well as suppliers, to play a key role in the relationship and the need for customers, in particular, to adopt and foster the appropriate mentality when constructing the outsourcing contract.

The legal foundations

Part VI deals with another outsourcing fundamental that is often badly handled – the legal and contractual aspects of outsourcing. Too often, lawyers unfamiliar with the complexities of an outsourcing transaction assume that it is just another supplier agreement. A badly drafted or negotiated contract will not only significantly increase the likelihood of a contract renegotiation within a short time of the contract commencing, but may also impact on the ability of the parties to successfully manage the contract and resolve issues as they arise. This can lead to costs increasing, and ultimately can cause deal failure. My chapter is aimed at providing a plain-English account of the major considerations for any outsourcing contract. It is well understood that an outsourcing contract is one of the more complex commercial agreements that an in-house lawyer or manager will come across. It is also likely to be one of the more time-consuming as the process from start to finish can take several months. My hope is that my chapter will make this process somewhat easier, and enable those tasked with managing the outsourcing process to have a meaningful discussion with lawyers, advisors and, most importantly, the supplier. To complement this, the chapter from Chiasson, Dexter and Wotherspoon takes the outsourcing of systems development and examines the processes that inhibit or promote vendor-client agreement on the changes that inevitably occur during the relationship. Alternative approaches to resolving outsourcing conflict are also discussed.

The future

The Final Section of the book takes a look at the future of outsourcing. There seems little doubt that what is now called 'utility computing' or 'on-demand computing', will be the basis for outsourcing services in the near future, and for those unfamiliar with the topic, or considering offers from one of the increasing number of utility computing service providers, should read Kaplan's chapter carefully. Secondly, the future of offshore outsourcing as a management tool is examined by Mark Kobayashi-Hillary. In particular, Mark focuses on the future drivers and inhibitors of offshoring, and makes some educated guesses as to what the key issues will be over the next few years.

This book has been more than 18 months in the making, and my thanks and appreciation go to the publisher, Palgrave, for having invited me to produce the book, to the authors for their diligent hard work in developing their ideas, to my colleagues David Barrett, Michael Sinclair and Claire Bodiam for their assistance, and finally I would like to thank my wife, Kylie and my two children Jack and Oscar for their support and patience.

Peter Brudenall, Editor

Part I

A Framework for Successful Outsourcing

1

From Fixed Contracts to Dynamic Partnerships: Successful Outsourcing in a Changing World

Darren Dalcher

1 Introduction

Following major outsourcing deals that saw many large organisations including AXA, BAA, the Bank of Ireland, Procter and Gamble, Barclays, the Inland Revenue and the BBC outsource their IT services, the trade magazine *Computing* named 2003 the *year of the outsourcer*. The trend towards increased outsourcing has continued throughout 2004 and into 2005. According to Meta Group more than 40 per cent of all new application development work is now outsourced. Indeed, over one-third of all European outsourcing deals take place in the UK making it one of the most developed outsourcing markets in the world.

However, according to the Gartner Group, European businesses wasted over £4 billion on poorly managed outsourcing contracts resulting in customer satisfaction with outsourcing falling from 81 per cent in 2001 to 50 per cent last year. The Meta Group released the results of a new survey in June 2004, showing that 80 per cent of businesses found that their outsourcing arrangements did not match their expectations. Gartner also estimate that as many as 80 per cent of outsourcing deals are unsuccessful with problems ranging from strained relationships to catastrophic failures and ultimately cancellations of service. Outsourcing advisory firm Morgan Chambers recently reported that only 22 per cent of the 157 UK organisations questioned in their recent survey felt that their suppliers had 'totally delivered' to their expectations. Moreover, the June 2004 survey from Meta Group reveals that 60 per cent of outsourced organisations encountered business-critical problems. A clearer understanding of the impact and implications of outsourcing is thus needed.

Outsourcing occurs when an organisation contracts external resources and professional services in order to develop or operate their information systems thereby meeting specific business needs. It typically involves hiring an external organisation that specialises in providing such competency, product or services. Outsourcing is generally viewed as a cost-effective way of controlling the costs of the information system function. Providers benefit from economies of scale related to mastering a professional service and investing in supporting infrastructure that enables them to offer a first class level of expertise and reputation in that domain. Outsourcing thus relates to the provision of services based on a mature technology rather than to the technology itself.

Fitzgerald and Willcocks (1994) defined outsourcing as 'the commissioning of a third party (or a number of third parties) to manage a client organisation's IT assets, people and/or activities to required results'. The focus is on the management of the IT activity by the outsourcer according to a **defined specification** or **service level** which needs to be agreed in advance.

The decision of whether to outsource or to perform the same functions internally can be crucial to the ultimate success and positioning of the organisation. While at surface level the decision resembles the classical make-or-buy choice, the implications relate to the profitability and sustainability of the core business of the organisation.

The main reasons for outsourcing relate to the buying-in of expertise, the greater efficiency that is obtained, the reduction in cost and the resulting focus on the core business of the organisation. The outsourcing decision is, therefore, part of a complex process of decision making that involves not one but rather a chain of linked decisions that begin with the identification of the core functions and purpose of the organisation, and an assessment of the level of service that is currently or that can potentially work towards achieving that purpose. The rule of thumb is not to outsource any operations that involve core competencies or any aspects that are critical to the core business strategy or to crucial business performance aspects. Following the identification of core functions it becomes possible to address some of the fundamental questions related to outsourcing namely:

- Should the organisation outsource some of its activities or services?
- If so, which ones?
- Which vendor to select?
- What type of contractual agreement is necessary to secure those services?
- How to secure and manage a stable and productive working relationship with the chosen vendor?

Outsourcing decisions impact regular operations and special projects alike. They address the core business, image and perception of the organisation and directly influence the product or service associated with the name. They are thus crucial to the success and the ultimate responsiveness of the organisation.

Outsourcing decisions are made by management not on a one-off basis but as a continuous stream of choices which are integral to maximising the value of IT, the support it provides to the core business, and the resulting overall position and stability of the organisation in the marketplace. An example of what could go wrong when the decisions are not made properly has recently been unfolding in the UK legal system. The case revolves around an £11 million dispute between the Co-operative Group, the largest UK retail company, and ICL, the service provider now part of Fujitsu Systems. In January 2004, following two years of legal battles, three appeal court judges threw out the January 2003 ruling by the Technology and Construction Court that favoured the vendor. The clients initiated the project without finalising the terms of the contract or considering the nature of the relationship with the vendor. The clients terminated the project weeks before the vendors were finally due to deliver the working version of the system. The disagreement revolved around the suppliers' refusal to agree on penalty clauses for the late delivery. The case highlights the importance of the initial decisions about the contract, the mechanisms for monitoring it, and the (in)ability of both sides to manage the communication, relationship and expectations.

The rest of this chapter focuses on exploring the questions posed above and recommending a framework for answering them. The chapter begins by addressing the potential for benefits, opportunities and risks in outsourcing. It describes a detailed case of a spectacular outsourcing failure where everything that could have gone wrong did. The case highlights the issues related to the balance between benefits and risks in outsourcing. The case is followed by a set of recommendations and lessons for improved practice. Outsourcing raises many special issues that need to be managed and these are addressed as a set of issues. The chapter ultimately proposes a framework for managing the outsourcing process which is explored in detail. The framework addresses the key issues and provides step-by-step guidance in leading and directing outsourcing efforts.

2 The outsourcing rationale

The concept of outsourcing is hardly new. The notion of sub-contracting particular services has been utilised in many industries to maximise efficiency and buy-in specialised resources and services. However, the link to the identification of core competencies and functions is much more recent. Subsequently, many organisations are focusing on identifying core activities and outsourcing any aspects that are not essential or related to that provision. The decision about outsourcing is thus becoming more tactical enabling a greater focus on risks, opportunities and potential benefits.

The first question posed in Section 1 was 'should the organisation outsource some of its activities or services?' Making a decision regarding whether 'to outsource or not to outsource' depends on many factors and is specific to an organisation at a certain point in time. Outsourcing offers a range of benefits that may apply to an organisation. It also opens up the potential for exploring new arrangements and benefiting from the resulting adjustments and realignments within the organisation. However, reliance on outsourcing also exposes an organisation to a range of new risks that need to be understood and considered. The remainder of this section explores the rationale for outsourcing in terms of benefits, opportunities and risks.

2.1 Outsourcing benefits

Outsourcing can offer numerous potential benefits focused on the economic, strategic and expertise-related nature of the activity. Table 1.1 lists some of the expected benefits.

The focus on core business is essential to understanding outsourcing. Organisations seek to maximise their internal efficiency by focusing on the skills and services that are essential to the delivery of their essential core activities. In the same way that an organisation will focus on streamlining their key activities, vendors who specialise in the delivery of outsourcing solutions will invest in improving their practice and benefit from the resulting economies of scale. Vendors are also likely to have increased security and more superior quality and operations standards.

Outsourcing organisations can thus benefit from hiring of specialists with proven expertise and skills, and an investment in best practice and state-of the-art technology. Many organisations will not be able to achieve best practice in every aspect of work but will be able to buy into the infrastructure required to support such practice. Moreover, as many organisations are unlikely to progress to the higher levels of the Capability Maturity Model (CMM, CMMi), the Project Management Maturity Model (PMMM) or to achieve certain quality standards, outsourcing provides an

Table 1.1 Benefits from Outsourcing

Access to proven expertise, skills, capability and competence
Access to state-of-the-art technology and best practice
Added flexibility and reliability
Transfer of risk to specialists
Improved quality of products and services
Focus on core business areas
Cost savings
Greater efficiency
Improved contribution of IT to business performance
Freeing up of internal talent
Creation of new sources of revenue and profit
Improved financial planning

easy way to secure and prove such attainment from a specialist who is already qualified at that level. The higher degree of specialism combines with the transfer of risk to lead to better quality products and services which are likely to be delivered in shorter development cycles. Furthermore, the investment in best practice should enable vendors to pass back savings from the adoption of the infrastructure and the maximisation of activities to all their clients.

Outsourcing provides access to rare skills that may not be available to individual organisations and to specialised technology (including advanced hardware and software). It directly helps in enabling access to innovative business practice and to state-of-the-art technology with minimal access costs (compared to the initial investment that would have been required to set it up). The result is an improved contribution of advanced information technology to business performance. It also frees up scarce and costly internal talent while creating new sources of revenue and profit.

Outsourcing carries the potential to improve financial planning in an organisation when contracts are clearly specified. Furthermore it may free the organisation from paying licence and maintenance fees for tools and resources as well as reduce some of the fixed costs and salary bills.

2.2 Outsourcing opportunities

Outsourcing can also be responsible for introducing a new set of opportunities. Outsourcing implies gaining access to rare skills, experience and specialised technology that may not be available to the organisation. It thus offers flexibility in covering for unavailable expertise and adding additional skilled staff especially during key periods.

With little reason to reinvent tools, approaches or solutions that are already utilised elsewhere, outsourcing leads to clear cost savings. More crucially, it enables the organisation to focus more closely on core business areas and to utilise all creative energy to improve the core provision. Selecting accomplished providers not only reduces the risk but also enhances the quality of products and services aligned to non-core activity (and indirectly leading to a reduction in the re-work needed in such activities).

Organisations are thus likely to release areas not viewed as core competencies. The improved flexibility in managing IT resources and the enhanced (and better focused) capacity for more productive allocation of scarce internal resources make outsourcing attractive to managers. Ideal conditions for outsourcing occur:

- when current services are ineffective, limited or technically inferior;
- when troublesome functions need to be eliminated;
- when the organisation is unable to keep pace with changing technology; and
- when the vendor is an acknowledged specialist in the general domain or the specific application.

Crucially, outsourcing underpins the organisational effort to improve by offering new capacity for growth and change. For example, outsourcing allows the organisation to pursue more projects with the same number of people (and resources). Moreover, it enables shorter project durations and faster application development leading to a general increase in the organisational capacity for change and general responsiveness. It may also provide a readily available source of consultancy and advice as part of standard support.

2.3 Outsourcing risks

Outsourcing provides an opportunity for a reduction of risk through the transfer of certain identified services to acknowledged experts. However, it also has the potential to expose the organisation to many alternative sources of risk. Table 1.2 depicts many common sources of risk associated with outsourcing.

The dominant feature gleaned from the table is the lack of control. Once the decision to outsource has been made, it is difficult if not impossible to reverse and is likely to lead to loss of control over various aspects of the organisation.

First of all, the contract binds the organisation to a supplier. Whilst the supplier is carefully selected on the basis of ability, skill and reputation, the organisation becomes bound to the supplier and to their business requirements. Changes to their financial position, redundancies and even loss of key personnel can have an adverse effect on the client's business.

Second, the technical dependence continues beyond the business aspects as outsourcing often involves ceding control of the information function. Changes to technology used by the supplier or to strategic decisions about technology can have adverse impacts on clients. As key technical aspects may now be under the control of external agencies, they may be in a position to

Table 1.2 Risks from Outsourcing

Dependency on supplier
Loss of control over the IS function
Loss of control over technology
Loss of control over IS direction
Loss of technical skills
Reduction in commitment
Vulnerability of information and intellectual property
Strategic vulnerability
Potential for escalation of contract (and costs)
Irreversibility of decision
Vendor lock-in
Legal, advisory and additional fees are often ignored
Long-term outsourcing contracts may complicate future mergers and acquisitions

increase costs and/or change basic systems forcing similar changes in the clients. (Paradoxically, the contract may also bind the organisation to older technology as specified in the original contract which may no longer satisfy their operational or business needs.)

Third, outsourcing may impoverish a company in terms of the technical expertise-base required for future operation and strategic decision making. Reliance on external skills may encourage diminishing internal attention and has the potential to lead to diminishing expertise, practice and capability in such areas.

Fourth, reliance on external suppliers exposes trade secrets, intellectual property, client details and strategic information. Moreover, as vendors are specialist in certain areas, they may be working for a number of competitors thus opening new potential strategic vulnerabilities.

Fifth, external providers may be viewed as having less loyalty and internal commitment to the organisation and to their key objectives. Furthermore, their understanding and commitment to some organisational issues such as uninterrupted service may conflict with those of the clients.

Generally, if things do not work out, the cost of recovering and restoring to the original position can be extremely prohibitive. The increasing complexity of many systems and the expectation of continuous operations are leading to the forming of consortiums of providers in order to deal with the inherently complex sets of expectations and needs.

Recognition of the dominant role of change and the corresponding emphasis on changing requirements also places a greater onus on the vendors to continue to assess needs, expectations and levels of satisfaction. However, the organisation is likely to have less say over projects and less control over the development direction adopted. Projects will not lead to additional growth in knowledge, expertise or skills available in-house and therefore the organisation may miss out on some learning opportunities and potential lessons which may have helped to shape its future. In other words, outsourcing functions may lead to a reduction in the potential for knowledge management.

Generally outsourcing seems to offer a mixed bag. The ultimate decision regarding outsourcing will be based on the balance between perceived costs, risks, benefits and opportunities. Many such decisions are based on a limited focus on the perceived benefits. The following section explores one such case from the perspective of a decision maker and shows the potential and the dangers inherent in outsourcing. The ensuing discussion will look into where the process of making the decision went wrong.

3 Mission impossible?

Imagine yourself sitting in the driving seat in front of the controls. Your new task, should you wish to accept it, is to lead/sponsor the implementation of a computerised despatch system for the Metropolitan Ambulance Service (MAS) in Melbourne, Australia. MAS is going for a state-of-the-art emergency despatch and communication system for one of the most complex ambulance systems in the world.

By way of background, the first plans for an ambulance service in Melbourne, the capital of the South East Australian state of Victoria, were made in 1883. By 1887 sufficient funds had been accrued to purchase six Ashford litters which were placed at the police station. In 1889, they were replaced by the first horse-drawn ambulance. This was the humble beginning of the Metropolitan Ambulance Service (MAS).

The current day MAS is responsible for providing emergency medical transport, pre-hospital care and non-emergency stretcher and clinic car transport services for around 3.5 million people throughout the Melbourne metropolitan and Mornington Peninsula regions, an area of almost 10,000 square kilometres. The service is the largest ambulance service within the State, with 62 emergency response locations, 763 staff (excluding non-emergency contractors), 56 emergency ambulance teams and 218 vehicles. It is also responsible for providing air ambulance services throughout the State. The service is an integral component of the local health care system and consequently a significant infrastructure is in place to enable a rapid emergency response and delivery of pre-hospital care to the community. Note that many but by no means all residents subscribe to the annual Ambulance Membership Scheme which entitles them to utilise the full services offered by MAS for free. In principle, non-subscribers are expected to pay for such services.

3.1 Are you ready to start?

In common with most ambulance services around the globe, emergency operations represent the primary function of MAS. In an average day, MAS ambulances attend to more than 600 medical emergencies and are also involved in transporting around 400 patients. Not surprisingly, there is a public expectation that the service will provide a timely, appropriate and professional response to all calls for emergency assistance. Emergency ambulances are despatched according to the information received from callers. Each call is assessed and given a priority code. Code 1 is a time critical emergency so that the despatched ambulance proceeds with lights and sirens. Code 2 is an acute non-critical case and the ambulance proceeds without lights and sirens. Code 3 is a non-acute or routine case.

There are one or two other things you need to know. MAS had undergone a turbulent period since the late 1980s with sustained criticism over poor ambulance response times highlighted by a number of events receiving extensive press coverage. Increased competition from the private sector further eroded trust in MAS. The service's financial performance had been poor with deficits recorded every year throughout most of the 1990s.

Furthermore, the intense public scrutiny required the local government to consistently increase its annual contributions but this did not lead to any direct improvements. Crucially for you, industrial relations between MAS management and the ambulance unions have always been poor. The last 15 years had been punctuated by strikes, mistrust and tension. The press coverage of ambulance inadequacies in a number of high profile cases and the willingness of individual crew members and union officials to provide the press with commentary and quotes further exacerbated an already strained relationship.

Your project journey is about to begin. The year is 1992 and MAS is utilising a variety of systems which are not integrated. There is also political change in the air as the election has just been won by the more aggressive Conservative Government concerned with eliminating the 'wasteful financial policies' of their predecessors.

A review of the service has just recommended significant improvement in the name of cost savings as a way of obtaining a reduction in the level of government contributions to the service. One of the suggestions was for improved technological systems to strengthen the despatch of ambulances which is where you come in. The new government was also quick to replace the MAS committee of management with a CEO with no experience in emergency services whose brief was to cut costs and break the union. (This is despite a number of coronial inquiries resulting from the high profile cases that recommended increased staffing). The key ingredients are now all in place for the countdown.

3.2 Oh, one more thing

Following a prolonged process, the contract was awarded by the government to the eventual winners. A consultant acting for the government during the evaluation was also employed by the winners. Following the submission of bids, the evaluation criteria were altered at the behest of senior ambulance service personnel. In the background, the media continues to offer significant coverage of delays in ambulance attendance and potentially related deaths.

The planned components of the state-of-the-art emergency despatch and communication system were:

- a despatch system for the automatic despatch of the nearest or the most appropriate vehicle;
- a satellite-based vehicle location system supported by a computerised mapping system;
- mobile data terminals to replace voice-radio communication.

Moreover, the system appears to be the first recorded attempt to computerise and completely privatise an emergency despatch system.

Implementation was scheduled to proceed in a Big Bang manner with a switchover to the full system scheduled for 24 August 1995. The fixed deadline was imposed by the clients without negotiation and was to become a major constraint on the project. What needs to be borne in mind is that MAS represents one of the most complex ambulance systems in the world, covering 3.5 million people over 10,000 square kilometres.

3.3   Ready, steady, go

Having chosen to accept your mission, you are in control of the Ambulance Service project. The project is progressing to the impossible deadline that was imposed. It is now mid-1995. Following media scrutiny of the contract-awarding story, an independent consultant is employed to assess the state of the system. His report identifies 50 faults labelled 'critical' or 'high priority' including:

- the volume of information handled by the automatic vehicle location system was causing it to bog down and report incorrect locations;
- allocation of a vehicle to a job could take up to two minutes during which the console was 'locked up';
- responses taking longer than sixteen minutes were required to generate exception reports but the system's measurements of its own response times were not accurate;
- the report generator, responsible for producing exception reports, contained critical faults;
- while no statistical tests had been applied, it was observed that even on simple tasks the automatic route recommendation facility often recommended routes heading in the **opposite** direction from an accident scene.

The MAS switch over took place as originally scheduled with many of the faults identified in the report still outstanding! Within a few days of the switch over MAS officers began complaining about the performance of the system and a heated row developed between MAS and the contractors. MAS internal documents recorded the fact that the system often 'teetered on the edge of disaster'. The media was quick to uncover evidence of frequent system shutdowns.

MAS claimed that the contractors had promised to deliver things that they never had a chance of delivering. Later investigation revealed that politics played a major part in the complex relationship between the state government (which had cut costs by using the contractors), the systems suppliers (who had agreed to an unrealistic time frame in which to introduce the system and which were about to provide similar systems for the fire and police services as part of a deal), the ambulance union (which would have liked its members to do the despatching rather than non-paramedic civilians), and MAS management (caught between the other three). Within two weeks of the switch over, MAS was complaining to the Health Minister. Government advisers suggested that ministers should claim that performance was improving.

3.4 In operation

System logs were now showing that ambulances couldn't be picked up by the system and that the system was locking up. Public pressure led the Victorian Auditor-General to approve an extensive performance audit of MAS. Meanwhile, the developers were trying to boost the performance figures and improve the system.

In February 1996, the head of MAS told a ministerial steering committee that he 'had evidence that the services provided to MAS ... are progressively getting worse' and 'the service was sub-standard and worse than what was previously provided at the old Communications Centre.'

An incident in August 1996 attracted particular attention. An emergency call to an address in South Street reported that a man was unconscious and thought to be suffering from a drug overdose. The despatch system failed to recognise the street name and 'corrected' the address from South Street to Sadie Street. The operator had failed to notice the error so the wrong address was passed to the ambulance crew. The ambulance eventually reached the right address but too late, and the patient died. It is significant that the system was known to be still confused between the two streets 10 months later.

MAS ambulance performance standards for serious cases stipulate that an ambulance should be despatched within 150 seconds in 80 per cent of cases. The actual figure for November 1996 was 78.7 per cent. The introduction of a new question-and-answer routine (AMPDS) for call takers in December 1996 resulted in this figure plummeting to 34.2 per cent. Early the following year the figure crept up to 36.7 per cent. (A commission of inquiry later discovered that calls were often re-started to boost performance time statistics.)

In January 1997, the head of MAS complained to the Department of Justice that MAS was asked to lower their required performance standards rather than expect the developers to improve the performance of the computerised system. He added that MAS 'was of the view that X-developers do not really understand or have not come to grips with operating in an emergency services organisation environment and are unlikely to do so unless there is a fundamental shift in approach.' A month later, he complained that it was 'no longer acceptable for MAS to rely on X-developers to eventually "get it right".' This would, once again, seem to be a good time for pressing the abort button.

Instead, when the use of imported 'trouble-shooters' failed to alleviate the problem, MAS and X-developers embarked on a protracted series of

negotiations culminating in agreement to lower the benchmark performance standards in return for reduced payment. Note that the recognition
of the trade-off between performance and cost followed the physical
implementation of the system.

3.5   Audit results are published

The Auditor-General's special emergency report on MAS contractual and
outsourcing practices was published in April 1997; that was several months
earlier than originally scheduled because of the 'discovery of extremely
serious matters identified during the course of a performance audit.' It enu-
merated serious deficiencies and highly dubious practices including huge
cost blow-outs, entangled relationships between managers in the service
and private companies, a biased tender, and inadequate supervision of contractual decisions by MAS management (who were said to have been
'derelict' in their responsibility).

Major flaws identified included:

- reliance on an unknown consultant without a formal contract and with
  no attempt to establish past experience or association;
- acceptance of the needs analysis submitted by the consultants in charge
  of the tendering process despite serious reservations about the quality of
  the analysis;
- serious functional and technical flaws, and shortfalls in the original tender
  document which was obviously written around the X-developers' system;
- the system specification document, which was hurriedly developed, was
  known to contain major shortcomings yet was fully utilised by the service;
- the absence of documentary evidence to substantiate how the
  34 registrations of interest were short-listed to four potential suppliers;
- the inability of the service to produce the evaluation criteria used in
  selecting X-developers and the informal approach used to eliminate the
  remaining bidders;
- failure to adequately satisfy a key condition set by the government for
  the new call and despatch system to be able to integrate into the state-
  wide emergency system, irrespective of the eventual supplier;
- failure to achieve the projected savings of $20 million;
- retrospective approvals freely granted by management for payment;
- easy acceptance by MAS management that all was well.

The audit also uncovered a technical memorandum that had been sent to
the MAS CEO by the service's manager of information systems prior to the
awarding of the contract, expressing the depth of his concerns and reservations about the proposed system and the selected contractors. It called for:

- withdrawal of the specification as it did not cover MAS requirements
  and a delay of four weeks to enable a team of specialist staff with

expertise in communications, information systems, technical services, ambulance procedures, and despatch systems to review and redraft it;
* review and redrafting of the schedule and especially of project milestones and phases to obtain a realistic schedule with 'practical implementable stages';
* review of the short-listed suppliers;
* appointment of a project manager, ideally with skills in computer-aided despatch and related technical areas.

Minutes from subsequent meetings reveal that these points were discussed and were shared by all key personnel with the exception of the chairman. These concerns were brushed aside and the tender process was allowed to continue unchanged.

3.6   Back to the present

Following the publication of the Auditor-General's report, the systems support manager resigned.

In May 1998, a police report compiled by the Major Fraud Squad was submitted to the Office of Public Prosecutions. Later that year, an independent auditor was appointed to investigate claims that the poor response times were boosted by phantom emergency calls to show response improvement in the achievement of performance targets.

During the initial stages, MAS computerisation was alleged to have resulted in a less efficient ambulance service plagued with technical hitches, loss of experienced staff and low morale. The performance of the emergency despatch system has caused much public concern as faults in the system have been implicated in a series of misadventures in which people have died while waiting for delayed or misdirected ambulances. Rod Morris, the Victorian secretary of the Ambulance Employees Association (AEA) is on record saying 'The worst aspect of the X-developers affair is not the cost but the fact that the government lost control of essential services and as a result people died unnecessarily.'

Following a win by the Labor party, a wide-ranging Royal Commission started an investigation into the affair. The commission appointed the former head of the Major Fraud Squad as its chief investigator.

In an attempt to improve ambulance response times, a new scheme was launched in May 1998 with trained fire-fighters dealing with ambulance emergencies as the fire brigade's response times are faster.

4   Recommendations and lessons: a baker's dozen

The MAS case raises many issues generally related to the sound management of projects. The key lessons are listed below in terms of a set of recommendations for improving IT practice. While the lessons apply to the MAS despatch system, they are also generic enough to apply as a set of lessons to most projects. The following section will look at some of the other issues from the perspective of outsourcing.

4.1 Contract in haste, repent in leisure

Ensure proper vetting and approval of all suppliers and sub-contractors. While MAS had detailed procedures, these were not strictly followed. The approval process needs to be independent and reliable (and subjected to risk assessment). Also watch out for changes to requirements and late adjustments.

4.2 Mistaking half-baked ideas for projects

Miracles rarely ever happen. A well articulated set of project goals and objectives is the essential starting point. Ensure the scope is well defined especially when a fixed fee is agreed to in advance and will bind the contract. MAS failed to apply proper risk management techniques to evaluate the dangers (and opportunities) associated with the project. Use risk management and cost/benefit techniques to establish requirements and feasibility. Detailed cost/benefit or feasibility or risk assessment should accompany each stage. Ensure you begin with a clear set of requirements. Continuously challenge assumptions and the project from multiple perspectives to ensure soundness, secure logic, and perceive alternatives. Establish a clear set of success and acceptance criteria.

4.3 Only ostriches bury their heads

The MAS case shows many danger signals that were consistently ignored during the first few years. Good management entails looking out for such potential signals. Organisations normally contain a variety of such signals requiring an active plan for issue identification: spot your sponsors, secure senior management involvement, don't ignore the environment, carefully assess the current technology infrastructure, identify the stakeholders, open communications throughout the organisation, try to uncover hidden agendas and watch out for internal politics. Try to avoid creating a blame culture.

Politics will often play a part in unfolding failure stories. In any new project it is worth the time to try to figure out some of these relationships. The MAS project manager should have ensured all stakeholders were involved in the deliberations by facilitating full consultation between management, staff, trade union representatives and information technology advisers as well as despatch and safety critical experts. The system must have total ownership by both management and staff to secure both commitment and priority. The system must be viewed from alternative perspectives (encompassing different stakeholders' perspectives) to expose omissions and preconceptions. Staff must also believe in the system which is only an option when trust is established through consultation, participation and involvement. A more participative approach is required to diffuse internal pressures and political climate. Lack of participation and communication with the stakeholders in the project can be debilitating as was witnessed in the MAS story.

4.4 Magic solutions do not come with warning labels

New technologies mean great opportunities but also unknown risks that must be managed. Despatch systems, including ambulance despatch systems, represent complex applications that often go wrong. Changing work practices through investment in new and often untested technology carries great risks to the project and the organisation adopting the new system.

4.5 The conservation of energy principle

Avoid the 'all at once' trap. MAS opted for a Big Bang implementation of experimental technology in a novel and complex application. When deadlines are tight, make maximum use of known technology and available solutions. Beware of deadline constraints which 'anchor' thinking. Balance solution and deadline – if the deadline is fixed in concrete and you fear getting stuck, consider changing the solution.

4.6 Small is beautiful

Large systems can be very challenging to implement. The MAS system should have been introduced in a stepwise modular approach thereby reducing the overall risk exposure while experimenting with new technology. Break every project into a series of smaller deliverables. This will reduce the risk, offer gradual functionality, and get users and stakeholders involved.

4.7 Plan for disaster

The MAS project assumed that everything would fall into place and the system would be implemented without any hitches. No attempt was made to predict problems or to allocate resources to solving such issues when they were highlighted. Use risk management, plan for all contingencies, and develop a series of 'what if?' scenarios. Use multiple levels of back-up procedures. Plan for late deliveries from suppliers.

4.8 The three monkeys – see no evil

There is a natural reluctance not to cancel runaway projects. Investment already made in the project feeds an escalation cycle and results in throwing more good money. Avoid the escalation trap!

In the MAS case, the project was called into question by technical experts on numerous occasions, yet despite specific protestations, the implementation process proceeded unchecked. In such high risk projects, frequent monitoring and feedback should be utilised to detect deviations from plans and problems. Use risk management to evaluate all consequences and threats. Concerns voiced by potential suppliers should not be ignored. Problems cannot all hide under the carpet – there is not enough room.

4.9 Follow me – The competent project manager

Surprisingly, many large complex projects like the MAS project do not employ an expert project manager to deal with problems and manage the project. Appoint a qualified and experienced project manager to lead from the trenches. Look for the ability to handle unexpected crises and deviations from plans. Use a strong, experienced and knowledgeable team of professionals. Technical know-how needs to be complemented by relevant application domain knowledge. Clarify all lines of responsibility and accountability. Keep the team motivated.

4.10 The plan of attack

Use a project management methodology to make sense of the overall project. Build on firm project foundations. Follow the feasibility study with carefully planned schedules, charts, deadlines, milestones and action lists. Secure the availability of adequate resources according to plan. Establish an effective configuration management and version control system to enhance visibility.

4.11 Estimation

Use a sound basis for both schedule and budget estimates and not arbitrarily adopted constraints (which can be hard to do in some environments including local government and the ambulance despatch sector). Ensure visibility is sufficient for effective progress tracking and rapid intervention. Plan for (independent) quality assurance of the system. When such assessments point to problems (as was uncovered by the independent consultant) the problems need to be analysed and the risk management framework re-applied to the entire project. The system must therefore be developed in a timescale and at a cost that allow for consultation, quality assurance, testing and rework! Ensure the system is fully tried and tested prior to release as stakeholders and the local population may react when a system such as an ambulance despatch begins to misbehave.

4.12 The balancing act

Decision making under multiple constraints is difficult. Make an effort to understand all the project tradeoffs including the concerns of different stakeholder groups. Never over-appreciate the ability of humans. Take time to consider all the implications in order to enable informed decisions. Use formal decision making techniques to quantify trade-off decisions.

4.13 People power

Changes to working practices introduced by the computer need to be carefully assessed and discussed with all concerned parties. This is particularly critical in environments where the computer will replace or augment and alter human activities meant to be carried out under extreme conditions. Get people in the right attitude for change. Ameliorate user distrust, based on earlier deliveries and proven results. Gain user confidence through safe warm-up projects offering small benefits.

Training should be followed by re-training to ensure that staff are familiar with all features of the system. The timing of the training should be met to ensure 'skills decay' does not occur. Recognise the importance of the person-machine interface and its potential role in initiating and exacerbating failure sequences. Try to perceive the interface from the most extremely 'pressured' perspective of potential operators and decision makers. Do not attempt to replace precious people's skills; build around them to support their decision making ability.

4.14 Just in case you break one – post-mortems and learning

Failures offer great, if somewhat costly, lessons. Over the years we have witnessed a host of great learning opportunities. Having made the investment, it would make perfect sense to reap the rewards. Failure offers the professional an insight and a true learning opportunity. Grab the opportunity to improve future competence. For the organisation, it offers a chance for long-term learning and improvement.

5 Managing key outsourcing factors

The previous section offered some general project management solutions required to effectively deal with projects and organisational undertakings with a particular focus on the MAS case. This section looks at the key issues related to the planning and implementation of effective outsourcing practices in light of the lessons from the MAS case. It also draws heavily on over 15 years of research into project failures. The focus therefore is on a set of critical issues that need to be considered to facilitate effective outsourcing arrangements.

5.1 Risk

Risk featured heavily in the lessons from the MAS case. Outsourcing offers a complex relationship. It starts with a focus on core skills and represents the transfer of risk to experts. However, outsourcing is not a transfer of responsibility. Activities and tasks may be delegated but in the case of failure, the service which is not performed may impact or even disable the core service offered by the client. Indeed, one may contend that outsourcing represents swapping one set of risks for another that assumes trust and reliance in the ability of the supplier to understand, respond and monitor the business needs of the client. In reality, the client still bears most of the risk as inability to deliver an infrastructure for a supermarket or a despatch system for an ambulance service means that they cannot continue to perform their core function.

5.2   Starting point

The introduction pointed out the importance of a defined specification and the agreed service level. As the client is ceding some control, they must have clearly defined requirements (and expectations). These are key drivers in the outsourcing relationship and must be monitored throughout the duration of the relationship. The service level needs to be monitored objectively to ensure strategic targets (such as ambulance despatch and arrival times) are achieved.

5.3   Contracts

The June 2004 Meta Group survey of 150 senior level IT managers revealed that most organisations fail to properly plan outsourcing projects and to employ legal protection to ensure that basic specifications and targets are actually achieved. Outsourcing offers great potential in a relatively stable environment or industry. Special consideration is required when the organisation is dealing with novel or unique applications or when the environment is unstable and rapidly changing as the original definitions may no longer suffice. Indeed, under such conditions, the contractor may be forced to rapidly adapt to constantly changing business realities or risk compromising the client's core business. However, many outsourcing relationships depend on the fixed price contract arrangement which prevents the vendor from having an incentive or even a justification to respond to changes and introduce additional efficiency measures. New complex undertakings, such as an ambulance system, should be matched by a dynamic contract that reflects the true nature of the undertaking. Moreover, the contract needs to be clearly and unambiguously defined (which was not the case in either the supermarket or the ambulance outsourcing relationships) especially when the final cost is agreed in advance.

The need to be able to fully specify objectives, targets and requirements is often assumed in an outsourcing relationship. In many cases, however, it is impossible to specify all parameters in advance. Changing conditions often dictate changes to pre-specified factors as the project progresses. Such conditions are not ideal for outsourcing unless one can employ a dynamic contract which offers increased ability to change service levels and related quality to adjust delivery outputs. Contracts should include incentives to encourage the supplier to improve efficiency and work together with the client to improve their services and, as a result, the client's business performance.

5.4 Relationships

The most suitable supplier cannot be selected on the basis of price alone. Most successful relationships are formed where there is mutual **trust** between the two parties in an open relationship. Indeed, trust supplemented by honesty and flexibility offers the foundation for successful partnerships under win-win conditions. Outsourcing relationships tend to evolve over time. In order to maintain a mutually beneficial relationship, the supporting contract should specify incentives that will encourage the contractor to make adjustments to ensure the clients' objectives are still addressed as a result of changes in the external environment and in the clients' internal requirements. Indeed, the key is to identify key performance targets – and structure the relationship so that there are incentives for both sides to meet them thereby maintaining their commitment to the relationship.

Some organisations now employ dedicated relationship managers to maintain dialogue and support the relationship with key partners. On larger projects dedicated teams are likely to work on monitoring performance, benchmarking, reviewing delivery and compliance, monitoring the original objectives and liaising with the supplier. Whatever the size of the organisation there should be sufficient staff to continuously manage the relationship with the provider. The typical rule of thumb for investment in relationship management with the supplier, to ensure the effectiveness of the relationship is maintained, is in the range of four to five per cent of the contract value.

5.5 Expectations

Different stakeholder groups will have differing perceptions and expectations which may ultimately derail the deal. Indeed, expectations need to be managed on all sides as suspicions grow and people need to feel reassured. Expectation management can help to reduce underlying tensions and flag potential problem areas. Planning, discussing and seeking agreement in the early stages help to clarify assumptions and expectations, and ensure that mutual understanding develops.

5.6 Communication

Partnerships are built through communication of needs and preferences. Managing expectations and relationships both depend on the key ability to keep communication channels open and convey perceptions. The ability to respond to change and the desired flexibility in outsourcing arrangement also depend on the level of communication between the participants in the partnership. Note that communication also relates to internal stakeholders who maintain their respective perspectives and agendas and who may need to be reassured about their position (as well as new roles and responsibilities) with regard to the outsourced services.

5.7   Ability to recover

Given the risks associated with outsourcing and the reliance on external suppliers, attention should be paid to devising possibilities and mechanisms for regaining control of the outsourced services. This should include clearly specified termination procedures that will enable rapid and structured uncoupling of the contract and the services thereby maintaining the interest of both organisations and avoiding the need for protracted negotiations and legal battles. Recovery provisions work best when they are negotiated early and placed in the contract.

In a recent landmark case, the UK's Inland Revenue transferred from a 10-year relationship with one supplier to a brand new supplier. The transition period was treated as a project and lasted for six months entailing transfer of staff, ensuring continuity of service from current systems and the handover of completed projects. The transition also entailed a rewriting and redefinition of the needs and service level requirements As part of the handover, more than 95 per cent of employees working on the original deal gradually transferred to the new supplier (under the European legislation to protect employees' rights – see further Chapter 11).

5.8   Selectivity

In some cases moving to an outsourcing arrangement may require the client to teach the vendor how to do something the client has more experience in. Besides not making any business sense, it opens up a vulnerability to the vendor sharing the knowledge with their new clients who may be in competition with the original client. There are other cases where outsourcing a service or capability may impact the organisation's ability to concentrate on key areas and deliver on target. Unless the supplier has clear and direct expertise in these areas, such functions should not be outsourced.

5.9   Plan to manage

The key factors required for effective outsourcing rely on many interpersonal skills. In order to apply the skills, participants need to allow for the time required to manage, control and balance the activities and costs associated with finding this time. In terms of resources, managing relationships, expectations, communication and flexibility will require an additional 10 per cent of cost and resource investment to ensure effective planning, control and monitoring of outsourcing (a small investment given the scale of failure described earlier).

6   The successful outsourcing process

Earlier sections discussed some of the lessons and described some of the critical issues related to outsourcing. This section draws on the earlier lessons and recommends a set of steps that builds on the key factors identified above and implements them into a comprehensive outsourcing process designed to address the issues covered in this chapter and offer a strategy for successful outsourcing. While many other sources offer a process for outsourcing implementation (see for example, Hui and Beath 2002), the perspective offered here builds on the lessons from earlier failures representing the next stage of our work on learning from failures and improving successful outcomes. The basic process relies on a set of twelve activities to address outsourcing concerns, issues and risks.

6.1 Situational assessment

Identify objectives, strengths and core competencies of the organisation. Success in outsourcing depends on the ability to focus on the business goals. Outsourcing services certain aspects of the business but it is there to serve the key business goals and this is the basis for judging the effectiveness of outsourcing in terms of the gains that have been obtained and the way they address business objectives.

6.2 Needs assessment

Define needs required to achieve strategic objectives (assess tactical and strategic impact of outsourcing on any of the functions). The definition should include the level of service that is appropriate for the needs.

6.3 Business case

Determine the business case for outsourcing: what, why, when, how. Given the core business competencies, this step is concerned with determining what functions outside the core speciality could be more usefully outsourced to specialists. This is achieved through the development of a detailed business plan including full consideration of all relevant options, different pricing policies, desired levels of quality, and the mix of skills and capabilities. How much face to face contact is needed? How much time will it take? How do skills get passed from the supplier to the business? Are you willing to lose them?

Making a good business case is crucial. The case should also define the degree of reliance on a single supplier. Making a mega deal with one supplier can be risky in terms of dependence. Organisations can also sign with a range of suppliers to mitigate the risk of total reliance. Thus, requiring the organisation to deal with multiple vendors which would be more difficult to manage but also providing a wider range of skills and expertise. Organisations have different preferences. Rolls Royce and the European Space Agency recently signed mega deals with one supplier in order to make cost savings, while Barclays Bank have signed a series of smaller outsourcing deals with different suppliers.

6.4 Buying in

Enrolment of stakeholders to ensure continuing understanding and support for the outsourcing process.

6.5   Requirements

Client requirements should be documented and specify the business and technical needs of the business.

6.6   Solicitation planning

Establishment of specific and objective criteria for selecting bids, minimising bias and development of mechanisms for establishing consensus between eventual assessors. Should include criteria for evaluating vendors and their performance.

6.7   Invitation to tender

Solicitation of bids requiring a specific Supplier Service Description as well as a complete development plan, and full explanation of approach. The purpose of the documents is to generate sufficient confidence in the vendor's ability to understand the business need and complete the work successfully. The documents should specify that the customer maintains some level of control over the project (or service).

6.8   Assessment

Ensure match between the requirements expressed in the Invitation to Tender and the supplier response in the Supplier Service Description. Client to use team nominated (during the solicitation planning stage) to review the proposed service and the match between the items. Assess the bids and select the most suitable. In recent years, many suppliers have been prone to financial instability during the term of the contract. The detailed investigation should include overall reputation, market share, responsiveness, expertise, skills and capabilities, flexibility in terms of contract arrangements, price and past history and the financial health of the supplier.

6.9   Communication

Establish a good relationship with the potential providers and clarify expectations. This relationship will need to be cherished and maintained by keeping the communication channel open to ensure the continued success of the relationship. The ability to communicate, coupled with the working communication links can thus be viewed as a growing resource developing alongside the project.

6.10   Contract negotiation

Establish a contract, including full scope, duration, type of relationship with the vendor, clear boundaries, clearly defined performance criteria, testing procedures, acceptance criteria, payment structure, incentive structure, change control criteria and provision for change, and adjustment on basis of altered objectives and revised organisational targets. It also requires precise delineation of responsibility, entitlement to changes and the likely costs. Establish the technical review process specified in the contract. Thoroughness and comprehensiveness are often cited as key objectives in a contract. It is useful to negotiate a sound contract (business requirements may evolve over a 10-year period) and complicated legal contracts are difficult to change. Additional conditions for revision and renegotiation can therefore be added to the main contract. Poorly written contracts often result in additional charges, consultants' fees and legal expenses as seen in the supermarket case. Indeed, as seen in the MAS case, starting work before all details are agreed to is perilous. Consider the most suitable form of contract that will allow the relationship to evolve as the nature of the business changes. Objective assessment of rewards and risks must be aligned with strategic intent for outsourcing and should be allowed to determine the most suitable type of contract. (If the project is urgent and cannot wait for the initial definition a starter time-and-material contract may be required to cover the interim period while the contract is being developed.)

Service level agreements should be stated in business terms rather than in terms of the technology used to service the business at any one point. This is particularly important in long-term contracts where technology is likely to change rapidly. The purpose of the contract is to achieve what both parties want and to avoid unnecessary legal issues. The negotiation should focus on maintaining the channels of effective communication to enable both sides to understand key issues and derive a win-win solution thereby providing incentives to all participants. Expectations can thus be formalised in the contract rather than remain as unuttered assumptions.

Note that the National Outsourcing Association in the UK is currently working on a new form of contract that will create a win-win situation for both parties. Under the new terms, suppliers will be obliged to reveal their profit margin on an agreed level of service. The profit margin will then be split between the supplier and an investment in creating new services and innovative ways of working thus offering a potential for improvement in customer service levels and an incentive to suppliers to find new ways of working together and addressing the evolving needs of their clients. The revised contract will be introduced as part of a revised code of practice which will be released towards the end of 2005.

6.11 Monitoring

Monitor performance and adjust. Continue to seek meaningful communication. Manage the agreement, monitor achievement and manage expectations.

6.12 Benchmarking

Provide detailed guidelines for measurement of performance. Different parties involved in a relationship often have completely different sets of expectations about the same situation. Measurement is therefore crucial to determine performance levels using agreed metrics specified in the contract. Benchmarking measures need to be applied regularly and include measures to determine stakeholder satisfaction, meeting of business requirements and effectiveness of relationship management in addition to traditional price and service levels. (Benchmarking should be defined in the contract so that standards and measurable items are agreed to by all stakeholders. This will enable effective collection and review of data which can be submitted for peer group review and detailed comparison prior to reporting.)

7   Summary

Outsourcing is a fundamental business trend that increasingly impacts many projects and services. Outsourcing relies on clear understanding of business objectives and the need to focus on and maximise key skills and abilities. Effective outsourcing requires a clear understanding of the impact of change and the benefits, opportunities and costs associated with the practice.

Many outsourcing projects fail to deliver the promised benefits due to an inability to handle some of the key factors associated with communication, expectation and relationship management. Outsourcing is not a short-term solution but a long-term commitment often likened to a marriage. Make sure you are ready for the next step and satisfied with your choice of partner. Would you go for the 'cheapest' partner?

The key skills required for outsourcing are related to establishing the relationship (finding the ideal partner), maintaining the relationship and closing the relationship using various formal mechanisms to ensure that the relationship works for BOTH partners. It ultimately calls for attention to detail, attention to your partner, mutual commitment and the realisation that everyone needs to work at the relationship to ensure its longevity.

Circumstances often change forcing the partners to work harder to keep the relationship going. By learning from your partner and responding to their cues, it is often possible to make the relationship safer and stronger so that sharing becomes a strength rather than a bind. Outsourcing, too, can feed on opportunity to translate potential into gain. The steps proposed in this chapter are offered as a framework for reducing the incidents of strained relationships and catastrophic failure and increasing the level of satisfaction of expectations in a period of growing demand for successful outsourcing partnerships.

References

G. Fitzgerald and Willcocks, A business guide to outsourcing information technology, a study of European best practice in the selection, management and use of external IT service (Wimbledon: Business Intelligence, 1994).

P.P. Hui and C.M. Beath, 'The IT Sourcing Process: A Framework for Research'. Working paper, University of Texas at Austin (2002).

Bibliography

R. Aalders, *The IT Outsourcing Guide* (New York: Wiley, 2001)

CIO, www.cio.com/research/outsourcing (accessed June 2004).

S. Cullen and L. Willcocks, *Intelligent IT Outsourcing: Eight Building Blocks to Success* (Oxford: Elsevier, 2003).

General Accounting Office, *Information Technology: Leading Commercial Practices for Outsourcing of Services*, GAO-02-214 (October 2001). http://www.gao.gov/new.items/d02214.pdf (viewed June 2004)

T. Kern and L. Willcocks, *The Relationship Advantage: Information Technologies, Sourcing and Management* (Oxford: Oxford University Press, 2001).

R. Kishore, H.R. Rao, K. Nam, S. Rajagopalan, and A. Chaudhury, 'A Relationship Perspective on IT Outsourcing', *Communications of the ACM*, 46:12 (2003) 87–92.

R. Klepper and W.O. Jones, *Outsourcing Information Technology Systems & Services* (Upper Saddle: Prentice Hall, 1998).

M. Lacity and R. Hirschheim, *Information systems outsourcing: Myths, metaphors, and realities* (New York: John Wiley, 1993).

M. Lacity and L. Willcocks, 'An empirical investigation of information technology sourcing practices: lessons from experience', *MISQ*, 22:3 (1998) 363–408.

M. Lacity and L. Willcocks, *Global Information Technology Outsourcing: Search for Business Advantage* (Chichester: Wiley, 2001).

J.N. Lee, 'IT outsourcing evolution – past, present and future', *Communications of the ACM*, 46:5 (2003) 84–89.

Y. Lichtenstein, 'Puzzles in software development contracting', *Communications of the ACM*, 47:2 (2004) 61–65.

National Association for Outsourcing, www.noa.co.uk (accessed June 2004).

R. Nellore, *Managing Buyer-Supplier Relations, The winning edge through specification management* (London: Routledge, 2001).

Outsourcing Institute, www.outsourcing.com (accessed June 2004).

D.J. Reifer, 'Seven hot outsourcing practices', *IEEE Software*, 21:1 (2004) 14–16.

R. Sabherwal, 'The role of trust in outsourced IS development projects', *Communications of the ACM*, 42:2 (2003) 80–86.

E. Sparrow, *Successful IT Outsourcing* (London: Springer Verlag, 2003).

L. Weinstein, 'Outsourced and out of control', *Communications of the ACM*, 47:2 (2004) 120.

Part II

Strategies for Offshore Outsourcing

2
Strategic Offshoring: Decision Analysis, Best Practices, and Emerging Trends
Dan (B.D.) Bhide

1 Introduction

1.1 Objectives

Any decision related to 'optimal sourcing' of business processes or IT functions is complex enough to arrive at and more so to implement successfully. This is because of the sheer multitude of options available – from in-sourcing to co-sourcing to outsourcing – and equally wide ranging objective and subjective factors that go into decision making and successful implementation of a sourcing decision – from strategic, tactical and operational to economic, political and competitive factors. Offshore sourcing ('offshoring') of business processes and IT functions adds several more layers of complexity and hence risks to the sourcing lifecycle (Figure 2.1), while, as one would expect, also offering significant potential competitive advantages if implemented correctly.

The objectives of this chapter are to:

- elaborate on the decision analysis process for evaluating offshoring options during the 'planning' phase of a sourcing lifecycle,
- discuss best practices for risk mitigation and value maximisation during management of the end-to-end offshoring lifecycle, and
- discuss some of the emerging trends in offshoring.

The intent is not just to discuss these aspects and factors from the 'outsourcing' perspective – there is a plethora of literature available in the public domain on outsourcing.[1–6] The intent is to emphasise the additional layers of risks, benefits, myths and complexities that 'offshoring' options impart (over and above non-offshoring options) to decision making and implementation of 'globally optimal sourcing' initiatives.

1.2 Evolution of services offshoring

The evolution of services outsourcing can be traced back to the good old mantra of success in business: *'Buy smarter, process more efficiently, and*

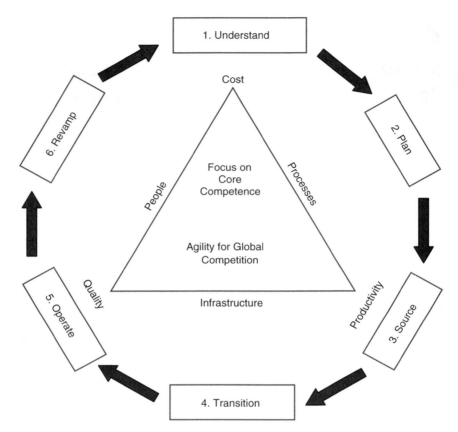

Figure 2.1 Objectives Based Management of Sourcing Lifescycle

sell more'. As far as 'smarter buying and efficient processing of *products'* is concerned, over the past four decades, many North American and European corporations have been successfully procuring raw materials from and moving or outsourcing manufacturing to lower cost locations in Asia and South America.

However, in today's globally competitive environment with perpetual pressures on margins, 'smarter sourcing and efficient processing of *products'* is no longer a sufficient and sustainable competitive strategic advantage. Realising this dilemma, global visionary companies started toying with the concept of 'smarter sourcing of *services'* in the last two decades. In the late 90s, many US and European companies tested 'offshoring' waters in a significant way for the first time while seeking low-cost solutions for the legacy work on Y2K-related initiatives. As the value of offshore IT programming skills became apparent, many US and European companies and their willing service provisioning counterparts wanted to move up the value chain to consider offshoring higher-value added IT functions and business processes.

Along came several other developments over the last decade that are forcing many global corporations to reevaluate what their core and non-core business processes and IT functions are:

- post 9/11 difficult global economic climate and increasingly global competition have necessitated globally competitive cost structure,
- workforce and demographic changes (aging population, decreasing birth rates and insufficient inflow of immigrants) in the US and Europe have created the potential for continued shortage of qualified work force,
- disruptive internet-enabled and telecommunication technologies and dramatic reductions in the cost of telecommunications have enhanced the
  - range of business processes and IT functions that can be delivered remotely and
  - distances from which such services can be delivered (evolving from on-site to onshore to nearshore to offshore),
- availability of cheap yet qualified offshore resources and enhanced capabilities and infrastructure of offshore suppliers have helped to partially mitigate the risks of offshoring initiatives.

Successful initiatives of global visionaries such as General Electric, Citibank and British Airways in offshoring their critical yet non-core processes have been well publicised. Consequently, offshoring has indeed emerged as a potential means of improving cost effectiveness, quality, and productivity of business processes and IT functions while achieving enhanced agility and focus on core competencies. Several Global 1000 companies have followed suit over the last five to 10 years to benefit from this emerging trend. What started as a trickle in the early 1990s has now become a tidal wave of offshoring business processes and IT functions.

1.3 What offshoring is and is not

'Offshore sourcing' does not necessarily mean 'outsourcing'. It is a different dimension (location/distance) of the 'optimal sourcing' decision as indicated in Table 2.1.

Offshoring, thus, encompasses a wide range of options, including offshore insourcing, joint venture/co-sourcing and outsourcing. Inherent to this dimension of distance/location are several factors,[7-9] such as below, that make offshore sourcing significantly different from onshore sourcing:

- The types and levels of risks with offshore sourcing are substantially different from those with onshore sourcing. For example, geopolitical risks of the 'so far unknown' location can be significantly different from the known onshore risks. Thus, disaster recovery planning is more critical for offshore sourcing initiatives.

Table 2.1   Dimensions of the 'Optimal Sourcing' Decision

Sourcing Dimension	Dimension Options
Ownership	• In-sourcing • Joint venture/alliance/co-sourcing • Build-Operate-Transfer • Outsourcing
Strategic/Tactical	• Core vs. non-core • Critical vs. non-critical • Transformational vs. traditional
Processes/Functions	• Business processes • IT functions • Other functions
Scope	• Piecemeal vs. incremental vs. big-bang • Parallel vs. sequential transformation
Chronology	• By business division vs. shared services • By geography • By business process or IT function
Duration	• Short-term – One-time/project based • Long-term – continuous/as needed
Location/Distance	• On-site • Onshore • Nearshore • Offshore
Type of relationship	• Customer-vendor relationship • Collaborative partnership
Number of relationships	• Multiple service providers • Strategic prime contracting

- Significant differences in business environment, culture and values necessitate different styles of managing people, processes and infrastructure to achieve planned business objectives.
- Fewer resources and assets (people and infrastructure) are transferred to the service provider during offshoring initiatives than during onshore outsourcing initiatives. Consequently, for the client, the potential to generate cash flow by offloading infrastructure supporting the offshored processes is minimal. Similarly, for the service provider, the upfront investment can be significantly higher. For both the parties, training and documentation requirements for knowledge transfer are more critical. Thus, in general, transition for an offshore sourcing initiative can be significantly more resource intensive from time, personnel and cost perspectives than that for an onshore outsourcing initiative.
- Differences in legal environment, such as intellectual property protection laws, privacy laws, labour and employment laws, and legal requirements for cross-country data transfers mean that 'offshoreability'

of a process or function can be significantly different form its 'onshore outsourceability'.

• The operating model can be significantly different with offshoring due to the possibility of 24 × 7 operation and its implications to changing working hours of the onshore resources engaging with the offshore team.

• Potential differences in the quality of offshore infrastructure and resources from their onshore counterparts imply greater criticality of due-diligence of offshore locations and service providers.

• Processes and methodologies for managing offshore sourcing lifecycle are less evolved than those for onshore sourcing. Similarly, the skills required to manage offshore sourcing is different and in less abundance than that for onshore sourcing.

Because of these differences, the value assessment process, best practices for risk mitigation, and strategies for value maximisation in offshoring also differ from those for onshore outsourcing. These factors also imply the need for a longer-term approach to offshoring initiatives and hence greater strategic consideration by management.

Reduced cost, higher quality and enhanced productivity are as much primary drivers for offshore sourcing as they are for onshore sourcing. However, the cost basis of onshore outsourcing is not much different for a service provider than that of continued insourcing by the client. Consequently, in an onshore outsourcing initiative, the main objectives of outsourcing are achieved primarily through the following means:

• marginal cost per additional client is less for the service provider than the internal cost to the client due to:
  • economies of scale resulting from spreading the cost of infrastructure over multiple clients,
  • greater standardisation, or
  • greater automation of customisation;
• higher quality through functional and industry expertise and higher process maturity levels,
• higher productivity through greater standardisation, automation and better process controls.

In case of offshore sourcing to locations such as India, Philippines, China or Russia, the cost basis itself is already dislocated substantially in favor of offshoring (vs. onshore outsourcing). Consequently, service providers intent on enhancing the relevance of offshore sourcing as a better strategic option for the clients (than on-site/onshore outsourcing), need to focus their consultative selling efforts and internal resources on better positioning of *other* critical factors such as quality, productivity, data security, IP protection and risk mitigation.

2 Decision analysis for offshoring

2.1 Overall process flow for outsourcing decision making

Any business decision, including one about optimal sourcing of business processes or IT functions, involves evaluation of multiple options for their alignment with strategic business objectives, financial impact, risk assessment and political effects. At a very high level, the decision making processes for offshore sourcing can be viewed as a '6WH' process as shown in Figure 2.2 below:

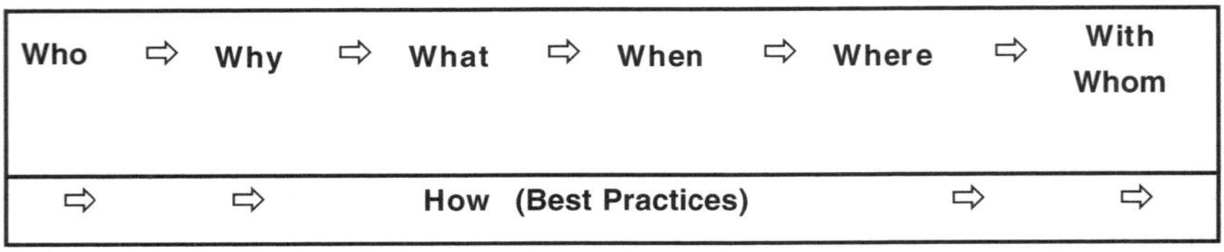

Who ⇨ Why ⇨ What ⇨ When ⇨ Where ⇨	With Whom
⇨ ⇨ How (Best Practices) ⇨ ⇨	

Figure 2.2 Process Flow for Decision Making on 'Optimal Sourcing' Initiatives

This decision process flow is not always necessarily sequential. In fact, several aspects of the process can and often do overlap each other. Inherent to the decisions about 'What' and 'With Whom' are the decisions related to the ownership model itself as to whether offshore in-sourcing, offshore co-sourcing/joint venture, offshore outsourcing or offshore build-operate-transfer model is the optimal sourcing option.

Offshoring should be viewed as consideration of offshore sourcing as a *component* of a 'globally optimal sourcing' strategy that also includes on-site and onshore/nearshore delivery. It should not imply complete offshore sourcing of business processes or IT functions.

2.1.1 Who – internal readiness assessment

So far, *Fortune 500* companies have embraced offshore sourcing of business processes and IT functions in a significant way and *Global 1000* companies are following suit.

In general, consideration of offshoring initiatives is appropriate for companies if:

- the senior management is committed to pursuing offshore sourcing as a strategic initiative rather than as a divisional/operational issue to be dealt with at lower levels,
- the management can offer effective involvement and sponsorship through focus, stability, time and other resources,
- the strategic direction and business objectives are well defined and no significant realignment of senior management is in the offing that

may question or redefine the business objectives behind the sourcing initiatives,
- other major restructuring without 'optimal sourcing' focus are not underway that can conflict with the business objectives behind offshoring initiatives,
- the core and non-core competencies[10] have been clearly identified, and
- internal costs, performance and maturity levels of processes being considered for 'optimal sourcing' are known and benchmarked.

An internal readiness assessment is necessary for detailed consideration of these issues before engaging in any serious strategic 'optimal sourcing' initiatives.

2.1.2 Why – business objectives

Understanding the primary motivations behind 'optimal sourcing' initiatives and how they are aligned with strategic business objectives is the next step in the decision analysis process. Some of the potential drivers/accelerators as well as concerns/inhibitors to 'optimal sourcing' initiatives are described in Table 2.2.[1, 2, 11, 12] The most often cited primary motivators for offshore sourcing initiatives revolve around cost savings, enhanced quality, productivity, customer service, focus and agility.

A well-developed business case based on a balanced strategic value assessment of 'optimal sourcing' should identify the primary motivators as well as define baseline criteria that must be satisfied by any sourcing option to replace continued in-house sourcing.

2.1.3 What – which business processes/IT functions

Before selecting specific processes that are appropriate for outsourcing, it is important to determine those that certainly should not be early candidates for outsourcing consideration.[1, 13] General guidelines for identifying such processes include:

- core competencies (see below),
- critical processes subject to unacceptable levels of political risk for reasons such as potential damage from data leakage, loss of intellectual property/proprietary information and so on,
- processes requiring regulatory compliance such as laws to protect privacy or transfer of sensitive data across international boundaries with significant potential for legal liabilities, diversion of management's focus and public embarrassment in case of non-compliance,
- broken processes that are volatile or unclear in scope, and
- processes with complex, ill-defined decision making logic requiring a last minute balancing act between conflicting objectives.

Table 2.2   Potential Benefits and Risks of Outsourcing

Potential Benefits/Drivers/Accelerators	Potential Risks/Concerns/Inhibitors
Strategic	
• Focus on the core competencies • Enhance agility for rapidly changing market environment • Enhance flexibility for M&A, divestitures and starting new businesses • Accelerate business transformation/ reengineering benefits • Match in-house support services of larger competitors • Reduce risks from changes in the market conditions, competition, industry con solidation, regulatory environment, financial conditions and technologies affecting non-core processes	• Opposition from management and lower level resources • Limited cost-effective mitigation options if relationship fails • High exit barriers • Leakage of proprietary/confidential information • Unknown locations/service providers • Uncertain legal environment
Financial	
• Convert fixed plus variable cost structure to a reduced, predictable and variable structure based on volume and performance • Achieve visibility, control and transparency of costs basis for outsourced processes • Conserve capital by avoiding current and future investments in the infrastructure for non-core functions • Grow revenue by moving released capital into revenue generating core processes and engaging in processes (such as claims collections at significantly lower costs) that were not economically viable earlier • Generate cash flow with reduction in resources and infrastructure • Create incentive for the service providers to reduce costs while improving quality, productivity and security by converting a client's internal cost centre to a supplier's profit centre • Positive market reaction for proactive cost cutting and improved ROI on the freed-up capital	• Exposure to service provider's financial viability • Cost overruns from out-of-scope services • Higher cost of services if usage projections are not realised • Additional one-time costs related to planning outsourcing initiatives and personnel payouts • Additional ongoing costs of relationship management

Table 2.2   Potential Benefits and Risks of Outsourcing – *continued*

Potential Benefits/Drivers/Accelerators	Potential Risks/Concerns/Inhibitors
People and Processes – Expertise, Quality and Productivity	
• Reorient quality internal resources to more valuable roles • Gain access to world-class expertise with business, industry and technical specialisation not available in-house • Engage quality labour at lower cost • Replace internal processes lacking controls, compliance and accountability with world-class processes at higher process maturity levels • Enforce process discipline through standardisation across business units • Focus on ROI and business benefit of processes • Improve turnaround times with 24 × 7 support	• Loss of in-house expertise • Loss of control over day-to-day decision making • Dependence on service providers • Employee relations and morale issues arising from threatened job security • Exposure to suppliers' lack of commitment – if larger or more strategic customers are obtained • Lack of supplier motivation for process improvement without incentives • Limited in-house processes and tools supplier management
Technology and Infrastructure	
• Reduce lead times to catch-up with latest technology without heavy investments and risks of the learning curve • Achieve economies of scale with service provider spreading the infrastructure costs over multiple clients	• Risk of disruption • Possibility of being tied to obsolete technology for supplier to achieve economies of scale

Interdepartmental, cross-functional or multidisciplinary processes also typically do not service as early candidates for offshore sourcing consideration.

Questions to ask while determining core competencies[1, 6, 10] include:

• Does this process define or defend a unique current or future competitive advantage that is hard for competitors to imitate?
• Is this process critical to meet current and long-term business objectives?
• Is the competitive advantage of this process sustainable with continued internal operation?
• Can future leaders of the company evolve out of this process?
• If starting afresh, would this capability be developed internally?
• Does this business process contribute directly to enhancing revenues or market share?
• Would other companies hire us to perform this process for them?

Processes that fit the above profile should not be outsourced. However, 'offshore insourcing' of such processes can be considered by companies that have earlier been through the learning curve of offshoring and if concerns such as protection of intellectual property/proprietary information can be adequately addressed.

Processes not eliminated by the above considerations (non-core processes) can be evaluated further as potential candidates for outsourcing and offshore sourcing[6, 11] if:

- the process need not be owned and performed internally,
- internal delivery does not meet business requirements or does not deliver world-class quality and productivity at a competitive cost,
- internal process cannot be improved at reasonable cost to become competitive,
- qualified external service providers are available with equal or better capabilities and can deliver the process in a more cost effective manner,
- the process can be serviced remotely and delivered over e-infrastructure without face to face contact with the customer or the end user,
- the process is repetitive and transaction or labour intensive,
- performance of the process can be measured, monitored and benchmarked,
- the decision making logic of the process is well-defined and requires minimal last minute judgment calls,
- capability to manage offshore relationship is available through in-house resources or third-party assistance or can be developed internally.

It is not necessary that all the criteria above be applicable to candidate processes and functions. However, they do help to identify early candidates and the chronology of sourcing strategy (Section 2.5). Some of the common factors to be considered during the analysis of 'what' processes and functions to outsource are listed in Table 2.3 along with those relevant for other aspects of decision analysis ('when', 'where' and 'with whom'). As would be expected, these factors influence multiple aspects of decision analysis and should be evaluated carefully through qualitative and quantitative analysis (discussed in Section 2.8).

Two-dimensional mapping of candidate business processes across critical evaluation criteria such as criticality ('core'ness) vs. complexity, maturity level vs. remote serviceability, labour intensiveness vs. transaction volume, process stability vs. decision ambiguity and so on can also help management identify 'offshorable' business processes and IT functions for further consideration of optimal sourcing options. Such processes and functions should then go through more extensive qualitative and quantitative analysis comparing in-house operations with other sourcing options.

In general, standardised business processes can be easier to outsource even for mid-size organisations. Unique and highly customised processes, on the other hand, may be 'offshorable' for larger corporations but not necessarily for their smaller counterparts if the processes lack critical mass of transaction volume or revenues. In addition, it is easier for larger corporations to support high initial costs and to develop resources and capabilities for managing offshore relationships. However, smaller corporations can level the playing field by seeking third-party assistance with advice for and management of offshoring initiatives.

2.1.4 When – scope and chronology

Critical decisions to make at this stage revolve around:

- the extent of scope (piecemeal, incremental or big-bang approach) and
- the chronology of implementing sourcing initiatives – by business division or type of shared services, by business process/IT function or by geography.

While offshoring business processes or IT functions, a greater strategic value of business transformation can also be achieved if existing business processes are also reengineered to enhance their efficacy and productivity. Depending on the maturity and utility of existing processes and the overall comfort level with outsourcing, some companies choose to achieve 'parallel transformation' (simultaneously outsourcing and reengineering) while some others choose to achieve 'sequential transformation' (that is, reengineering followed by outsourcing or vice versa). Qualitative and quantitative value assessment (Section 2.8) of these and other factors will help determine a long-term 'optimal sourcing' roadmap.

Piecemeal, incremental and big bang approaches to 'optimal sourcing' have their own advantages and risks.[11] In general, the 'big bang' approach is exponentially more complex even for the veterans of outsourcing. Hence, 'starting small, prototyping extensively and scaling-up rapidly' is a better option for novices and experienced companies alike to mitigate risks and maximise value from 'optimal sourcing' initiatives.

2.1.5 Where – location analysis

Typically, country/location and service provider evaluations happen in tandem since one cannot be assessed rationally without consideration of the other. Location specific factors, in general, revolve around the current and future trends in the quality and cost of labour pool and infrastructure, legal and cultural business environment, support and incentives from local government, geopolitical risks, and distance/time zone related aspects.[14] The evaluation method for country/location analysis is described in more detail in Section 2.8.

Among the offshore locations, based on the above criteria, India and Philippines are considered preferred locations in general, with China, Russia, South Africa and Eastern European countries emerging as competitors. Currently, India is clearly ahead of the competition by a significant margin. Canada and Ireland have been popular 'nearshore' sourcing locations for quite some time. However, over the last five years, significant cost advantages of offshore locations have clearly tilted the balance in favor of these offshore locations.

2.1.6   With whom – service provider analysis

Considering the high financial and political costs of reversing an offshore sourcing transaction, it is extremely critical that a well-rounded methodology for due-diligence of service provider be developed and adopted. Critical factors for such an assessment (see Table 2.3) revolve around the following four key areas:

- overall cost (TCO – total cost of offshoring) and financial stability,
- expertise and capability,
- ability to collaborate, and
- cultural fit.

The evaluation method for service provider due-diligences is described in more detail in Section 2.8. Again, many of the top-tier offshore sourcing companies from India have an extensive presence and established infrastructure in the US and Europe over the past decade. Due to their involvement in offshoring of legacy work on Y2K-related initiatives in the 90s, some of these companies have better processes in place for managing the *offshore* sourcing lifecycle than some of the top US firms that have started their offshore presence for outsourcing in a significant way only in the last two to five years.

Certification standards for quality management and software development such as ISO 9001 and Capability Maturity Model (CMM) have been around for a while. More recently, in response to the growing trends in 'optimal' sourcing, new models such as COPC-2000[15] and eSCM (eSourcing Capability Model)[16] for assessing capabilities of customer contact centres and IT-enabled sourcing service providers respectively, have emerged.

Table 2.3   Evaluation Criteria for Decision Analysis of Offshoring Options

Category of Criteria	Relevance for Sourcing Decision Analysis			
	What?	When?	Where?	With Whom?
Evaluation Criteria (Internal and External) ↓	Processes and IT Functions	Chronology and Scope	Country/ Location Analysis	Service Provider Analysis
Cost				
Total cost of ownership	X	X	X	X
Transition and termination charges	X	X		X
Cost of labour and management	X	X	X	X
Cost of infrastructure	X	X	X	X
Cost of real estate			X	X
Cost of living			X	X
Corporate tax rates	X		X	X
Exchange rates	X		X	X
Federal and local tax incentives and subsidies	X		X	X
Cost benefit analysis	X	X	X	X
Sensitivity analysis of critical assumptions	X	X	X	X
Quality				
Process maturity levels	X	X	X	X
Current and planned certifications (CMM SEI, COPC, etc)	X	X		X
Continuous processes improvement methodologies in place	X	X		X
Productivity				
Implications of possible 24 × 7 operations	X		X	X
Work culture/ethic			X	X
Commitment to base-line response time	X			X
Location				
Geopolitical risk	X	X	X	X
Economic stability	X	X	X	X
Governmental support			X	X
Industry association support			X	X
Cultural compatibility			X	X

Table 2.3   Evaluation Criteria for Decision Analysis of Offshoring Options –
continued

Category of Criteria	Relevance for Sourcing Decision Analysis			
	What?	**When?**	**Where?**	**With Whom?**
Evaluation Criteria (Internal and External) ↓	**Processes and IT Functions**	**Chronology and Scope**	**Country/ Location Analysis**	**Service Provider Analysis**
Geographic proximity/time difference			X	X
Entrepreneurial environment			X	X
People				
Quality of workforce	X		X	X
Language proficiency	X		X	X
BPO and ITO experience and skills	X		X	X
Understanding of business objectives	X	X		X
Well-defined governance structure	X	X		X
Size of labour market	X		X	X
Employee turnover rates and retention policies	X		X	X
In-house political opposition	X	X		
Processes				
Candidate processes for optimal sourcing				
Criticality ('core'ness)	X			X
Complexity of decision making logic	X		X	X
Labour and transaction intensiveness	X	X		X
Level of standardisation/ commoditisation	X	X		X
Acceptable base-line performance	X			X
Process maturity levels – internal and external	X	X		X
Understanding of process interdependencies	X	X		X
Sourcing Lifecycle Management Processes				
Ability to evolve and manage global service delivery	X	X	X	X

Table 2.3   Evaluation Criteria for Decision Analysis of Offshoring Options –
continued

Category of Criteria	Relevance for Sourcing Decision Analysis			
	What?	When?	Where?	With Whom?
Evaluation Criteria (Internal and External) ↓	Processes and IT Functions	Chronology and Scope	Country/ Location Analysis	Service Provider Analysis
Solution architecture capabilities	X			X
Project management skills	X			X
Transition management capabilities	X			X
Maturity of transition management processes	X	X		X
Extent of process automation Maturity of governance processes	X	X		X
Reporting processes and capabilities	X	X		X
Issues identification, escalation and resolution processes	X	X		X
Processes for data security, protection of intellectual property and privacy	X		X	X

Infrastructure (Availability, Reliability, and Redundancy)

Telecommunications Infrastructure	X		X	X
Other infrastructure – water, electricity, public and private transportation (roads, airports) and so on			X	X
Legal infrastructure – Intellectual property protection, Data Privacy laws, Labour laws, Visa regulations	X		X	X
Data backup and Disaster recovery capability	X			X
Ability to ramp-up infrastructure	X			X
Availability of basic services			X	X
Understanding of infrastructure interdependencies	X	X		X

Other Vendor Specific Criteria

Financial stability	X			X

Table 2.3   Evaluation Criteria for Decision Analysis of Offshoring Options –
continued

Category of Criteria	Relevance for Sourcing Decision Analysis			
	What?	When?	Where?	With Whom?
Evaluation Criteria (Internal and External) ↓	Processes and IT Functions	Chronology and Scope	Country/ Location Analysis	Service Provider Analysis
Access to capital			X	X
Experience/track record	X			X
Quality of references				X
Size of business	X			X
Ability to collaborate	X	X		X
Flexibility in service delivery	X	X		X
Business analysis capabilities	X			X
Knowledge transfer and value addition capabilities	X	X		X
Transition planning, Implementation, and support capabilities (including at the end of the contract)	X	X		X
Ability to match resources with varying demand	X			X
Willingness to share risks and rewards	X	X		X
Compatibility of corporate cultures	X			X
Understanding of issues specific to industry verticals	X			X

2.2   Qualitative and quantitative analysis

In order to make sound 'globally optimal sourcing' decisions, qualitative analysis (involving subjective assessment of non-financial criteria) and quantitative analysis (of financial aspects and Key Performance Indicators) should be conducted in parallel for all sourcing options.

2.2.1   Qualitative analysis

The examples of criteria commonly considered for qualitative and quantitative analysis of outsourcing decisions (what, when, where and with whom) are indicated in Table 2.3. Initially, the number of criteria chosen for any evaluation should be kept to a bare minimum[2] reflecting only those that are essential to rule out unacceptable options based on predefined critical success factors (CSFs). Secondary criteria should be considered only for more detailed comparison of options that pass through the primary filtering criteria.

Decision and risk analyses of multiple qualitative criteria that may not be convertible to dollar amounts (to signify their implications on the overall decision making process) are often made using software solutions based on Multi Criteria Decision Analysis (MCDA) techniques such as Analytic Hierarchy Process (AHP)[17, 18] and Simple Multi Attribute Rating Technique (SMART).[19–21] In a nutshell, these techniques involve weighing the criteria based on their importance to the decision maker and rating the alternatives based on each criterion. The overall 'score' of an alternative is the weighted sum of its rating for each criterion, as shown in Table 2.4.

Since the rating of multiple criteria in such an evaluation is relative, it is very important that the baseline (pass/fail cut-off mark) and the meaning of ratings be clearly determined, understood and communicated in advance to all evaluators of options. Ratings of each evaluator should also be discussed later in detail to ensure consistency in the assumptions made by the evaluators

2.2.2 *Quantitative analysis*

Financial analysis of all sourcing options should be based on multi-year financial models covering the entire planned duration of the sourcing initiative. The true impact of all one-time and ongoing costs and benefits such as the following[1, 3, 22] needs to be considered:

- direct and indirect costs from operating, overhead and capital budgets,
- additional one time and ongoing costs such as payouts for displaced resources, initiative planning, travel, transition, governance, cost of third-party advisors and so on,
- intangible costs such as temporary productivity shortfalls from loss of morale, schedule/requirement changes, scope creep, legal hurdles and so on,
- tangible benefits such as improved productivity, quality and revenue, effects of reinvestment of released capital, and
- intangible benefits such as new growth opportunities for revenue and market share, effects of business transformation and so on.

Some of the methods commonly used for evaluating sourcing options include:[3]

- Net Present Vale (NPV)
- Internal Rate of Return (IRR)
- Payback Period (PP)
- Return on Investment (ROI)
- Net Cash Flow (NCF) and Cumulative Cash Flow (CCF)
- Economic Value Added (EVA)
- Total Business Return (TBR)

Table 2.4 Qualitative Evaluation of Multi-Criteria Options

#	Criteria Group	Group wt %	Criteria wt %	Criteria Weight Factor	Explanation of Ratings		Explanation of Minumim Requirements Whom	Minimum Pass/Fail Rating	Actual ratings (1–10) of Sourcing Options for What, When, Where & With			
					Rating 1	Rating 10			Option A In-source	Option B	Option C	Option D
i		G_i	W_i	$Z_i = G_i * W_i$					A_i	B_i	C_i	D_i
G1	Criteria Group 1	25%										
1	Criteria 1		20%	5.00%				6	6	8	6	5
2	Criteria 2		15%	3.75%				7	8	9	7	6
3	Criteria 3		20%	5.00%				6	6	8	8	6
4	Criteria 4		10%	2.50%				7	7	9	7	7
5	Criteria 5		35%	8.75%				6	6	8	8	6
			100%	$\Sigma G_i * W_i = 25\%$								
G2	Criteria Group 2	40%										
6	Criteria 6		15%	6.00%				6	6	8	8	5
7	Criteria 7		35%	14.00%				7	8	7	7	7
8	Criteria 8		50%	20.00%				7	7	9	8	8
			100%	$\Sigma G_i * W_i = 40\%$								
G3	Criteria Group 3	35%										
9	Criteria 9		20%	7.00%				6	7	8	7	6
10	Criteria 10		35%	12.25%				7	8	7	8	7
11	Criteria 11		30%	10.50%				7	8	8	7	6
12	Criteria 12		15%	5.25%				6	6	9	8	7
			100%	$\Sigma G_i * W_i = 35\%$								
		100%		100.00%								

Total Composite Score of a Sourcing Option >>>

$\Sigma Z_i * A_i$ = 7.11	$\Sigma Z_i * B_i$ = 8.05	$\Sigma Z_i * C_i$ = 7.52	$\Sigma A_i * D_i$ = 6.63
Baseline	Select	Back-up	Discard

Each of these parameters reflects on different aspects of the financial implications of the sourcing options. Net Present Value is the most common means of comparing different sourcing options since, unlike some other parameters, it reflects on all current and future annual cash flows and also takes into account the opportunity cost of capital. A simplified sample worksheet comparing multiple sourcing options is shown in Table 2.5. All assumptions made while comparing 'optimal sourcing' options should be clearly stated upfront. In addition, extensive sensitivity analyses of effects of variations in critical assumptions on relative merits of multiple options should be carried out. While comparing the responses of service providers to RFPs, it should be ensured that all responses are compared under the same set of assumptions of transaction volume growth, service level requirements and so on.

3 Best practices for value maximisation

In spite of best intentions and extensive preparation, not all 'optimal sourcing' initiatives achieve all the planned objectives. Ultimately, the long-term success of a company in achieving planned business objectives from any offshore sourcing initiative hinges on its ability to manage the distant relationship across multiple time zones with significant differences in business environment and culture.

In order to maximise value and mitigate risks from any offshore sourcing initiative, it is necessary to adopt and follow a methodology for proactive management of the entire sourcing lifecycle (Figure 2.1). There is sufficient literature in the public domain[1, 2, 11, 23] detailing best practices to be followed during outsourcing initiatives in general. Following are a few of the critical best practices that can be adopted to avoid common pitfalls *unique to 'offshore sourcing' initiatives*:

3.1 Understand

- Treat offshoring as a strategic initiative with extensive executive (CXO and XVP) level involvement. Offshore visits by executive sponsors to see the ground realities help sensitise them to rational decision-making.
- Understand that optimal offshoring initiatives can and should also have on-site/onshore components.

3.2 Plan

- Since cost benefits of offshore sourcing may be easier to prove than onshore outsourcing, greater emphasis during value assessment should be on maintaining or enhancing quality, productivity, customer satisfaction, data security, IP protection and risk mitigation.
- Do not underestimate the contributions that experienced third party advisers, including sourcing strategy consultants, financial advisers and

Table 2.5 Financial Analysis of Sourcing Options

Sourcing Options >>>	Option A On-site–In-house (As Is)					Option B Offshore Sourcing Vendor B				
Year >>>	Year 0	Year 1	....	Year N	Total	Year 0	Year 1	....	Year N	Total
Annual business process costs										
Direct costs										
Indirect costs										
Contract related costs										
Business unit costs										
Planning										
Training										
Business reengineering etc.										
Intangible costs										
Project cancellation										
Scope creep										
Requirements/schedule changes etc.										
Total costs										
Total costs in today's $										
Tangible benefits										
Quality improvements										
Productivity improvements etc.										
Intangible benefits										
New revenue opportunities										
Market share growth opportunities etc.										
Total benefits										
Total benefits in today's $										
NET of costs & benefits										
NET in today's $										
Net present value (NPV)										
Total cost of ownership (TCO)										
Return on investment (ROI)										
Payback period (months)										

Table 2.3 Financial Analysis of Sourcing Options ■ *continued*

Sourcing Options >>>	Option C Offshore Outsourcing Vendor C				Option D Offshore Insourcing			
Year >>>	Year 0	Year 1	....	Year N	Total	Year 0	Year 1	....	Year N	Total
Annual business process costs								
Direct costs								
Indirect costs								
Contract related costs								
Business unit costs								
Planning								
Training								
Business reengineering etc.								
Intangible costs								
Project cancellation								
Scope creep								
Requirements/schedule changes etc.								
Total costs								
Total costs in today's $								
Tangible benefits								
Quality improvements								
Productivity improvements etc.								
Intangible benefits								
New revenue opportunities								
Market share growth opportunities etc.								
Total benefits								
Total benefits in today's $								
NET of costs & benefits								
NET in today's $								
Net present value (NPV)								
Total cost of ownership (TCO)								
Return on investment (ROI)								
Payback period (months)								

lawyers can make. This is especially true if there is no sufficient prior experience and in-house capability for planning and implementing offshoring initiatives.

- Larger companies with previous offshoring experience should not exclude the consideration of 'offshore insourcing' and 'offshore co-sourcing' options in their 'globally optimal sourcing' initiatives.
- Companies without significant offshoring experience should shy away from the big bang approach and instead pursue the 'low-hanging fruit' strategy-phased (incremental or piecemeal) approach starting with stable, low-risk and well-documented processes requiring minimal oversight.

3.3   Source

- Location and supplier due diligence are even more crucial for offshore sourcing since the legal environment, geopolitical risks, infrastructure capabilities, business culture and work ethics are often significantly different from those on shore.
- Spread risks across two or more locations if feasible. Sourcing from multiple service providers depends on many factors including transaction volumes, qualifications of service providers and achievable benefits on the cost–quality–productivity–security fronts.
- Offshore suppliers with onshore subsidiaries can provide better relationship management and more robust contracts (say, US to US contracts) based on familiar local laws.
- Develop a mutual sense of partnership during the sourcing phase itself. Exploring local culture together – food, movies, festivals, monuments and so on – can go a long way in building a rapport that will be crucial during the governance phase.
- Plan for additional hidden ongoing expenses such as travel expenses, redundant infrastructure, communication costs and so on.
- Ensure that the contract spells out the process, costs and support requirements for the transition at the end of the contract (revamping) with all three possibilities in mind – renewal of the contract with some changes, transfer of services to another service provider and bringing offshored operations back on shore (begin with the end in mind).
- Incorporate sufficient flexibility in the contracts for changes in business environment including scope and transaction volumes.
- Define clearly the right (if any) of either party to walk away and its impact on finances and transition support requirements.

3.4   Transition

- Transfer of fewer, if any, resources (employees and infrastructure) to the offshore service provider should be proactively countered with more extensive training of service provider's resources, management of infrastructure and documentation and prototyping of processes.

- Plan for access to requisite systems and software from Day 1.
- Pay special attention to intellectual property/privacy protection, data security, disaster recovery planning and international laws for cross-country transfer of sensitive data such as patient's health records.

3.5 Operate

- Remember that offshore does not mean off the radar screen of management. Proactive management of internal inputs to and performance of service provider deliverables by qualified and well-trained internal resources is mandatory.
- Put in place processes for frequency, format and scope of synchronous (meetings, telephone calls, videoconferences) and asynchronous (fax and emails) communications, and guidelines for response times and documentation of issues raised and decisions made in informal communications.
- Proactively address communication gaps arising from cultural differences. In some eastern cultures, supervisor – subordinate or customer – service provider relationships hinder communication of bad news or difficulties in implementing infeasible suggestions of the boss/customer.
- Retain the authority to approve critical changes in resources (people, processes and infrastructure) of offshore service provider.
- Plan for changes in incentives, working hours and after-hours availability of on-site/onshore resources to interact with their offshore counterparts.
- Integrate the delivery of offshore and in-house teams to ensure seamless service delivery to end users and customers.

3.5.1 Application of lean manufacturing principles

Principles of lean manufacturing, such as those described below, can be as valid for repetitive servicing of standardised processes with well-defined steps[24] as they are for repetitive manufacturing of products on an assembly line:

- Placing linked processes near one another rather than in separate functional departments eliminates idle time between processes and delays in transferring paper work.
- Standardising procedures such as formats of documentation and locations of file storage avoids idiosyncrasies of individual choices and reduces training requirements as well as productivity losses during coverage in one another's absence.
- Eliminating loop-backs avoids having the same employee process the same transaction/item twice and thus also avoids confusion and idle time.
- Setting a common pace ('tact' time) reduces idle time further downstream in the processing cycle and enables performance measurement of individual team members.

- Balancing loads evenly amongst teams reduces process delays and allows for comparison of team performance.
- Segregating complexity helps reduce the turnaround time for simpler cases/transactions and enables establishment of complexity-based performance standards for different teams.
- Posting performance results in common areas encourages productivity improvements through competition and identifies weaker links for further training.

Application of such lean manufacturing principles can thus reduce processing time, rework, idle time and other inefficiencies, thereby, enhancing productivity and competitiveness of business processes. They also force adoption of customer-centric performance standards (the person next in the processing chain being the customer) and help streamline the process before potential automation in the future.

3.6 Revamp

- Start planning for the revamping phase about six months to a year before the end of the contract.

4 Evolving trends in offshoring

Offshoring of business processes and IT services has evolved very rapidly over the past decade as a strategic and tactical management tool and is inevitable and irreversible for creating globally competitive service delivery capability to serve increasingly global customer base of growing corporations. Gartner reports that by the end of 2004, 80 per cent of companies will have held high-level discussions about offshore sourcing while 40 per cent of companies will have already completed some pilot programmer or will be actually using nearshore or offshore services. Some of the critical emerging trends in offshore sourcing are briefly summarised below:

- **Distinction between BPO and ITO will disappear.** In the past, this distinction between business process and IT outsourcing was supplier-induced (based on their delivery capabilities) rather than customer-driven and hence will not be sustainable. The focus in the future will be on the delivery of integrated end-to-end process solutions requiring competing service providers to collaborate to meet the divergent needs of a client.
- **Mid-market offshoring will emerge.** The success of larger corporations with offshore sourcing has sensitised mid-size companies to its potential benefits and challenges. Over the next five years, mid-size companies will shed their psychological barriers to loss of control and explore offshoring possibilities with greater vigour.

Offshoring service providers that can evolve business models and processes in line with smaller transaction volumes of mid-size customers will benefit the most as the critical mass of offshoring from mid-size companies evolves. This evolution will require innovative financial models, and higher levels of maturity, standardisation and automation of offshored processes as well as sourcing lifecycle management processes. Selling to the price-sensitive mid-size companies will also require smarter consultative pitching of the 'value' of offshoring beyond lower costs.

Initially, mid-size companies will more likely go for offshore *outsourcing* rather than for offshore *insourcing or joint ventures*, considering their limited exposure to offshore sourcing and lack of mature internal processes, infrastructure and resources to manage the same. For the same reasons, they may rely on third-party advisers to a greater extent (than their *Fortune 500/Global 1000* counterparts) to manage their early ventures in offshoring.

- **Outsourcing backlash and restrictive legislation will slowly dissipate.** Even the 2004 election-year media hype in the US about offshoring has only helped increase its awareness among executives. Eventually, politicians and affected employees will realise that, in free-market societies, global competitors not affected by restrictive legislations of a state or a nation can create a potentially sustainable advantage for themselves relative to their competitors affected by such legislation. This threat alone will prompt affected companies to relocate to areas without such restrictions on their ability to effectively compete in the global environment. This can result in even worse dislocation of jobs than proactive enhancement of skill sets to move up in the value chain. Just as water has the tendency to seek sea level, businesses look for globally competitive cost-structures while serving their global customer base. No one has yet built a dam big enough to hold all water at high altitudes and the global economics of offshoring will be no exception.

- **Disappearance of service jobs due to automation will be a much bigger phenomenon** around the world in the coming decades than the job losses in the service sector due to offshoring. Automation has resulted in the loss of more than 10 million labour-intensive and repetitive jobs in manufacturing in the last decade alone.[25] Similarly, smart interconnected applications with embedded intelligence and collaboration capabilities will continue to automate (and hence replace) repetitive service functions such as directory assistance, customer service and Help Desk. As these 'servbots' (service robots) evolve and mature, they will replace even more service functions involving advisory functions, reference and interactive assistance.

- **Business process standardisation will spark a revolution in services sourcing** over the next decade, similar to the one ignited by interchangeability of components during the Industrial Revolution two hundred years ago. It will accelerate 'virtualisation' of corporations – converting cost centres of non-core functions at clients to profit centres of core functions at service providers. In the process, it will also make 'services outsourcing' more feasible for small and medium enterprises (SMEs).

- **Criticality of enterprise outsourcing strategy will be better appreciated.** Piecemeal outsourcing of interdependent business processes will suffer from lack of integration and can be more harmful in the end unless it is part of a well thought-out enterprise-wide outsourcing strategy.
- **Consolidation among service providers is unavoidable.** The offshoring market is highly fragmented but rapidly evolving from the service provider perspective. Considering the cost of presence in potential client locations (typically in the US and Europe) during the long sales cycles, and the cost of infrastructure, processes and resources required to support offshored processes and sourcing lifecycle management processes, the presence of some of the smaller players is not sustainable even in the near future. Smaller players with a viable business model or focus on niche markets will have to either build critical mass rapidly or be acquired by the bigger fish. The rest will simply fade away.
- **Improved management of offshoring lifecycle will come of age.** While maturity levels of offshored processes have evolved rapidly, those for managing the sourcing lifecycle itself have significant room for improvement. Fortunately, the migration from resource utilisation-based or process-based pricing to performance-based pricing will force service providers to enhance the maturity level of processes for managing offshoring lifecycle.

  Greater automation, live monitoring, instant reporting, automated alert triggering and proactive response systems will need to be embraced quickly by service providers to stay competitive and enhance the comfort level of clients wary of losing control. Software solutions and service portals for managing the supply chain of service delivery will evolve to provide the necessary infrastructure and tools.
- **On-Demand services will be in demand.** Service delivery as a pay-per-use business utility will evolve in the near future, providing further impetus to converting fixed plus variable cost structure of services to variable (volume/performance based) cost structure. Initiatives of larger service providers such as IBM ('e-business on demand') and HP ('adaptive infrastructure') are clearly accelerating this trend.
- **Offshoring of government services will remain minimal.** Offshoring of government services constitutes an insignificant fraction of global offshoring volume due to its implications to local politics. Considering the anticipated growth rate of offshoring of corporate business

processes and IT functions, any ban on offshoring of state or federal government services will have no material impact on the offshoring market as a whole. Local taxpayers, however, will either pay more taxes for government services or receive fewer services for their taxes.

Conclusion

Offshore sourcing of services is an irreversible trend that will grow even more rapidly over the next decade than in the past. When practiced as part of a 'globally optimal sourcing' strategy, offshoring has the potential to fundamentally change some of the existing facets of corporate structure and business models such as vertical integration. It will accelerate 'virtualisation' of corporations driven by a focus on core competencies and agility to serve an increasingly global customer base with a globally competitive service delivery capability.

Offshore sourcing can level the playing field among organisations of different sizes in the sense that it can enhance the agility of larger corporations (today, smaller companies, in general, are supposed to be more agile) while giving smaller companies the benefits of economies of scale (perceived today to be an advantage for larger companies with deeper pockets for capital investments).

Taking a strategic approach to 'globally optimal sourcing' of business processes and IT functions can help a corporation create a sustainable competitive advantage. On the other hand, failure to comprehend long-term implications of offshore sourcing trends can endanger its very existence in the end. The decision analysis process, best practices and emerging trends elucidated briefly in this chapter are meant to avoid such an eventuality.

Notes

1. M.F. Greaver, II, *Strategic Outsourcing: A Structure Approach to Outsourcing Decisions and Initiatives* (New York: American Management Association, 1999).
2. Rob Aalders, *The IT Outsourcing Guide* (Chichester, UK: John Wiley and Sons, 2001).
3. Daniel Minoli (1995) *Analyzing Outsourcing – Reengineering Information and Communication Systems* (New York: McGraw Hill Inc., 1995).
4. S. Elliott, (ed.), *Outsourcing: A Strategic Framework* (A Productivity Quality Center – APQC – Publication, 1997).
5. White Paper by Mayer Brown Rowe and Maw LLP, '*Outsourcing: Maximising Value and Avoiding Pitfalls*', retrieved on February 3, 2004 from http://www.mayerbrownrowe.com/Outsourcing/primer/index.as.
6. M.F. Corbett, '*Corbett's Core Competencies Test*', retrieved on September 3, 2001 from http://www.firmbuilder.com.
7. D. Davison for Meta Group, Inc. '*Offshore Outsourcing Subtleties: Outsourcing and Service Provider Strategies*', 13 March 2003.
8. Offshore Insights White Paper by neoIT, October 2003, '*Onshore versus Offshore Outsourcing: Significant differences require unique approaches*', retrieved on September 17, 2003 from http://www.sharedxpertise.org.

9. C. Ford and T. Newman for Alston & Bird, *Offshoring – the Pros and Cons of Outsourcing Abroad*, Sourcing Interest Group, retrieved on November 9, 2003 from http://www.sourcinginterests.org/ArticleReprints/OffshoringProsCons.htm
10. C.K. Prahlad and G. Hamel (1990) 'The Core Competence of the Corporation', *Harvard Business Review*, 68 (3) (1990) 79–91.
11. Queensland Government, Australia, *'The Queensland Government Guide to Best Practice in IT Outsourcing'*, Government Information and Communication Technology, June, 1997. Retrieved on January 7, 2004 from http://www.iie.qld.gov.au.
12. J.B. Quinn, 'Strategic Outsourcing: Leveraging Knowledge Capabilities', *Sloan Management Review*, Summer (1999) 9–21.
13. Bierce and Kenerson, P.C., 'What and when you should not outsource', retrieved on August 11, 2003 from http://www.outsourcing-law.com/articles/what-should-not-be-outsourced.asp.
14. M. Betts, 'Offshore Buyer's Guide', *Computer World*, September 15, 2003, retrieved on December 7, 2003, from http://www.computerworld.com/managementtopics/outsourcing/report
15. Customer Operations Performance Center, *'Release 3.3 – COPC-2000 CSP Gold Standard'*, retrieved on February 7, 2004 from http://www.copc.com.
16. The IT Services Qualification Center, *'The eSourcing Capability Model for Service Providers eSourcing Capability Model (eSCM-SP) v2'*, School of Computer Science, Carnegie Mellon University, retrieved on July 27, 2004 from http://itsqc.cs.cmu.edu.
17 T.L. Saaty, *'Multicriteria Decision Making – The Analytic Hierarchy Process'* (Pittsburgh: RWS Publications, 1992).
18. T.L. Saaty, *'Decision Making for Leaders'* (Pittsburgh: RWS Publications, 1992).
19. W. Edwards, 'How to use Multiattribute Utility Theory for Social Decision Making', *IEEE Trans. Systems Man*, Cybern. 7 (1997) 326–340.
20. R. Kamenetzky, 'The Relationship Between the Analytic Hierarchy Process and the Additive Value Function', *Decision Sciences*, 13 (1982) 702–716.
21. D. von Winterfeldt and W. Edwards, *'Decision Analysis and Behavioral Research'* (Cambridge: Cambridge University Press, 1986).
22. B. Redman, W. Kirwin, T. Berg for Gartner Group, Inc. RAS Services. 'TCO: A Critical Tool for Managing IT', 12 October 1998.
23. Excerpt from Sourcing Interest Group research report, 2003, 'Best Practices in Procurement Outsourcing', retrieved on October 2, 2003 from http://www.sourcinginterests.org.
24. C.K. Swank, 'The lean service machine', *Harvard Business Review*, October (2003) 123–129.
25. H. Cohen for Strategy Analytics, 'The Threat of Intelligent Capital', May 2004, retrieved from June 26, 2004 from http://www.strategyanalytics.com.

3

The Politics of Offshoring: Trends, Risks and Strategies

Paul Morrison

1 Introduction

The most striking result of the rapid growth of offshoring has been the noisy public controversy it has generated in the UK and US. For many executives, this is a source of exasperation as the 'offshore backlash' appears to them to have been driven by the wrong-headed whingeing of the economically illiterate. In my discussions with businesses considering offshore, I often detect a sense that a business should just 'get on' with doing business and let the concerns of the media, politicians and society evaporate as they get used to the idea of offshoring. Many of the fears about offshoring are indeed exaggerated, even sensationalised. But, a business would be well advised to take the offshore debate seriously.

Offshoring simply relates to the cross-border relocation of service activities – either in-house or outsourced. Globalisation in the extractive and manufacturing sectors has been around for a long time, so why is the offshore debate significant? To some extent, offshore is indeed 'business as usual'. The pioneers such as British Airways and General Electric have been 'offshoring' for decades, even if they labelled it as something else. Yet, as the globalisation of services gathers pace, it is clear that offshoring represents a profound revolution in how services are provided. Offshore redefines where business is done and how it is done opening up new opportunities and new risks along the way. These shifts in the status quo are too significant to occur uncontested.

Any look at past episodes in globalisation show that they have almost always been controversial – through union activism, customer boycotts, legislative restrictions or media controversy. The same friction has and will continue to affect offshoring – despite the controversy of recent months, the offshoring debate is not over. As the trend accelerates and broadens into new activities and industries, political and reputational skirmishes will continue to limit the boundaries and speed of offshoring strategy – whether the criticisms of offshoring are misguided or not.

The thesis of this chapter is simple: there are business benefits to understanding and addressing the wider concerns regarding offshoring. Many organisations have not embraced this approach, assuming that offshoring will simply become uncontroversial. This may turn out to be correct in the long term but it represents a poor risk management strategy. If the aim of your organisation is to develop a best practice global sourcing strategy from day one, you need to understand the offshore debate, its implications and the options that are available to address the risks.

2   Dissecting the offshore debate

In order to address the reputational risks posed by offshoring, an understanding of the key themes underlying the debate is essential. Offshoring first hit the headlines in late 2002 in the US and UK. During 2003, the volume of press stories, web chat and TV coverage grew substantially, and 'offshore' gained common currency as a term relating to the location of jobs and businesses – rather than oil rigs, wind farms or tax havens.

As with all complex controversies, the offshore debate has been driven by a web of interlinked issues – perceptions, events and concepts that bring the interests of different groups into conflict. The profile of offshoring can be partly explained by the fact that it overlaps so many different themes – including corporate strategy, corporate social responsibility, trade and investment policy, competitiveness, unemployment, education and skills, immigrant labour, national security, intellectual property, globalisation, international development, and developing country exploitation. But, in order to get an understanding of the major drivers of the offshore debate, a few recurring angles stand out – the economic impact, quality, security and exploitation.

2.1   The economic impact

The timing of the emergence of offshoring as a public issue in 2002 is significant. At that point in time, steady growth in global sourcing was coinciding with the prolonged economic fallout from the technology boom. This naturally focused attention on the dominant theme of the offshore debate – the question of the economic impact and, in particular, the jobs impact of offshoring.

Whether based on fact or speculation, the growing offshore trend was seen by many as a direct cause of the widespread layoffs that affected many business sectors particularly the information technology sector, from 2000 onwards. At a time of a perceived 'jobless recovery', press and TV coverage of offshoring in the US focused almost exclusively on the impact on employment. This is typified by the CNN 'Lou Dobbs Tonight' news programme which, has for several months, featured critical coverage of the economic impact of offshore projects. The CNN website features 'a list of companies we've confirmed are "Exporting America". These are U.S. companies either sending American jobs overseas or choosing to employ cheap overseas labour instead of American workers.'[1] In the UK, most of the early coverage of offshoring focused on the impact on the call centre industry, a dynamic sector that had grown rapidly from the 1990s, with particular significance in many poorer communities in post-industrial regions.

Other economic questions remain, particularly regarding the effect on higher value activities, the nature of 'next generation' service activities, and the 'hollowing out' of strategic sectors such as R&D, pharmaceuticals and biotechnology.

To some extent, the cruder 'jobs exodus' economic allegations against offshoring have receded, in the face of a growing body of analysis such as the research reports of McKinsey and Evalueserve that identify the net economic gains of offshoring.[2] Many observers are predicting an end to the offshore debate altogether as they perceive the US economy is emerging from its jobs slump. But even so, the tangibility and timing of the economic benefits of offshoring remain an issue. According to Alok Aggarwal, Chairman of Evalueserve, although 'high-wage countries will ultimately benefit from this trend, it is not yet known when these benefits will begin to accrue. Whether these benefits will trickle down to the working population or be restricted to wealthy shareholders is yet to be seen.'[3]

2.2 Quality

Quality of service has also been an important subject of contention. To offshore vendors, quality of service has long been a key marketing message. Quality accreditation was a major aspect in the building of India's credibility as an IT destination where, for example, adherence to rigorous CMM 'level 5' software development processes has been widely adopted.[4] As a result, many offshore strategies are now justified on the basis of the quality capabilities that can be accessed – not just on cost reduction. For Jonathan Chevallier, BPO Market Development Director of Xansa, the technology and business process outsourcing company, quality is a major issue: 'we all want good service and good products. If [offshoring] service quality is there, customers and investors will be happy.'[5] This mindset is reflected in the proliferation of other quality methodologies and standards such as Six Sigma, ISO and eSCM.

Yet, anecdotal accounts of poor quality from a range of offshore locations have been widely circulated in the media such as stories of bug-ridden IT development or poor customer service at call centres. The call centre quality debate has focused on questions of accent, cultural clash and lack of local knowledge despite the language neutralisation and induction training provided to call agents. In a widely cited story, it was claimed that a technical support help desk for Dell was recalled from an offshore location back to the USA, allegedly as a result of poor service quality.[6] Significantly, quality certification is not enough. According to Julie Rowden of Bluerock

Consulting, a management consultancy specialising in financial services: 'In the area of IT development, clients of Bluerock have noticed variable levels of quality from their offshore providers and between projects within the same provider, even where each provider is quality certified to the same level.'[7] As the economic controversy, the initial driving force behind the backlash, loses some of its potency, questions about quality of service have gained increasing prominence in the UK and US debates. Although cases remain isolated or anecdotal, these perceptions are powerful and widely held, as underlined by a number of market research reports. According to research by Intervoice, a voice-recognition software firm, three quarters of surveyed call centre managers have a negative perception of the quality of offshore call centres.[8]

2.3 Security and regulatory compliance

Concerns have also been raised about the security and data protection implications of offshoring. Offshoring shifts business activities to new jurisdictions but how well are the security requirements observed? Can offshore facilities meet the regulatory requirements of the European Data Protection Directive or Sarbanes Oxley section 404? Offshore facilities have aimed to address such concerns through extensive employee vetting, secure infrastructure, paperless offices and the rollout of standard global security technologies and processes.

Nevertheless, a number of stories about misconduct and the disclosure of sensitive financial or medical data have emerged in recent months, raising questions about the integrity of offshoring sensitive activities.[9] As a result, much public sector work will remain emphatically onshore, and private sector offshoring could face increasing regulatory requirements in the future. A significant amount of the legislative activity in the US currently focuses on tightening the security requirements for private sector offshoring. In America, these concerns have linked up with the issue of national security and the vulnerability of distributed global sourcing networks to terrorist sabotage.[10]

Sensitive to these perceived shortcomings, NASSCOM, the industry association for Indian software and service companies, has launched initiatives to identify and fill any potential security gaps.[11] And as Jonathan Chevallier notes, although 'it is important to continue to be compliant, there is also an element of raising the bar for offshore facilities' – for example, the electronic fingerprint recognition systems used for one Xansa financial services client in India are seen to be well ahead of the security systems in place at typical onshore BPO facilities.[12]

2.4 Exploitation

Finally, the offshore debate is being fuelled by the emotive issue of exploitation based on the idea that lower costs in offshore locations rely on poor working conditions. This theme has been highlighted by some union groups and builds on the anti-globalist thinking previously directed against extractive and manufacturing businesses. Of the four themes identified here, exploitation has been the least salient in the media, but as with other episodes in globalisation, it could gain potency with time.

Applying the 'sweatshop' label to offshoring could appear to be farfetched. Services generate theoretically 'clean' jobs. Offshoring firms often provide promotional videos and tours of their high-spec facilities. The large number of applicants for each vacancy also suggests that offshore jobs are often extremely attractive locally.[13] According to Silicon.com, 'Tata Consulting Services and Infosys Technologies Ltd., among India's largest IT services companies, had one million job applicants each in 2003 – and offered jobs to fewer than one percent of them.'[14] The leading service companies in India have high profile corporate social responsibility values and programmes, and their leaders are often highly respected social figureheads.

Yet, criticism of offshoring does not often extend to crude allegations of 'sweatshop' conditions. Instead, there has been a questioning of general levels of wellbeing and why, in some cases, standards appear to be lower than in the West. For example, the small size of workstation cubicles, excessive shift length or the 'psychological stress' for a call centre agent of maintaining a US-friendly persona are cited as examples of inappropriate pressure on offshore workers.

Indirectly, offshoring could also be discredited through association with the poor human rights record of a 'destination' country. For example, many predictions about the future of offshoring point to China, a country with a number of obvious human rights issues, not least of which is the poor levels of union representation which directly contradicts fundamental International Labour Organisation human rights conventions. In addition, in India, unions and international bodies such as Union Network International have made an issue of perceived low levels of unionisation, arguing this has been and will be a basis for exploitation.

The alleged mistreatment of employees, both those onshore and offshore, could also contribute to another perception – that offshoring is inconsistent with Corporate Social Responsibility (CSR) commitments. At a time when businesses are striving to demonstrate positive impacts on society, being seen to 'take advantage' of workers at home or abroad could certainly undermine an organisation's CSR credibility.

It is difficult to predict how the offshore debate will develop in the future but it seems highly likely that offshoring will remain controversial based on two rather obvious facts. Firstly, all analysts predict that offshoring will continue to grow in terms of *scale* – more companies will adopt it, in more countries (for example, France and Germany), on a bigger scale. Secondly, all the evidence indicates that the *scope* of offshoring is everwidening, moving up the value chain to more sophisticated activities such as design, journalism, legal services, equity analysis, accountancy and possibly also moving into previously out-of-bounds activities (notably in the public sector). This means that offshoring will continue to encounter new sets of vested interest. Every time offshoring advances, it will face debate, criticism and opposition.

2.5 Business risks

So, why is the offshore debate relevant to businesses considering new offshore plans? Exponents of the 'business as usual' school are correct in noting that despite the backlash offshore sourcing has been continuing to grow rapidly. But, even though the debate has not stopped or reversed offshoring, this does not mean it has had or will have no impact. *Perceptions will continue to determine how far and how fast offshoring grows.*

The questions raised by the offshore debate (such as unemployment, quality, security) are potentially significant issues for the company's stakeholders. In the case of offshoring, the three most important groups are employees, customers and government. These groups are the levers by which the debate becomes a real business risk – a business will face major problems if employees, customers or the government are opposed to such a strategy.

For *employees*, actual or imagined offshoring plans can generate fears about redundancy, loss of opportunity and long-term employability – even though an offshore strategy could be a crucial step in safeguarding a company's employment potential. This anxiety goes beyond damaging the motivation and productivity of employees working in departments that are transitioning work offshore. Uncertainty can spread amongst other areas, particularly where the scope and nature of the global sourcing strategy is poorly communicated. These issues could damage productivity, retention, recruitment and morale. In addition, more severe disruption could be caused by confrontation with unions through protests and strikes action. According to Marc Vollenweider, CEO of Evalueserve, many 'employees are likely to feel insecure and dissatisfied, leading to an increase in union activism, and which could result in an organisation-wide decline in productivity and service levels.'[15]

Regarding *customers*, offshoring could damage brand positioning and reputation. This could ultimately impact sales and profitability. If an offshore strategy were to be unpopular with consumers (for example, through a perceived impact on quality of service), it is not difficult to see some form of negative sales impact even without a coordinated consumer boycott. Offshoring could particularly undermine a brand with a strong emphasis on 'community' or 'national' values. For example, a retail chain or bank that has built up a reputation as a local, community-focused organisation could alienate customers if sourcing work from overseas were perceived as damaging to local employment prospects.

Politicians have the power to curtail offshoring via legislation and public policy. As with all multinational activity, offshoring is only possible because it is allowed to happen by a regime of national and international legal and political permissions. Both home and foreign governments have the ability to modify how or whether offshoring is conducted – using tools such as taxation, subsidies, new technical specifications, workforce standards or sectoral prohibitions.

2.6 Assessing the impact so far

So, if these are the potential levers of impact – employee, reputation or regulation – what has been their impact so far?

Regarding *employee relations*, there have been only a few examples of outright disruption caused by offshore plans.[16] Amongst unionised workforces, there were protests by the union Amicus at Prudential in late 2002, which later modified its plans to relocate activities to India.[17] BT was affected by similar protests in March 2003.[18] In the US, telecoms operator SBC faced four days of strikes by the Communication Workers Union of America (CWA) in May 2003, partly as a result of offshore issues.[19] Bank of America's plans to transfer facilities away from the Bay Area generated national and local press attention, heightened by the suicide of worker Kevin Flanagan apparently after losing his job and completing a 'knowledge transfer' with his offshore replacement.[20]

At the less conventional end of the spectrum, CWU launched a 'Pink Elephant' campaign against offshoring in mid-2003, and Amicus sang anti-offshore Christmas Carols outside Aviva's office in December 2003 – both with questionable impact.[21]

However, it should be noted that the degree of collaborative engagement between employers and unions has been more striking than any confrontation, particularly in the UK. This is illustrated by the Connect union's agreement with BT and by UNIFI's agreements with HSBC and Barclays (see case study box).

Looking beyond the union dimension, in private many executives continue to flag the employee relations impact of offshoring as a major headache – how can an offshoring strategy be effectively yet sensitively communicated to our workforce? How can I prevent an offshoring strategy demoralising our remaining onshore teams? The evidence for these issues is anecdotal, but unsurprisingly so, as employee anxieties are both qualitative and seldom disclosed in public. One source of information on this perspective is through employee and website chat rooms where offshoring has been a topic of very obvious concern.

Consumer attitudes have not yet significantly mobilised against offshoring. Blue-chip offshore clients are clearly concerned about how global sourcing could influence brand perceptions as indicated by the highly secretive nature of most offshore strategies. Most big brand organisations have chosen to keep a very low profile on offshoring and vendors complain in private about their inability to get client references for external marketing purposes.

In addition, a number of leading consumer brands such as Nationwide and Alliance & Leicester in the UK have publicly adopted 'non-offshore' positions, choosing instead to emphasise their commitment to local operations. For example, Phil Williamson, CEO of Nationwide, observed that his organisation has 'strong links to the communities in which we operate and we have no plans to desert these local communities in favour of overseas call centres'.[22]

A number of surveys suggest there is broad consumer disapproval about offshoring, for example, with the Lloyds TSB union suggesting that 55 per cent of Scottish customers would consider changing bank rather than having their accounts managed in India.[23] Despite such strident predictions, there is no evidence to indicate that this reaction has yet occurred. Exactly how 'onshore' strategies will play with consumers remains to be seen and many commentators view them as highly risky. According to financial analyst and writer Alpesh Patel, when a UK bank recently said 'they would not offshore, and tried to spin that as an act of caring and patriotism, all that happened was that they damaged their customers with poorer services and more costs, damaged their employees because job losses would follow to allow for the higher cost base, and damaged their shareholders because of the smaller return on equity'.[24]

The *legislative* dimension has been a focus of the offshoring debate in America where politicians have been quick to tap into widely-held concerns. There have been dozens of proposals against offshore, focused on measures such as the restriction of public contracts, new visa limits and 'right to know' proposals. In particular, Senator John Kerry has made an issue of offshoring in the 2003/4 Presidential campaign, lambasting 'Benedict Arnold' CEOs for undermining the US economy and proposing federal 'right to know' legislation to moderate offshoring. By April 2004, politicians in 36 states had introduced 100 bills to restrict outsourcing and offshoring with numerous initiatives at a federal level.[25]

Yet, despite this intense debate and lobbying, the enacted policy measures against offshoring have not been substantial. The one federal bill passed into law, the Thomas-Voinovich amendment (January 2004), only applies to Treasury and Transportation budgets, and it has been estimated to impact only an estimated one to two per cent of Indian offshoring revenues. The White House has followed an increasingly pro-offshore line, despite the controversial reception of Gregory Mankiw's Economic Report of the President published in February 2004.

Similarly, state level legislative activity has been noisy but limited, focusing in particular, on specific areas of public procurement. For example, the state of Indiana cancelled a $15.2 million contract with Tata Consultancy Services (TCS) in November 2003, requiring that the project be supplied by local vendors.[26] This was symbolically significant but not material in terms of overall offshoring flows.

Furthermore, the UK has seen no legislative activity at all. Relatively high levels of employment have reduced the political temperature regarding off-shoring and a strong free market argument has been widely broadcast by the government, both by the Department for Trade and Industry and the Prime Minister.

Yet, significant political intervention is not inconceivable. As off-shoring grows in new sectors (such as R&D or public services), there could be renewed pressure to redefine the boundaries of what should be sourced globally. Similarly, legislation in the US regarding security and

A recent Percept straw poll of business opinion gives a snapshot of corporate views on offshoring and the relative weight of concerns. Ninety per cent of respondents indicated that business was not doing enough to tackle the off-shore backlash and that it would continue to be a problem in the future. Heading the list of concerns, 87 per cent of respondents showed concern about the potential impact of offshoring on workforce morale. In addition, 57 per cent of respondents cited the potentialfor corporate brand/reputational damage, and 43 per cent identified the potential for damage of corporate social responsibility credentials (see Figure 3.1). Thirty-three per cent saw negative perceptions of offshore sourcing potentially damaging customer demand.[27]

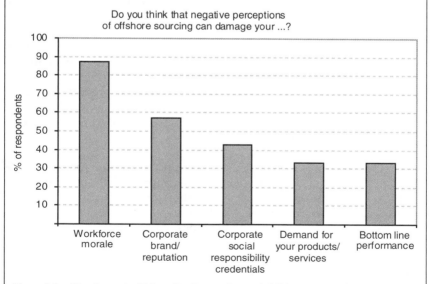

Figure 3.1 The Impact of Negative Perceptions of Offshoring
Source: Percept Risk & Strategy 'Offshore Perceptions 2004'

the requirements for offshore contractors to comply with Sarbanes-Oxley show that offshoring is still subject to political control. As a result, the political climate could yet hold back the offshore development of certain sensitive sectors and activities.

Drawing these three angles together at a macro level, the impact has so far been limited. Worker disruption has not been widespread; there is little evidence of sustained consumer activism on offshoring; anti-offshore legislative moves have been minor in scope. Although the offshore backlash has had a limited impact overall, individual companies are deeply concerned about avoiding potential damage and becoming 'flashpoint' companies. Offshoring has not been a systematically damaging reputational issue for business – but executives are nevertheless alert to the potential pitfalls. There remains scope for reputational damage and responsible business leaders are managing these risks accordingly.

2.7 Strategies

There are three basic choices for a business to handle the reputational risks of offshoring:

- Firstly, a company could delay or reject offshoring altogether. The popularity of this type of reaction is reflected in the extensive anecdotal evidence that offshore plans have been scaled back, delayed or cancelled, and by the 'pro-onshore' strategies adopted by some UK financial services organisations.
- Secondly, a company could choose to evade reputational issues by conducting 'offshoring by stealth'. This is no longer a viable strategy for many organisations, particularly global players or leading national brands. The low, first-mover profile of the pioneers of offshoring such as British Airways, General Electric and American Express is no longer available.
- Thirdly, a company can choose to understand and address the concerns of stakeholders systematically.

This final choice will be the only appropriate choice for most businesses in globalising industries. The specific approach will obviously vary significantly according to the type of offshoring, industry and the profile of the organisation. But, there will be a set of common considerations for any organisation considering developing or ramping up an offshore strategy:

1. Understand current and future stakeholder concerns

A systematic analysis of the perspectives of all stakeholder groups is an invaluable tool. This involves identifying all key stakeholder groups (such as employee, customer, media, regulator, community) and sub-groups and then mapping against each the relative importance of different offshore issues (such as security, quality, economic impact). This issue-stakeholder map can then form the basis for a plan of action to address the offshore debate. This tool should be dynamic as the make-up of your stakeholders and their concerns will evolve with time. Timing is critical: according to Xansa, 'It is very important to think about stakeholder strategy early, so as to mitigate the risks from the start.'

2. **Develop a plan for displacement management**
Offshore sourcing does not necessarily entail employee retrenchment. But, in the many situations where this is the case, carefully considered plans will dramatically reduce the potential disruption caused by offshoring – firstly, by avoiding displacement where possible and secondly, by supporting displaced workers where avoidance is not possible. Avoidance strategies include retraining, voluntary redundancy schemes and active redeployment programmes. Support strategies for displaced workers include retraining allowances, compensation and outplacement assistance. In addition to measures applicable to displaced individuals, consideration should also be given to communities where substantial numbers of redundancies could result in more systemic displacement problems. In such cases, liaison with local and national public bodies will be valuable.

3. **Make the case for offshoring**
Effectively communicating the rationale for offshoring is crucial. This is a complex task relying on a detailed understanding of the offshore plans, the perspectives of stakeholders and clear thinking regarding mitigating strategies for the potential downsides of offshoring. Communications need to combine a recognition of the concerns that offshoring can generate, with a clear dismissal of the 'myths' of offshoring and a reaffirmation of the company's core commitments – such as the development and welfare of the workforce as a whole. Communication should, of course, be in terms that are meaningful to the end audience (an employee communication should avoid the jargon that infests offshore business cases or the macro-economic terminology of the business press). But, at the same time, any realistic communication needs to underline the powerful business factors that drive offshoring. The mode of communication may well take a number of forms according to the audience in question (such as internal memos, speeches, articles, white papers and press releases). In many circumstances, it will be appropriate for your organisation to make use of industry associations as a collective voice but in all cases this should always complement, not replace, your own bespoke internal and external communications activities. By aiming

for communications that are clear, comprehensible and honest, you will be taking steps to minimise the scope for misunderstanding, anxiety and uncertainty, both inside and outside the organisation.

4. **Ensure the highest standards**

   Failure to comply with expected standards could be exploited by off-shore critics and result in significant reputational damage. Therefore, any offshoring plan will need to build in mechanisms for maintaining operational standards such as quality of service, security, business continuity and data protection. This applies equally to an in-house facility (via processes, methodologies and corporate culture) as an outsourced facility (via contractual and service level agreements). Service level expectations must be defined and monitored, both during transition and ongoing operation. Significantly, offshoring provides opportunities to realise major performance improvements rather than merely maintaining the same standards. According to Tim Lloyd, Managing Director of ALS Consulting: 'Going through the discipline of carefully defining then relocating processes can result in improved service levels and help businesses get to grips with new compliance issues like Sarbanes Oxley.'

5. **Align offshore plans with your CSR strategy**

   Given the significance of offshoring, both for groups in developed and developing countries, your CSR teams should be involved at an early stage to advise on the implications of different offshoring options. Ensure that the offshore rollout and operations do not compromise your CSR commitments such as minimum labour standards, environmental impact or (in the case of exit management) community support. This will involve audit activities to ensure compliance, consultation with local stakeholders (such as community groups and NGOs) and identification of strategies to mitigate negative local impacts such as changes to working patterns and pressures on traditional family life. Although the CSR angle of offshoring has not yet been widely scrutinised in public, it is likely that it will form an increasingly significant risk area, especially for leading brands.

Many executives will have skipped this chapter altogether. For those who have not, many may now be foaming at the mouth – surely all the above suggestions get in the way of 'just getting on with it?' However, I have tried to show that although there are a range of complex and deeply held concerns about offshoring, there are also practical options to help address the reputational risks. No doubt, the future will provide a rich case history illustrating where companies have clearly appreciated the reputation risks of offshoring – and where they have not.

Case Study 1: BT

BT was one of the first UK companies to experience an offshore backlash, despite long standing sourcing links with India. In 2002, BT announced plans to source several hundred call centre jobs from India following a period of rationalisation in BT's UK call centres. The Communication Workers Union (CWU) led to vocal protests across the UK in March 2003, falling short of strike action. The local and national press picked up the story with one tabloid labelling BT as 'British Delhicom' and others criticising the short-sightedness of offshoring.

This reaction quickly showed the emotive power of offshoring plans and emphasised the need for careful management of the issues. As well as engaging with the CWU, BT reached a significant agreement with Connect, the managerial union. This laid the basis for a more collaborative approach to offshoring, in which essentially BT undertook to avoid compulsory redundancies as a result of offshoring whilst making assurances regarding redeployment, consultation and ethical standards in offshore locations. In return, BT gained the positive involvement of Connect in the development of offshoring plans.

In addition, BT chose to openly explore the political and reputational questions raised by offshoring in a detailed whitepaper 'Good Migrations'.[28] Prepared independently, this was released in early 2004 and provided a social impact assessment of offshoring both in the UK and India. By recognising stakeholder issues, it provided a detailed appraisal of global sourcing contrasting sharply with the 'offshore by stealth' approach adopted by many other businesses.

Case study 2: Barclays

One of the UK's leading banks, Barclays Bank announced in January 2004 that it had reached a major agreement with the union UNIFI to work collaboratively on offshoring 'designed to minimise job losses and the consequent impact on people and communities, which will result as Barclays continues to reshape its business'.[29]

Barclays and UNIFI reached agreement on a range of activities including a redeployment programme, a £2 million fund to provide training for displaced employees, outplacement support, plus an agreement that all staff whose jobs are potentially to be offshored will be given 3 months advance notification of potential displacement plus another three months if they are actually displaced. In order to minimise compulsory redundancies, the agreement also included provision for a 'voluntary redundancy register' and 'job matching' to be administered by an HR team at an annual cost of £250,000. In addition, Barclays agreed to provide clear visibility of its global sourcing plans, providing full details on new offshoring projects at least six months in advance.

Regarding the question of exploitation in developing countries, Barclays repeated its commitment to the human rights standards of the UN Universal Declaration of Human Rights and the ILO conventions and agreed to refer to these standards as part of a third party supplier evaluation process.

Significantly, this deal was in place in advance of significant offshoring plans that where announced in June 2004 in which Barclays outsourced several hundred application development jobs to the technology consultants Accenture. In part, as a result of this proactive engagement policy, the announcement was accompanied by limited media interest unlike the criticism that has greeted similar announcements by some of Barclay's high street competitors.

Notes

1. CNN website: http://www.cnn.com/CNN/Programs/lou.dobbs.tonight/.
2. McKinsey Quarterly, 'Who wins in offshoring?', 2003 (Number 4); Evalueserve-Nasscom report, 'Impact of Global Sourcing on the UK Economy 2003–2010', 2004.
3. From correspondence with the author, July 2004.
4. The Capability Maturity Model®, devised by the Carnegie Mellon Software Engineering Institute.
5. From an interview with the author, August 2004.
6. Computerworld, 'Signs of offshore backlash growing', Ryan B. Patrick. See http://www.computerworld.com/managementtopics/outsourcing/.
7. Correspondence with the author, July 2004.
8. The Economist, 'Now hiring', 27 May 2004.
9. The Guardian, 'Calls for outsourcing inquiry as Capital One drops Indian firm', Heather Tomlinson, 26 March 2004.
10. For example, see CIO magazine, 'Should We Outsource Programming to Less-Than-Friendly Nations?', 9 Jan 2003. See http://comment.cio.com/soundoff/010903.html.
11. For example, see http://www.nasscom.org/trustedsourcing.asp.
12. From an interview with the author, August 2004.
13. 'The fact that there is a long queue of highly trained graduates hoping to join the industry would appear to mitigate the sweatshop allegation. Progeon claim to have over 20,000 graduates in their recruitment pipeline at any one point in time.' Julie Rowden, Bluerock Consulting, correspondence with author, July 2004.
14. Silicon.com website, 'Offshoring dos and don'ts', Bundeep Singh Rangar, 8 July 2004.
15. From correspondence with the author, July 2004.
16. But the economic impact of sourcing work overseas to India is no stranger to controversy. As long ago as the late seventeenth century, English commentators lambasted merchants for sending increasing quantities of cloth to the subcontinent to be finished, for fear of undermining England's industrial base. See David Landes, *The Wealth and Poverty of Nations* (Abacus, London), 1998, p. 228.
17. ComputerWeekly.com, 'Legal action on Pru's India deal may stall outsourcing', Nick Huber, 3 October 2002. See http://www.computerweekly.com/Article116283.htm.
18. ZDNet UK, 'Workers protest over call-centre outsourcing', Andrew Swinton, 20 March 2003. See: http://news.zdnet.co.uk/.
19. Reuters News, 'SBC, Union Reach Deal After 4-Day Strike', Justin Hyde, 25 May 2004.
20. The Economic Times, 'Outsourced: Death in Silicon Valley', Chidanand Rajghatta, 27 May 2003.
21. See http://news.bbc.co.uk/1/hi/business/3329807.stm.
22. Nationwide Press Release, 'Nationwide says no to sending call centres abroad', 12 January 2004.
23. Lloyds TSB Union News Release, 'MORI poll attracts extensive media interest', May 2004. See: http://www.saveukjobs.com/news.php.
24. From correspondence with the author, July 2004.
25. National Forum for American Policy, 'Exporting the Law: A legal analysis of state and federal outsourcing legislation', Shannon Klinger and M. Lynn Sykes, April 2004. See http://www.nfap.net/.

26. The Economic Times, 'India alarmed by Indiana's cancellation of software deal', K.C. Krishnadas, 11 December 2003.
27. Percept Risk & Strategy, straw poll of offshore perceptions, 2004. Percept contacted 200 organisations in the six months to June 2004. 30 responses were received from US and UK business leaders, policy makers and think tanks.
28. See http://www.btplc.com/Societyandenvironment/.
29. Barclays press release, 'Barclays and UNIFI announce offshore agreement', 5 January 2004. See http://www.newsroom.barclays.com/news/data/927.html.

4
Offshoring: Hidden Benefits and Hidden Costs
Paul Davies

1 Introduction

It is relatively easy to stumble badly when working with India and not only because of the cultural differences and the different approach to business. In addition to these real twin perils, you will find that there are any number of hidden costs and business issues that will hit you unexpectedly. If you aren't prepared properly and the hidden costs do strike home, then, the undoubted similarly hidden benefits of working with India will pale into insignificance.

You may be partly prepared for the existence of hidden costs by the various stories about working offshore which are becoming urban myths. While you are getting to understand the offshore world, you will probably often hear that all the business processes that went overseas are coming back to the West. The unstated presumption will be that this is happening because the promised benefits didn't materialise and the hidden costs defeated everything people tried to do. You may even find people who will quite authoritatively state that data protection is such a huge and undefined problem that no one can actually deal with it effectively. If that doesn't scare you, there are people who proclaim that your domestic employment legislation will follow you to the ends of the earth with disastrous results. You may even hear horror stories of people getting the service they specified but with calamitous results as their specification was so full of holes.

As with all urban myths, there is probably at least a grain of truth behind every story, especially the latter one, in just the same way that inevitably some Indian call centre workers must watch the odd western soap so that they can chat authoritatively to western clients although it is pertinent to observe here that I have yet to meet a westerner who has ever done so. Yet, these examples of the generation of fear, uncertainty and doubt (the well-known FUD factors) are not what should be in the forefront of your mind when contemplating going offshore to India. The real hidden costs are worth examining in detail as a preparation to realising the equally real hidden benefits of going offshore.

Some of these hidden costs will seem obvious once they have been introduced but it is worth saying that many companies have gone offshore without the first thought about at least some of them. If we remember that ordinary, domestic outsourcing projects often fail (up to 50 per cent according to the industry analysts, Gartner), and that there are a good deal more variables going offshore, it won't be surprising that the failure rate can be even higher going to India.

For obvious commercial reasons, you will not hear much about specific companies who suffer these failures, with the added fact that companies are so sensitive about offshoring now, that you rarely hear about the successes either.

2 Hidden costs

I look at a range of examples of hidden costs here. Though it isn't exhaustive, it is firmly based on experience. I first cover what many companies find a surprising paradox that the procurement department often runs into, then one example of how costs can run away in the selection process, some issues with travel costs, an unexpected result of using expatriates, the gap between training and production, recruitment for service centres, the siren-like qualities of pilots offshore, and making proper allowance for the effects on your existing staff when you decide to go offshore. Finally, I look at the potential for avoiding hidden costs by having a sourcing strategy (not just a strategy to source some work offshore), the effects of your internal political issues on costs, and I take a look at drawing up the right specification – partly as an introduction to the hidden benefits.

2.1 A procurement paradox

In any offshore exercise for a company of any size whatsoever, you will quite properly find your procurement department involved. There are two aspects of the way your procurement department will behave that lead to hidden costs here and although they sound contradictory at first, they are, in fact, complimentary. They are rooted in a paradox that says that what you immediately feel comfortable with should not be trusted, though it is immediately attractive because it seems so normal.

Your procurement department will not initially know much about going offshore or specific country issues. Many, but not all, of your potential Indian suppliers will know a great deal about western procurement practices. Out of this apparent contradiction, have come many unforeseen mistakes.

The result is that your procurement department will set out to tackle an apparently difficult task but one that misleadingly will appear in practice as quite straightforward with an obvious answer when they deal with Indian companies that major on what appeals to western business people. Against that, if they encounter Indian companies that are not so well versed in appealing to western business prejudices, they will find it extraordinarily difficult to appreciate and differentiate between such companies and the tendency is to go with what they feel safe with, rather than the best company for the job. When they are presented with a company that seems to be very normal and comfortable and just what your procurement department is used to, the result is usually predictable and, equally usually, unsatisfactory.

The first important hidden cost in any offshore procurement is therefore either to train members of your procurement department in how to deal with what is an alien business culture or employ a consultancy which is experienced in dealing with these issues. Cynics will also, probably rightly, explain that even selecting just the right consultancy for your business is an extra additional cost, and if the cost isn't apparent in money terms, it will be in time and that is often just as important.

If you don't either train your procurement staff in the way to address the differences in going offshore or use bought in expertise, you will find that your selection process, no matter how apparently objective, strategic and inexorable, will not give you the results you want. It will, however, give your potential Indian suppliers who are aware of how procurement works in the West what they want and your procurement people will feel that they have done a good job, perhaps regardless of the actual outcome.

This example illustrates a real truth about many of the hidden costs and issues in going offshore. If you always keep in the back of your mind that offshore companies probably understand you better than you understand them, you will have a much better perspective and approach. To summarise this, you need to be able to see the difference between a company that has worked hard to understand you in order to provide you with just the right solution for your needs and a company that will just tell you what it knows you will find easy to hear and appreciate. This might seem no different from your experience with potential suppliers in your domestic market. It is quite different in quality, however, once you see how attractive and compelling the latter proposition will seem in contrast.

On any number of occasions, I believe that I have more than earned my consultancy fees just by being able to demonstrate to my western clients what is actually happening in front of their eyes and ears as opposed to what they are perceiving.

2.2   Casting a wide and expensive net

Another hidden cost – often hidden because it doesn't figure in the budget properly as it occurs too early in the process – also relates to the selection of an Indian supplier or partner. For many years, I have focused on the criteria for selecting a supplier as selecting one across cultures is so fraught with difficulties. Do not be tempted, however, to cast your net wider and wider when faced with the difficulty of choosing a supplier or partner in the belief that by doing so you will reduce risk. You will only pile cost on cost.

There is a real example of a western insurance company that started by seriously considering over 200 suppliers – after deskwork had reduced the list to that number. This is obviously absurd. Yet, any number of major western companies have abandoned the approach that they would apply onshore and created short lists of 20. I have come to the conclusion that this means that the western company doesn't trust Indian companies and also doesn't trust its ability to select. There are simpler and much more cost-effective ways of going through this process.

The insurance company example above was actually worse than it looks because this in-country exercise only kicked in after an exhaustive process of identifying the right country that had selected India.

If you can't trust your own normal processes to select the right supplier or your judgement because you find the business culture so challenging, abandoning common sense and going for such extensive and expensive assessments won't help, though it might seem reassuring at the time. You may well be right to be wary, if only for my first reason above, but throwing money at the wrong problem won't help and the hidden cost can be enormous. It might seem too obvious to say that if you feel at all uncomfortable, take advice, but my example above is real and it clearly wasn't obvious to the insurance company.

2.3 Some extra travel costs

A large cost in offshoring, and one that will not immediately appear to be hidden, is travel to your offshore country. The reason why it becomes a hidden cost is that it is so often under-estimated. Western business people's travel and subsistence costs, in even, say, India, are such that it doesn't take much extra travel for your original budget to look decidedly optimistic. This is, of course, without considering opportunity costs associated with your people being out of the office.

Rather than detail the way that extra travel usually builds up, which are fairly obvious, let me look at ways of mitigating those extra costs. There are some straightforward and legitimate approaches that will immediately save you money such as for example, buying air fares in India. The cost differential is surprisingly large. If, for example, you have two return journeys to make in a limited time, buy the middle trip in India. While this type of tactic is worthwhile, it is best to take a more strategic approach to reducing travel costs and, incidentally, budgeting for them properly in the first place.

The following advice may appear hardly incisive but I have found that prudent company after prudent company has fallen into this trap when dealing with India when it would never happen in the European or American market. Try above all to avoid *ad hoc* trips. Inevitably, during any project, they will become what the project team calls essential but you have procedures for dealing with this in the normal way. Because India is so different, reason can be overwhelmed relatively easily and you will find such trips building up.

The trips are usually very expensive, not only because you have to buy the tickets at short notice but because they are incredibly disruptive. You will find that while someone is offshore putting out some forest fire, other problems will build up at home. You will lose time and you will lose momentum. You will know how disruptive such events can be if you have ever outsourced a project in your home market. Going offshore multiplies the costs and the bad effects, and yet going offshore seems to make them more easily justified. In truth, my experience is that the opposite is the case.

In your planning phase you will have to make some allowance for these trips but, much more importantly, you may find that my experience can help reduce them to the minimum. Once your in-house project team has worked out what it is doing and how it will do it, that is a good time to make a team trip. It may not be appropriate for your circumstances but I have seen an apparently huge up-front cost for a team visit pay dividends. These largely come from the shared understanding that is usually created that will reduce the need for unexpected trips. That doesn't change across cultures though the apparently high initial cost may make you forget it.

I made the point about budgeting properly for this cost line. Whatever you do, don't turn an expected and important overt cost into a hidden one by underestimating how much travel will inevitably cost. You should allow something over $7000 per week, including business class air fares and subsistence, for a trip. I am by nature a pessimistic business planner and always try to allow for more travel than seems reasonable. If you take a more optimistic view of travel requirements, you won't need many surprise trips to ruin your budget.

2.4 An expatriate trap

Having expatriates in a country is often rightly seen as a requirement and it won't look like a hidden cost as it will appear quite properly in your projected budget. It will often become a hidden cost as it, too, will usually be more expensive than it looks. This is not because, for example, real estate rents are very high in the main cities and the metros, as this can be allowed for. The hidden costs are actually subsidiary to that and insidious in my experience. Let me give but one real example. Having that one person, even if absolutely essential, will provide a magnet with inevitable results. He or she will have to be reviewed. He or she will need back up. There will be any number of reasons why a trip is necessary and some of these will be genuine and valid, and the trips will not be *ad hoc* but they will build up into huge costs. The first answer is not to underestimate the extra travel that will be generated by having your own person on-site.

2.5 Training and productivity

There are other costs that also become hidden costs if they are not properly appreciated. You will readily understand them but even so, these can easily move from open costs to hidden costs. Training, for example, will be obviously important, and you will probably, very happily, concentrate on training people in your processes and procedures and, to some extent, appreciate that you have to train people to understand your domain issues. Translating that training into productive work will broadly take the same amount of time as in your home country. One domestic call centre that I was associated with, focused on technical support, and the training programme lasted two months. Becoming properly productive took another six weeks of hard work on the phones.

The difference offshore is that while those time scales will remain broadly similar for a technical environment, a service centre will take an increased time from finishing formal training to on the job productivity. This will be masked to some extent by the more highly qualified people that will probably be taking on your tasks offshore. They will make astonishing initial progress but you will find that the moment when real productivity is achieved and the time when hidden benefits start to accrue takes longer than onshore.

2.6 Recruitment for service centres

Look carefully at recruitment costs, too, whether these are direct costs to you or indirect costs, especially since these may impact on your costs in an unexpected way. Recruitment in the Indian information technology world is slick and brilliant, relying on networks of people who can find the right skills quickly. It works astonishingly well. Indians engaged in business process outsourcing themselves typically assume that the same recruitment capability lies in this new world, and you may find that this is an aspiration rather than a reality. Although providing the right staff quickly enough has rarely been an issue in the software development environment, it has proved quite an issue in setting up business processes and has cost more time than might be expected.

My advice is always to be wary about projected recruitment costs for call centres and other business processing environments. Allow a good contingency in your business plan for recruitment as it can often cause big surprises.

Your supplier may well have all the right skills and capabilities but do not overestimate the ability of your supplier, even if they are experienced in this area, to identify the right sort of recruits. It will be more of a cost to you but do take the lead with your supplier and provide more help with job profiles and descriptions of skills that are needed than you might expect. While the immediate cost may seem high, this can quickly be quite a substantial cost – and it is often hidden even during the development of a project.

2.7 Dropping the pilot

A further hidden cost here is the propensity to believe in pilots offshore and pilots that have to build up slowly. If you are offshoring a process that works – to whatever extent – think carefully about whether you will need a pilot. I am sure they must have a use. I just haven't found one for a pilot where there is an existing process or service. You will find overtly risk-averse companies go in for them but they are much more expensive than going live with a full service. They seem to me just to be a hidden cost that is thought necessary by project managers to protect the project manager's continuing career. I am perhaps too cynical but regard any request for a pilot with a jaundiced eye. You will usually also find that the cost of the pilot will not have been properly allowed for, especially since they generate the need for extra trips, but that is a different issue.

2.8 And then, morale

In your own country the hidden costs of outsourcing will often be related to the costs that you will have allowed for but not allowed for enough. Once again the answer is to look searchingly at your assumptions. Most business people moving jobs offshore will understand the costs involved in making people redundant or in retraining staff in new areas of business. The hidden cost here usually arises from the effect on morale and productivity. If you do nothing about this effect, you will suffer from reduced customer satisfaction which may lead to a decline in revenues, poorer quality, work being done twice or more or any combination of effects that a disenchanted work force can create. The opposite way of dealing with this issue will also cost money – probably less than the unmitigated effects – and will still often be a hidden cost.

Whatever solution you use, whether it is, for example, paying terminal bonuses for a good handover or putting in place a retraining programme, you will have to think carefully about this cost. Do not ignore, for example, the effects on the people who – perhaps for the moment, at least in their own minds – are not immediately directly affected because they are working in a completely different department. You may find that your attrition and recruitment costs go up elsewhere in your business and while that won't necessarily figure in the project's budget, this will inevitably hit your bottom line.

The second hidden cost related to this, that very often becomes a very public and damaging cost, is closely related to the first. There may well be a backlash amongst the local community. There may be a resistance amongst customers to dealing with an offshore processing centre. I suspect this is, as yet, more of an urban myth than reality but it may happen. Ignoring a potential public relations disaster, and they have been real enough, will be expensive. Anticipating it and mitigating its effects will also cost money. In a number of well-publicised cases these costs have been rather higher than anyone inside the company had reckoned on. Whatever else you do, don't let this be a hidden cost.

2.9 A sourcing strategy

You will also need to budget for a contingency plan, perhaps, for example, leaving enough of a remnant of your process in your domestic market so that you can, in an emergency, provide some service locally. You might want to have the option of rebuilding your service provision if all goes wrong offshore, either through incompetence or through matters, like a natural disaster, beyond anyone's control. Remember it might be cheaper to build a disaster recovery site offshore but still extra cost will come into this.

What is required here, and only you can say whether this is a cost to be attributed to any one project, is a sourcing strategy which will be a necessary cost if you are going offshore. One reason is that you will encounter all manner of nostrums. You will find, for example, people who say authoritatively that no more than a certain percentage of any process should go offshore. When I have questioned these statements I have found that they are usually based on a specific example from which some general rule has been extrapolated. I don't think there are hard and fast rules here – but it is important to know how much you can put offshore without creating risk of not being able to service your customers.

2.10 The corporate political dimension

Another real hidden cost that even some of the best regulated companies suffer from domestically, and which often remains hidden because it is not apparently part of the project, is the internal politics that will surround any offshore project. You will find those who are implacably opposed to it, some of whom may be worried that it will be successful. You will find those who are zealots for the project, and some of those will be worried that it might fail and they will be associated with it. There will be shifting alliances in between. In my experience these political issues are far more costly when engaged in an offshore project, probably because the potential rewards or levels of blame are more pronounced. As in your domestic operations, you will have to be aware of what is going on and deal with whatever manifestations there are in the appropriate way but do go out of your way to monitor such political issues, otherwise you will find that this becomes a huge hidden cost.

Other hidden costs will not be that different from those of any project. There may be cost overruns on start up expenses. There may well be – almost certainly will be – the usual costs from delays and unexpected hitches. These may be more significant because it is offshore but they won't be any different.

2.11 The specification

In this light, as an introduction to hidden benefits, let me introduce the hidden costs involved in agreeing to a specification. Although this issue has reached the status of an urban myth, as I said earlier, the germ of the urban myth is still important, and if you are not aware of it, a poorly created specification will cause you immense costs. A thin specification for an onshore project will cause enough problems. An inadequate specification for an offshore project will cause the same budget overruns but worse.

Mitigating this problem by developing a proper specification in the first place will cost you extra work at the beginning and probably much more expense than you would normally set aside but it will save enormous costs later. My answer is both to allow more resource and funding than you think sensible for an equivalent onshore project and to welcome the process. The discipline involved in getting a good specification is worth more as the project unfolds and you may find that what starts as a hidden cost becomes one of the hidden benefits of going offshore.

3 Hidden benefits

Just as there are hidden costs, there are hidden benefits in going offshore, just as there are in any project that is well-conceived and run. The usual issue is whether you can be flexible enough to take full advantage of the benefits that need to be brought out into the light.

As an introduction to those benefits, I look at the speed with which your process or processes can be brought to life, what a new workforce of highly educated people can contribute, how to gain strategic insights, eliminating technology for business benefit, the potential for differentiation of service from offshore, and how business agility can be increased by going offshore. This last quality will also help you overcome corporate inertia and that is a much needed benefit.

3.1 Speed gains

In my experience, the major hidden benefit of going offshore provides a platform for a number of successive hidden benefits and is the opposite of some of the costs that I have outlined above. The speed with which a functioning process can be brought to fruition is astonishing. That speed means that the return on your investment can kick in faster than you might imagine, especially if you build in the right incentives. I have witnessed a processing centre move from a supplier's accepted proposal to a functioning service in less than six months (the process of taking the initial concept forwards and eventually accepting the proposal actually took nearer 18 months but that is another story of a procurement process that wasn't tightly controlled).

If you make a survey of companies that have gone offshore and ask them how long before their new facility offshore was fully functioning, you will get a range of answers and sometimes a range of answers from the same company about one project. The truth is that this is commercially extremely sensitive and more importantly internally politically-sensitive. As a prudent business planner, it is wise to suggest that from the moment the project starts offshore it will take 24 months to reach the same level of efficiency as you had in your local service centre. This is not only because it might take that amount of time but because it is usually wise to set expectations in the right way and be pleasantly surprised. You will, after all, find any number of companies which will proclaim that the in-house standard is *no surprises*. I have yet to find one that has found too much fault with a pleasant surprise.

Empirically, I think that the real time to match the efficiency of the original process carried out in the West is between 12 and 18 months. This is quite astonishingly quick and this time frame will be for your first process taken offshore. Succeeding projects will achieve maturity even faster. This is very definitely a hidden benefit – and one that wise business planners do keep hidden!

3.2 Fresh eyes

That often hidden benefit of a fast return on an investment is dwarfed by another that is enabled by it. Taking six months as the time that will elapse before you have a functioning centre, it will need another six to 12 months to become a mature business environment. During that time, you will discover that fresh, well-educated and intelligent eyes looking closely at all aspects of your processes will start to make subtle and then probably more dramatic improvements. In short, you will find that to match the original productivity of your service centre onshore takes the amount of time I have shown above but you will gain other benefits in the course of that period.

You will possibly find, for example, that your data is being analysed in unexpected ways – especially unexpected when you are only paying for data capture and reporting – and these insights will reveal cost-cutting opportunities that you hadn't contemplated. You will have suggestions about making your processes faster and less complicated. I have always found this a further compelling argument for offshoring a process just as it is rather than trying to improve it before putting it offshore.

In short, as with any outsourcing project, you will be examining what you do and how you do it in greater detail than you would normally apply to your usual business processes, with the additional benefit of fewer pre-suppositions and more disinterested analysts. Your new staff will be trained in your processes but they will still be new to them. This might be a wasting benefit but, properly handled, it won't be. You will find that if you and your supplier or partner create the right environment, you will reap the benefits of an engaged, committed, intelligent, highly qualified workforce.

3.3   Strategy, strategy

The next hidden benefit of this aspect of going offshore is related to strategy development. At the time of writing, this is often a well-hidden, not to say submerged benefit, but it is nevertheless an opportunity that is already being exploited by companies. It is commonplace that most corporations spend a great deal on developing their strategy and keeping it up-to-date. Properly done, this strategy development relies on research – market research, product research, demographic projections and associated areas of focus, and research into regulatory changes. Offshoring gives you access to much more inexpensive sources of such research capability.

Already some management consultancies are putting significant elements of their strategic research offshore and finding that, in addition to reducing the cost, they can produce more information more quickly. There is at least one new management consultancy that has sales and marketing in the west, and almost all the research, analysis and reporting provided from India, with substantial cost savings. One or two ordinary commercial companies are also experimenting with this opportunity and what might have been an expensive option, if starting from scratch, becomes far more affordable once you already have access to a service centre offshore. Because of the cost advantage of using offshore resources, such companies can experiment and explore different areas much more cost-effectively. Setting up a marketing campaign onshore is obviously a good deal more expensive than developing that capability offshore and already the use of outbound Indian call centres is becoming a benefit, hidden at the moment from most analysts' reports.

3.4   Reduced technology

In another area, I have been particularly struck by some experiments that seem to be turning the tables on the whole concept of going offshore. For tax benefit reasons, business process outsourcing is known in India as IT Enabled Services or ITES. Yet it was by removing the technology that a western company was able to gain a huge benefit. It involved removing that bane of many people's experience of call centres, the automatic voice response system – the one where a number of menus are presented and the client has to select the appropriate service using a telephone key pad. I have seen these so-called intelligent voice response too – but it didn't make the experience any more satisfying. By taking this technology out and putting people in, at a higher cost but still far cheaper than an equivalent call centre in the West, customer satisfaction increased dramatically. Going back to a human response may seem retrograde and it certainly was, in terms of absolute cost, but in terms of benefit, it was an astute step.

3.5 Processed in India

It is for reasons like this that I do not believe that it is fanciful to anticipate a time when providing a service offshore is seen as a marketing asset. There is a backlash developing against offshoring. There have been undoubtedly rather public glitches in services being put offshore with none too good results. Nevertheless, it is salutary to consider how far the offshore industry has come in a short period of time, a matter of a few years, and what it can achieve building on its undoubted success. Revenues would not be going up at a compound annual growth rate of more than 40 per cent unless there was a great deal right with the way the industry is developing. Extrapolating that growth with the increasing maturity of the offshore world, suggests that the attitude towards offshoring will change over the next few years. It is not fanciful to anticipate the time when the label 'processed in Hyderabad' or 'answered in Chennai' can clearly be seen as a potential unique selling proposition.

3.6 Agility

These benefits, hidden and virtually submerged in some cases, are significant enough but there is a final hidden benefit that may eventually be worth more than all the others combined.

Modern western corporations have taken to trumpeting their flexibility and fleetness of foot when addressing new markets. As with any brave claim, this often disguises just the opposite. Anyone who has much experience of corporate life knows, however, how long it takes to push a new idea to the point where it even achieves visibility, let alone implementation, in a mature corporate environment.

Your Indian supplier or partner, however, will be very different. If you watch Indian business people as closely as I do, your respect will grow and grow. This is not just because you will be watching an extremely successful group of people. You will probably soon become aware of a quality that will be initially alarming and then amazingly important.

For a number of reasons, not least the importance of the trader and the entrepreneur in Indian business, Indian companies are remarkably flexible. And they change as quickly as circumstances change.

For a start, they watch each other like hawks and any discussion with an Indian business person that brings into focus a third party Indian company will generally excite opinions and observations that are well-based. They also watch their markets closely and respond to changes very quickly indeed. When call centres first began to have any visibility at all in the Indian business community, it was a matter of weeks before a whole range of new companies were in the field, some, in my experience, having mastered the new vocabulary and little else. The capability, often enough, soon matched the presentations, however. As I have shown above, most Indian business people also monitor what is going on in the West and western business with a degree of attention that you will find surprising.

If you in turn watch your Indian partner carefully and discuss trends with him or her, you will have a lightning rod into market development both in your domestic market and in India. Watching how India Inc or India Ltd responds to western markets will give you insights into your domestic market in a way that only very expensive research will approach. You will have an insight into what your domestic competition is about to engage in very early in your competitor's planning cycle.

3.7   Corporate inertia

I have come to regard this very much hidden benefit as significant and likely to become more important over time. There is an additional reason for this. Working with your Indian supplier or partner will help you overcome corporate inertia and enter new markets or create new propositions much more effectively. If you can see your Indian partner or supplier gearing up in a particular direction and then you see that it is starting to take off, it is a great deal simpler to add to your existing contract in India and keep up with a new market trend than to go through the business development hoops internally.

This leads me full circle back to the issues with your procurement department and gives another reason why you should approach going offshore with a keen awareness of the differences involved. If you select as a partner or supplier a company that is just apparently geared up to address your needs but is really some sort of pragmatic hybrid, you may well lose this aspect of working with India as a benefit. If you can work with an Indian company that can actually understand your requirements but still retain its distinctive Indian qualities, its value to you will be that much more, even if in the short term it is more difficult to work together or it is uncomfortable for the procurement department.

4   Finally

Over the years I have been getting underneath the range of hidden costs in going offshore and analysing the hidden benefits. Because of that experience and because of the way that Indian business is maturing, it is becoming easier to see how to turn what are initially hidden costs into hidden and then overt benefits. This process will speed up and as the business world becomes more homogenised I expect that some of the benefits from cross-fertilisation will weaken. Yet, there is still an excitement in this environment that means that every business person has to be aware of the hidden benefits and the hidden costs – and know how to deal with both sides of the equation.

As companies start to discover the hidden benefits, and how to appreciate and then mitigate the hidden costs, the secrecy surrounding most offshoring activities becomes more intense. The secrecy starts because of fears of a backlash or other unwanted attention, and then becomes more profound. The number of companies that are happy to tell of their experience is reducing rather than increasing, and in this case, it is definitely a case of no news is good news – or at least no news is coming out because it is good news.

To make a success of going offshore, you will have to be very rigorous in challenging your normal assumptions. If you do so properly, you will find that there is a hidden cost even here, and one that is difficult to quantify, as it may largely result in lost time. Yet, I am convinced that not long after you have absorbed this hidden cost, you will start to find that it has enormous hidden benefits, not just in your current project, but in encouraging you to take the same approach to all your business issues whether in your domestic market or offshore.

Part III

Understanding Business Process Outsourcing

5

Business Process Outsourcing: A Manager's Guide to Understanding the Market Phenomenon

Ashok C. Devata, Rachna Kumar and Theophanis Stratopoulos

1 Introduction

Faster, cheaper, better has become the mantra for business success in today's economy and business process outsourcing (BPO) has become one of the means by which this goal may be achieved. BPO is defined as the *long-term contracting out of information technology enabled business processes to an outside provider to help achieve increased shareholder value* (Devata and Stratopoulos, 2004). With market analysts and researchers reporting significant benefits in terms of cost reduction, quality improvement as well as gains in flexibility and ability to focus more on the company's core competencies, companies of all sizes are contemplating the pros and cons of the global outsourcing of business processes. The global BPO market grew by 13 per cent between 1999 and 2000 to $119 billion and is estimated to reach $234 billion by 2005 (Whinston, 2004). The Americas lead in terms of BPO spending, with the US accounting for over 59 per cent of total worldwide expenditure. Europe is the second largest market for outsourcing services, accounting for 22 per cent of the market.

As with any market, the BPO market has a product, demand, supply, and business strategies. The **product**, which is any IT enabled business processes or any part of it, covers a wide spectrum, from customer relationship management to research and design projects. The **demand** for outsourcing is mostly from companies in developed nations or high-cost geographic areas such as North America, countries in Northern Europe and Japan. Whilst cost reduction is the most frequently sought after benefit through outsourcing, other benefits such as increased focus on core activities contribute to the growth of this demand. The **supply** side of outsourcing consists of a wide variety of players. Developing nations such as India and China or smaller developed nations such as Ireland, where wages for high quality English-speaking technical workers is only a fraction when compared to that in the US or UK, have a good number of companies that offer outsourcing services. The business **strategies** adopted by companies range from utilising their own subsidiary, a completely different offshore vendor, or a combination of both.

A novel product, and rapidly changing demand and supply functions, makes it an evolving market. Obviously, the development and growth in the BPO market has the potential to upset the competitive environment in a multitude of industries. As such, it is of great interest for managers and businesses to understand before they decide on any outsourcing strategy.

This chapter is the first to attempt to analyse and study BPO as a market phenomenon, that is, to examine simultaneously the behavior and strategies of buyers and suppliers of outsourcing services. In particular, we are analysing the factors driving and enabling the business process outsourcing market, the companies outsourcing (buyers and providers of outsourced services), what processes are being outsourced, how and why? Combining these aspects gives us a comprehensive view of the outsourcing market.

This knowledge is a valuable starting point for the development of a best practice guideline for managers in both buyers and providers of outsourcing services.

2   BPO: The product

In the early 1990s, Information Technology (IT) outsourcing was in the news when Kodak outsourced all its data centre operations in a 10-year, $250 million deal to IBM Corp, Digital Equipment Corp and Businessland Inc. This deal is perceived as the curtain raiser for the IT outsourcing industry and the precursor to BPO. Though it started with outsourcing hardcore IT activities such as data centre maintenance and software development, the current IT outsourcing industry encapsulates a wide range of IT services such as application development and testing, and even creative services such as animation development and content development. Similarly, today's BPO market deals with a wide variety of services. Customer service functions, human resource activities, finance and accounting services, as well as back-office transactions are just a few of the activities that are now being actively outsourced. In the following section we are going to outline and illustrate with examples the spectrum of outsourced processes.

According to Kennedy (2002), the most commonly outsourced business processes are from the finance and accounting departments (Table 5.1). Outsourcing deals in finance and accounting typically involve management of activities such as accounts payable, general ledger, fixed assets, accounts receivable, accounts reconciliation, billing, and reporting and analysis. British Petroleum was among the first companies to outsource

Table 5.1   Global Outsourcing Market

	1999		2003	
	Billion $	**Per cent**	**Billion $**	**Per cent**
CRM	33.2	23%	89.7	30%
Finance and accounting	90	62%	144	49%
HR services	3.9	3%	12.3	4%
Transcription	5.4	4%	10.8	4%
Engineering design/GIS	6.1	4%	10	3%
Animation/Content	6	4%	30	10%
Total	144.6	100%	296.8	100%

its finance and accounting functions to Accenture in the early 1990s. Finance and accounting functions such as item processing, in-clearing, corporate cheque fraud prevention, and pension and expense administration were included in the BPO deal. A few years later, in 1993, GE Capital Services opened its first service centre in India. The centre's 12,000 employees handle accounting, claims processing and credit evaluation services for more than 30 General Electric divisions. In a similar fashion, Ford has over 400 people in their Business Services Centre in India doing accounting for Ford worldwide. More recently, in 2001, Rhodia, a $7 billion maker of specialty chemicals headquartered in France, entered into a six-year contract with Accenture to transfer the bulk of its financial and accounting functions to a shared service centre in Prague (McKee, Garner and Abu Amara, 2000).

The next process to gain popularity in global outsourcing has been Customer Relationship Management (CRM). This involves all people, technology and business processes related to finding, attracting, retaining, or servicing and expanding a company's customer base. While telephone call centres, web-based technical support, and sales and marketing are typical CRM activities that are outsourced, CRM also includes non-technical customer support through e-mail response and instant messaging (live chat) services. Inbound and outbound call centre outsourcing is one of the fastest growing areas in BPO. For inbound calling service, which is purely a customer support division, call centre operators answer customers' calls to clarify their technical and non-technical questions. In outbound call centre divisions, operators either make calls to prospective customers or make cold calls to generate leads as part of a telemarketing strategy (Kennedy, 2002).

Numerous organisations have outsourced their CRM processes. American Express's call centres in Gurgaon and Delhi with more than 2000 employees, handle credit risk management and authorisation of payments. AOL's call centre in Bangalore employs more than 1200 workers. HP Compaq funded a fully owned subsidiary (Global E-Business Pvt. Ltd.) in Bangalore,

India. HSBC's centre in Bangalore provides transaction support for operations in the UK, Europe, and Australia. British Telecom is setting up two call centres in India, which are slated to have approximately 2200 employees. During the 1999–2000 period, outsourcing began to catch up with Human Resources (HR). Pioneers such as BP Amoco, Bank of America, British Telecom and BAE Systems began to hand over their HR operations to external service centres. Bank of America signed a 10-year deal in November 2000. Unisys Corporation signed a seven-year deal in August 2000. India has generated revenue of $7 billion in 2001 by offering services for HR outsourcing and stands as the leading destination for HR outsourcing and is estimated to generate revenue of $25 billion by 2006. HR includes payroll processing, benefits administration, tax fillings, employee database management, and hiring and firing practices. The Fortune Global 500 corporations employed more than 47 million people in 2001. The median number of employees for these corporations was approximately 63,000 (Kennedy, 2002). Quite frequently the employees are in multiple locations and countries. These figures offer a glimpse to the size and complexity of HR services in companies. Some functions such as payroll processing are more independently structured and easier to outsource, while other functions such as hiring and firing functions or employee database management are more difficult to outsource. But as Table 5.1 shows, HR Services represent only four per cent (4%) of total global outsourcing currently being undertaken and presents an opportunity for managers. Outsourcing human resources related services has the potential to lighten organisations' burdens by helping them screen, choose and manage employees more effectively.

Another popular segment for outsourcing is back-office transactions. Back-office transactions in any company are the routine fundamental activities that are required to run the business. Companies depend on the results of these back-office operations to administer core activities. Outsourcing these back-office transactions allow companies not only to save costs but also to gain flexibility and focus on core activities. Sales order entry and chequeing, contracts reconciliation, quotations generation, management of billing, invoicing and payments, insurance claims, document management, third party and fourth party logistics, transportation management and warehousing are a few examples of back-office activities that are generally outsourced.

It is clear from our discussion that the range of outsourced business processes is becoming extremely broad. Processes, which might have been considered sacred and not appropriate for outsourcing a few years ago, have become a standard part of outsourcing today. The traditional division between core and non-core competencies has become far more difficult to identify. Every process, unless providing a company with a competitive advantage, is now arguably subject to consideration as a candidate for outsourcing. In addition, for large companies outsourcing is beginning to become an almost seamless way of expansion. In such cases, the companies *add* resources and expand process and operations via global outsourcing but do not close or curtail their current level of process operations in their parent country. Utilising outsourcing in offshore, low-cost locations, or even within your own country for business expansion is also useful to study as a form of BPO because lessons derived are useful for managers planning various BPO strategies.

The most recent addition to this roster of outsourced activities is that of R&D departments. Recent announcements, such as those of General Motors, J.P. Morgan Chase and Google, pertaining to the outsourcing of R&D activities are now quite common. General Motors announced in 2004 that it is setting up a $21 million technology centre in India to carry out computer-aided design and engineering research. J.P. Morgan Chase & Co is offshoring some of its stock market and equity research to India, signalling possible new arenas for the offshore outsourcing trend. J.P. Morgan Chase expects to hire Indian MBAs who will do the heavy-duty number crunching, freeing up the American employees to focus on higher-level financial analysis and to spend more time with customers. Similarly, Google announced the creation of an R&D centre in India in December of 2003 (*Wall Street Journal*, 2003).

3   Drivers of the market: demand for BPO

Drivers of BPO are similar to the factors creating demand for BPO services. Demand in any market is defined as the willingness and ability to purchase a commodity or service, given market prices and available choices. In the BPO market, the demand is to purchase a service from companies which claim that they can administer certain business processes at lower costs and improved efficiencies. The outsourcing trend we are currently witnessing is a result of a series of economic, geopolitical and technological changes across the past decade. Analysing the current BPO market, we have identified two main drivers responsible for the BPO demand: Economic Forces and Business Practices.

3.1   Economic forces driving demand for BPO

It is not surprising that the two spikes of interest in the outsourcing market are associated with recessions in the US and by extension to the global economy. The first of these spikes was during the recession in the early nineties, while the second one coincided with the recession which started with the bursting of the dot.com bubble. During economic recessions companies tend to shift their focus to cost reduction and productivity improvements and away from business growth and expansion. This pressure on companies to become more efficient led them in a search for new avenues to reduce costs. Outsourcing non-core business activities to low-cost geographic areas emerged as a feasible solution.

Global giants likes GE, IBM, Texas Instruments and American Express were already taking advantage of low-cost geographic areas such as Ireland and India to process their business activities. What began as a ripple of activity with these companies and others is becoming the accepted way to achieve cost saving. Though the direct cost reduction and potential benefits through BPO have been reported to go as high as 60 per cent, 20 to 30 per cent cost reduction is more practical after considering transaction costs and costs incurred due to process control and monitoring (Morstead and Blount, 2003). Cost savings vary based on the outsourcing model – inshore outsourcing vs. offshore outsourcing – where inshore outsourcing refers to the scenario where the outsourcing vendor utilised is located in the same country as the client company, and offshore is where the outsourcing vendor utilised is located in a foreign country for the client company. Analysts report that inshore outsourcing can save around 10 and 20 per cent in costs whereas offshore outsourcing can save up to 40 per cent (McLean, 2003).

Cost reduction mainly comes from the difference in wages, for the same work, between developed and developing nations. Salaries for white-collar jobs such as HR administration, content development and call centre operation in developing nations are only 10 to 15 per cent of the salaries in the US. When it comes to jobs such as call centre operators, which are considered as educated jobs for graduates in India, the annual salary is $4000 whereas a call centre operator in the US would cost around $30,000. Figure 5.1 provides a graphical representation of the salary differential between US and India across a wide spectrum of jobs (BusinessWeek, 2004; Thondavadi and Albert, 2004).

Business process outsourcing has the potential to help companies shift from fixed to variable costs and thereby have the capability to be flexible to follow economic downturns very closely. Cost savings are secured by the variable cost structure that accommodates fluctuations in labour and equipment needs. Lowering costs results in increases in cash reserves. In addition to the benefit of lower cost and better service for the customer, it is the increase in cash reserves that has the potential to foster innovation. Several theoretical and empirical studies have found a strong correlation between increases in reserves and innovation and new product or service development.

The above discussion deals with the effect of economic downturn on the demand side of BPO. However, there was another equally important effect on the supply side of the BPO market. During the late nineties, IT workers primarily from India were attracted to the US and Western Europe in order

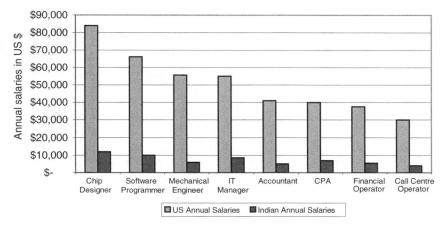

Figure 5.1   Comparison of US and Indian Wages

to deal with the Y2K issue and in response to the Internet explosion. By 2001 both these reasons disappeared and a pattern of repatriation occurred. These IT workers, with significant experience in the business processes and needs of large multinational companies, became the initial seed for companies offering outsourcing services in India and China. The economic downturn had a dual effect; it boosted, simultaneously, the demand and supply side of the BPO market.

3.2   Business practices driving demand for BPO

Companies aim to focus on their core competencies in order to offer better products and services. It is this desire to reduce non-core business operations that drives companies to consider BPO. Outsourcing non-core activities allows a company to focus on core competencies instead of investing resources on managing routine back-office operations. It is a 'do what you do best and outsource the rest' strategy.

As a differentiating strategy, companies desire to offer their products or services faster than their competitors or provide them more efficiently. For this, the support systems within the company have to provide faster or more efficient services. By outsourcing business activities to a location in a different time zone, companies can attain 24-hour operational cycles. This time difference in countries acts as an advantage for companies outsourcing their business activities to increase the pace of their internal business operations. The benefits of a virtual 24-hour operational cycle are clear in insurance and finance industries where the time it takes to process a credit application or insurance claim plays a major role in differentiation of services offered by a company (Thondavadi and Albert, 2004; Lacity and Willcocks, 2001).

Another business driver for BPO is the desire of companies to gain knowledge of technology, to access better processes or efficiencies and to learn about more efficient management procedures. Outside companies might be specialists in different business activities. By outsourcing, a company can gain access to this superior knowledge and capability. Companies are lured to outsourcing not just by the cost factor but also for the high quality service offered in some offshore companies. For example, when it comes to software development and process methodologies, all top-tier Indian vendors are certified at CMM Level 5, which is the highest level on Carnegie Mellon University's Capability Maturity Model. In fact, half the Level 5 CMM-rated organisations in the world are in India (Vijayan, 2003). Wipro, a company with more than 18,000 employees and $1 billion in revenue, and TCS, a company with 27,000 employees are just two of such high quality companies offering outsourcing services.

There are also companies that outsource for capacity. They know how to make a product but don't have capacity, or they don't want to invest in the technology and equipment to make it (Knowledge@Wharton, 2004). In light of these facts, outsourcing becomes a very attractive strategy for companies to expand and increase revenues. Companies that do not outsource are forced to outsource to save costs and compete in the market. Outsourcing, therefore, becomes a necessity rather than a strategy.

4   Enablers of the market: supply side of BPO

While the role of economic and market forces as drivers of the BPO market are important, this market explosion could not have been at its current status without the geopolitical changes and technological advancements that took place across the globe over the past decade.

4.1   Geopolitical changes enabling supply of BPO services

Since the mid-eighties, more than 60 countries – accounting for more than half of global population – opened their physical and economic borders to the global economy. For instance, after a serious financial crisis, India opened its economy in 1991 and since then liberalised rules for foreign companies to set up offices in India. This gave foreign companies access to a large, well-educated, English speaking workforce. Similarly, after a radical change in national policy, China opened its economy and unleashed the forces of modernisation in 1978 under the leadership of Deng Xiaoping. Continuing social and economic reforms in China led to significant development in technology infrastructure in the nineties, and increased the available pool of educated workforce. This resulted in new low-cost human resource for foreign companies to explore. Similar economic reforms along with political changes in countries such as Russia, Brazil and Argentina have exposed an availability of low-cost educated labour for companies in

Table 5.2 Comparison of Countries

	Country	Geopolitical Risk	Infrastructure	Annual Salary IT Programmer	English Proficiency	Cultural Compatibility	Govt. Support
Leaders							
	Canada	Low	Good	$23,174	Good	Good	Good
	India	High	Poor	$ 5,880	Good	Fair	Strong
	Ireland	Low	Good	$28,500	Good	Good	Good
Rookies							
	Argentina	High	Fair	$ 2,400	Fair	Good	NA
	Venezuela	High	Fair	$ 2,556	Poor	Poor	Poor
	Chile	Moderate	Good	$ 1,781	Poor	Good	Fair
	Pakistan	Very High	Fair	$ 4,860	Good	Fair	Good
	Thailand	Low	Fair	$11,124	Poor	Poor	Fair
	Egypt	High	Fair	$ 400	Good	Poor	Poor
Up Comers							
	Brazil	Moderate	Good	$ 1,308	Poor	Good	Fair
	Mexico	Moderate	Good	$ 1,400	Poor	Good	Good
	China	Moderate	Fair	$ 8,952	Poor	Poor	Fair
	Poland	Low	Good	$ 6,400	Poor	Fair	Fair
	Hungary	Low	Good	$ 6,400	Poor	Fair	Fair
	Bulgaria	Low	Fair	$ 4,800	Good	Good	Fair
	Czech Republic	Low	Good	$ 6,400	Poor	Fair	Fair

developed nations. This availability of low-cost educated workforce in various developing nations served as a vast supply segment for BPO services. US, European and Japanese corporations that were searching for new avenues to reduce costs and gain access to new talents took advantage of this vast educated workforce. These companies started shifting their back-office operations to developing countries, primarily to reduce costs and in the process created the BPO market. Table 5.2 compares various countries that are active in the outsourcing market on several factors (Overby, 2002).

4.2   Technology changes enabling supply of BPO services

BPO is a form of e-business and as such it implies the existence of a virtual market place. When a company in the US outsources its call centre activities to a company in Ireland, the transaction takes place through the information technology optical cables laid across the Atlantic. The information technology backbone becomes the transaction medium in outsourcing. The exponential development in information technology and communication systems all over the world is another key enabler for the BPO services supply.

These changes should be analysed under two different aspects of technology: technical feasibility and technology affordability. From the BPO perspective, technical feasibility is the ability of technology to continuously allow back and forth transfer of the outsourced business activities of a company to a different location; technology affordability is the ability of the companies to financially afford this technology to reduce costs. In the past 10 years, both these aspects of technology have seen vast improvements and have contributed to creating the supply side for BPO services.

Technical feasibility: Until recently, most business processes such as accounting, sales records, and payroll were performed manually with paper records. In the past decade, the IT revolution brought networking into companies and this resulted in a rapid shift toward digitisation of records and computerisation of processing. This digitisation of business activities allows companies to transfer the processing of work to any location with proper technical infrastructure.

The tech boom in the late 1990s has resulted in a major increase in information technology infrastructure primarily in US, Europe and South-East Asia. Thousands of miles of optical cables were laid deep below the oceans and form a strong information and communication backbone. This communication infrastructure allows companies to seamlessly transfer back and forth their digitised business activities to any desired location. Though lagging behind the US and Europe, developing nations are significantly increasing their communication infrastructure to foster supply in the BPO market. For instance, in India the amount of fibre in the national telecom backbone was estimated to grow to 430,000 km in 2003 from 170,000 km in 2000. This represents a growth in excess of 250 per cent in less than four years. The Indian international submarine cable capacity grew from 11 Gbps in 1997 to an impressive 541 Gbps in 2003. Also an 8.4 Tbps Singapore to Chennai international link was established in 2002 with which India has established global connectivity with the greatest capacity pipe in the world (Morstead and Blount, 2003). Figure 5.2 shows the large increase in information communication capacity related to the Indian subcontinent.

The Internet also plays a vital role in enabling the BPO market. Companies in developing countries including those in India and China are just a click away and are highly accessible for the corporations in developed nations wishing to outsource. The Internet has made worldwide communication easy and has also enabled very sophisticated remote monitoring. For instance, call centre applications can remotely monitor call centre representatives in India and watch the performance of the agents. This level of real-time performance monitoring is new and only happening because of CRM technology. Technology is facilitating the success of outsourcing as a business model. With that success, the quality and value added are only getting better (Robinson and Kalakota, 2004; Thondavadi and Albert, 2004).

Technology Affordability: Availability of technical possibility does not necessarily mean a business possibility. Communication from high-cost geographic areas to various low-cost geographic areas across the oceans has to be highly economical for companies to outsource their digitised business activities and save costs. In recent years, the cost of communication has radically dropped, allowing companies to economically transfer business processes to offshore locations. Regular uninterrupted communication channels, which were highly expensive in mid-90s, are now available to companies at affordable prices. For instance, the cost of a 2 Mbps

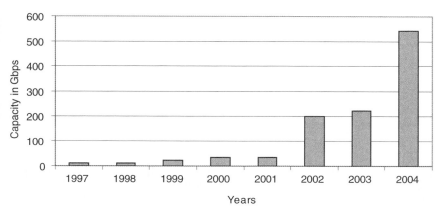

Figure 5.2 Indian International Submarine Cable Capacity

leased line from US to India in 1997 was close to $1 million per year whereas in 2002 that cost was close to $100,000. The availability of reliable and relatively cheap communication services has enabled the BPO market to expand at an overwhelming rate. If not for the financial feasibility of available technology, the BPO market would not have witnessed double-digit growth rates.

The combined effect of the interaction of these drivers and enablers was the creation of a booming BPO market.

5   Managerial relevance: business strategies for BPO

Though outsourcing strategies are still evolving, outsourcing deals such as GM and EDS, Xerox and EDS, Kodak and IBM, are more than a decade old. Economic and technological changes over the years are transforming the outsourcing market. The BPO segment now has a few strategies that companies are exploring actively. As the offshore BPO market is relatively new, it is hard to conclude one strategy to be superior to others. While deciding on a BPO strategy, companies normally choose captive centres, external vendors or hybrid models. These are further segmented as shown in Figure 5.3. Models have their own pros and cons and choosing a model depends on the company's current status, strengths and global stance.

Also note that when discussing trends in the BPO market, strictly following the definition of 'outsourcing' as *contracting out of business processes to an outside provider* allows us to only discuss external vendors. However, the offshoring phenomenon is so strong and of such managerial relevance today that some of the strategies pursued in the offshore context for business process projects have elements of outsourcing merely because of the countries chosen or the similarities in the issues to be handled. So for

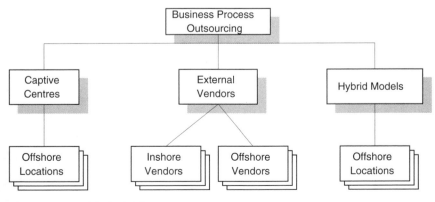

Figure 5.3   Models for BPO

example, when companies have opened captive centres in India and moved large portions of their business process transactions there, strictly speaking, the captive centres are subsidiaries and there is no BPO actually occurring. However, the choice of India as the location, the issue of hiring from a pool of culturally diverse but English-speaking and educated local talent and issues of remote management in a location where the companies have no historical experience have allowed the industry to loosely club offshore business process projects and offshore BPO projects into the same category of BPO. From a manager's perspective, this makes practical sense because the lessons for management and the risks and pitfalls to guard against are similar. As the BPO market matures and as the off-shoring market matures, these principally differing practices will be studied separately.

5.1   Organisational structures for BPO projects

Captive Centres: A captive model allows a company to retain its business processes within the company's global four walls. When a company chooses to outsource its business activities through a captive model, it is similar to opening a new office in a foreign location or setting up a sub-sidiary – both of which have been common business strategies for global-isation for the past three decades. But the fact that these setups undertake business processes, have heavy technology reliance as a basis for existence, need almost seamless technology and people management – sometimes round-the-clock – make captive centres for business processing different from past globalisation practices. Managers have found it more relevant to study and understand these in the context of offshore outsourcing of business processes.

A company can develop a long-term relationship with its intellectual resources and personnel in a foreign country by direct employment instead of contracting business process to a third party service provider. This model gains full independence in company policies, infrastructure development, business process and quality measures. Captive centres are relatively expens-ive as the company has to incur office setup costs, infrastructure costs, and other development costs and has somewhat higher risks as well.

Companies also have to deal with cross culture and business logistics issues. Table 5.3 lists some of the biggest captive centres of American cor-porations in India. As is evident from Table 5.3, captive centres are widely chosen models for corporations with global presence and experience.

External Providers: Instead of investing in a captive centre to transfer business activities to low-cost geographic areas, companies can choose to outsource their business activities to an external vendor often called a Third Party Service Provider (TPSP). Generally, companies restricted to a single nation that do not have overseas exposure choose TPSPs to out-source business activities and save costs. These TPSPs or external service

Table 5.3   Captive Centres in India

Company	Location	Employees
Morgan Stanley	Mumbai, India	1,600
DELL International Services	Bangalore & Hyderabad, India	3,800
American Express	India	4,000
GE	Bangalore, Gurgaon, & Hyderabad, India	12,000
Citibank	Mumbai & Chennai, India	2,500
Bank of America	India	1,000
ABN Amro (ACES)	Gurgaon & Delhi, India	2,000
e-serve International	India	3,149

providers can be inshore companies (i.e. within the parent company's country) or offshore companies. Companies, such as IBM, EDS and Accenture with global presence are active inshore service providers in the US whereas companies such as Progeon, Daksh eServices and Office Tiger are some of the many active offshore service providers. Most of these offshore service providers also have offices in the US and Europe primarily with sales and marketing operations. The offshore third party service providers market is relatively cluttered with point and partial solutions, whereas inshore BPO service market has big one-stop service providers such as Accenture, IBM, EDS and ACS. Teaming with the right provider is a critical factor in determining success in BPO deals when adopting the TPSP model. To date, few vendors have provided complete, end-to-end BPO solutions.

The third party service providers market in low-cost geographic areas of the global market is emerging rapidly. A number of leading software service companies are making a foray into the BPO domain, either directly or through the mergers and acquisitions route. Most Indian IT leaders today, such as Wipro, Patni, Satyam and HCL have a presence in this market. Active financial support and funding from US and European venture capital firms for offshore BPO service providers is not only increasing the number of service providers but also helping these service providers expand rapidly.

Some offshore service providers are themselves expanding to other countries for two reasons – to increase business and to take advantage of low wages in other developing countries. Progeon, the BPO wing of Indian software giant Infosys, apart from its four business offices in UK and US, has recently started developing its operations in the Czech Republic primarily to take advantage of low-cost labour. A \$900 million company, Wipro, for instance, has more than 18,000 employees and operates software development centres in the US, Canada, the UK, Germany and Japan. TCS, India's largest IT services exporter (\$1 billion), employs more than 24,000 people and has nine development centres outside India including one in China.

In a typical BPO deal with an inshore TPSP, the service provider takes care of all issues related to the transfer and administration of operations to the provider. The responsibilities of the company outsourcing business activities are relatively simple as it does not have to deal directly with BPO issues such as cross-cultural management, language barriers and technology concerns. The inshore BPO provider could be conducting its own operations either inshore or offshore. Accenture, based in the US, is a good example of such an inshore outsourcing provider for US companies. However, much of Accenture's operations for its clients are performed in India. Accenture's Bangalore office and IBM's office at Chennai are two leading operational centres for TPSPs which may be classified as inshore TPSPs for US companies desiring to get their business processes outsourced. (The Bangalore office of Accenture and the Chennai office of IBM would strictly be called captive centres of these service providers.) Though the companies outsourcing through these inshore TPSPs save less, the model is relatively secure and simple. The options in this model are explained in Figure 5.4.

When a company desires to have a direct relationship with a TPSP overseas, the cost savings can be relatively high. Table 5.2 had given some of these comparative costs. Cost savings could be in the range of 40 per cent to 70 per cent depending on several factors within the project. The company has to initially choose a country and then choose a service provider specialised in specific business activities before finalising the BPO deal. In March 2001, Guardian Life Insurance Company of America began

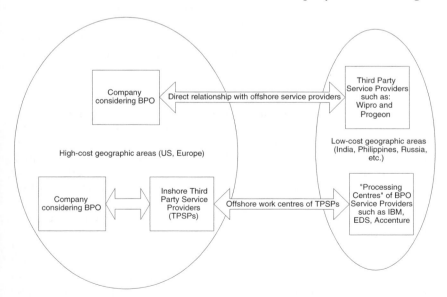

Figure 5.4 Models for Third Party Service Providers

outsourcing IT to India. The company later expanded its outsourcing scope to include help desk assistance, personal computer repair assistance and a disaster recovery operation. The result was an annual savings of $12.5 million. Though India is the leading destination for outsourcing, Ireland, China and Brazil are other countries often considered. Most Asian countries stand competitive in the outsourcing market, providing high quality service for low costs. HSBC plans to export 4000 British finance jobs to China, India and Malaysia to slash costs by 2004. UK based companies such as Lloyds TSB, Prudential and Aviva have already moved thousands of positions to Asia.

Hybrid Models: The hybrid model – as the name indicates – is a combination of the captive centre model and third party vendor model. In this model, a company outsourcing its business processes forms a partnership with an offshore service provider to start a pseudo-captive centre in the low-cost geographic area. As a globalisation strategy, this is similar to a joint venture. But as explained earlier, in the context of off-shore outsourcing, managers have found it more instructive to study these setups as a BPO endeavor. The third party service provider, in addition to its partial investment in the pseudo captive centre, also offers local business and management expertise in managing the centre. Generally, companies in high-cost geographic areas prefer these hybrid models before fully investing in a large-scale captive centre. The strategic alliance between TRW, a US based automotive and space technology company and Satyam Computer Services, an Indian IT company, to establish a centre to process business activities of TRW is an example of such a hybrid model. Satyam's other strategic alliances include companies such as GE, Computer Associates, Venture and Jasdic Park (Satyam Media Room, 2000).

5.2   Practical managerial steps for BPO projects

When companies decide to utilise the BPO route, several questions need to be answered. These range from what to outsource, who to outsource to, where to outsource, who will manage the new structures, how will the new arrangements be managed, how should the new organisation be structured, and so on. In fact, the decision of whether to outsource or whether to stay in status quo is the simplest one. It is the planning and the execution phase where the key challenges and successes occur.

Our discussions and understanding of the BPO market gives some guidelines for managers wishing to consider outsourcing. Since outsourcing is a complex business strategy, much of the particulars will depend on the individual company involved, the industry involved and the processes involved. But in every case, the very first step would be to conduct an internal evaluation. The internal evaluation should be aimed towards answering the question regarding what should be done internally and what should be outsourced. The general wisdom in this regard is that the core processes should be kept in-house and the non-core processes should be outsourced. The core competencies of the organisation can then be leveraged for business advantage. However, this distinction of core versus non-core for BPO is not a definite prescription because several companies have outsourced core processes such as customer relationship or product design and development, and are doing very well. Still, this provides a very good starting step to help frame a manager's choices (Scholl, 2003).

Assuming that the BPO decision has been taken, the second step would be to decide the location and vendor to outsource to. A SWOT analysis of the different countries that are popular outsourcing destinations (Table 5.2) helps in this analysis. However, once again, the particular global and local profile of the company being evaluated for BPO will decide the specific of the SWOT analysis. Vendor selection is crucial in this second phase and larger vendors with past record for successful outsourcing deals are usually preferred. However, often smaller or medium sized companies prefer to go with smaller vendors because they get better deals and more customised service. Choice of organisational structure for the BPO arrangement in terms of captive centre versus external vendors versus hybrid arrangement would be included in this phase. It is a good idea to establish an offshore steering committee to manage this step.

The next step is the planning phase where managers clearly define roles and milestones, negotiate rational contract foundations, and document reporting relationships. In case of offshore BPO, an offshore programme management team with an office in the relevant remote location is useful. Communication mechanisms, performance metrics, reporting frequency, and goals of the BPO projects are all specifics that have to be laid down at this stage.

The final step is the actual execution and programme management. The transition of work is considered to be the most challenging stage. Analysis and re-engineering of the process being outsourced helps in clear demarcation and documentation of the processes and in getting the outsourced unit up and running. In addition, knowledge transfer has several people issues and issues of proper change management which are crucial for the success of a BPO endeavor.

These managerial guidelines have higher chances of insightful application when based on a good understanding of the background, enablers and drivers of the BPO market. Managers will be able to ask the right questions, question the appropriate prescriptions, and learn from early movers and past experience of the industry. However, each of these steps and phases has many nuances and several variations depending on the specific nature of the organisations participating in the BPO deals.

6   Conclusion

In the context of this chapter, Business Process Outsourcing was defined as the long-term contracting of information technology enabled business processes to an outside provider to help achieve increased shareholder value. This definition was loosely expanded when studying BPO strategies to include conducting business processes with subsidiaries and with joint ventures in offshore, low-cost geographic locations. This delegation of business processes to an outsourcing vendor or to an offshore location is made under the understanding that the provider can manage the processes, provide services according to defined metrics and do this at a lower cost. We analysed the factors driving and enabling the BPO market, examined the processes that are being outsourced, and reviewed the strategies that are being employed. Combining these aspects gives us a comprehensive view of the current state of the outsourcing market.

In the future, however, we are likely to see more 'value added' business models. Currently, outsourcing service providers gain expertise in administering business activities and slowly institutionalise change while continuously improving the processes over time. In the future, BPO providers would not only take on the responsibility to manage the function or business process, but also re-engineer the way the process has been traditionally done. In addition to this evolution of the BPO models, more companies are entering the supply side of the BPO market. The increased competition will force suppliers to become more efficient and creative in terms of the spectrum of products and services that they offer.

The effect of the above changes in the supply side of the BPO market is dual. First, in the past and even today, the market for BPO services was mostly demand driven; we expect that this will change and the market will become more supply driven. Second, as the supply side is evolving and providers are more creative in the services that they offer, we are going to see more companies on the demand side lured to the BPO market in order to take advantage of these offers. Companies will also re-evaluate what processes are to be outsourced and what are not to be outsourced. This will bring us closer to the creation of the virtual company envisioned in the early days of the IT revolution.

From this, one can conclude that companies that have prior, successful experience in terms of managing outsourcing deals will be more prepared to deal with the challenges of managing a virtual company and take advantage of the opportunities that this model has to offer to improve their competitive position.

References

BusinessWeek, 'Going Abroad', *BusinessWeek*, February 3, 2004.
Devata, A. and T. Stratopoulos, 'The Life Cycle of Business Process Outsourcing', *Global Information Technology Management*, San Diego 2004.

Kennedy, R., *Exporting IT – Enabled Services from Developing Countries*, Harvard Business School, 2002.

Knowledge@Wharton, 'It's Time to Talk Sense about Outsourcing', The Wharton School of the University of Pennsylvania, March 10, 2004.

Lacity, M. and L. Willcocks, *Global Information Technology Outsourcing: In Search of Business Advantage*, John Wiley & Sons, January 15, 2001.

McCarthy, J.C., 'Offshore: The good, the bad, the ugly', *Forrester Research*, March 19, 2003.

McKee, D.L., Garner, D.E. and Abu Amara, Y., *Offshore Financial Centers, Accounting Services and the Global Economy*, Quorum Books, July 30, 2000.

McLean, H., 'What outsourcing can do for you', *Times Online*, March 31, 2003.

Morstead and Blount, *Offshore Ready: Strategies to Plan & Profit from Offshore IT-enabled Services*, American Productivity & Quality Center, 2nd edition, 2003.

Overby, S., 'A Buyer's Guide To Offshore Outsourcing', *CIO*, November 15, 2002.

Robinson, M. and Kalakota, R., *Offshore Outsourcing: Business Models, ROI and Best Practices* (Mivar Press, 2004).

Satyam, 'Satyam JV awarded $200 million contract from TRW', http://www.satyam.com/mediaroom/pr1dec00.html, 2000.

Scholl, R., 'Offshoring BPO: A Framework for Getting Started', *Gartner Research*, June 26, 2003.

Thondavadi, N. and Albert G., *Offshore Outsourcing: Path to New Efficiencies in IT and Business Processes*, Nandu Thondavadi Authorhouse, March 2004.

Vijayan, 'India Inc., Still Going Strong', *Computer World*, September 15, 2003.

Wall Street Journal, 'Google plans to open an engineering research and development center in India,' *Wall Street Journal*, December 11, 2003.

Whinston, A., 'Offshoring Statistics – Dollar Size, Job Loss, and Market Potential', http://www.ebstrategy.com/Outsourcing/trends/statistics.htm, 2004.

6

Offshore Business Process Outsourcing: Strategies to Minimise Failure

Jonathan Chevallier and Hilary Robertson

The huge prizes that can be gained from outsourcing business processes to low-cost offshore locations such as India have been well-publicised. However, getting to the prize is far from simple and can all too often seem like navigating around an iceberg: you can only see part of the problem; the rest of the hazards lie hidden. And to complicate the picture further, the risks are constantly moving and vary from one outsource to the next. To put it prosaically, there isn't a convenient A to Z to help anticipate the challenges of offshore business process outsourcing (BPO). Different companies will require different solutions, shaped by a variety of factors including the firm's strategic objectives, the processes it intends to outsource and its risk threshold. This chapter highlights some major but often hidden hazards and issues that need to be addressed when formulating and executing a strategy to realise the undoubted commercial advantages of offshore BPO.

The economic logic of offshore BPO, of course, isn't hard to grasp. How many CEOs wouldn't want to cut their processing costs by up to 60 per cent, especially when shareholders are knocking on the door demanding even higher returns? In fact, as we've seen in earlier chapters, many companies have already gone down this avenue and generated massive savings, setting the cash tills ringing in even more CEOs' heads and leading to forecasts that the offshore BPO market will mushroom into an industry worth well over $100 billion by 2008 (Agrawal, Farrell and Remes, 2003). These predictions are feasible. Nearly all the ingredients required, including the technological infrastructure, low telecommunications bandwidth costs and a more welcoming global regulatory environment, are already in place, underpinned by the most important ingredient of all – a vast pool of low-cost, skilled labour in the India's, China's and Philippines' of this world. However, there's one major problem that not only stands in the way of the long-term growth of BPO but also threatens to undermine the ability of companies to unlock the true potential of offshore outsourcing.

And, ironically, the source of this problem is the reason why so many companies are now considering offshoring – the ability to dramatically cut operating costs. The difficulty is that many firms are viewing this opportunity, which is sometimes euphemistically called 'labour arbitrage', as the sole raison d'etre of offshore outsourcing. This view has been reinforced by numerous widely-publicised reports from leading consultancies and research companies claiming cost savings of up to 80 per cent (for example Hoch, 2003). The practical reality is that most firms do not reap efficiencies on such a large scale, at least not in the near to medium term. The much bigger problem, though, is that figures like these, coupled with shareholder pressure to deliver swift returns, have led to a fixation on the cost side of the offshore outsourcing equation. This has had two detrimental impacts.

First, it has encouraged firms to ignore the significant opportunities to improve the quality of their service – and their revenue streams – via outsourcing, as discussed later. Second, it distorts and poisons the relationship between the client and supplier. It relegates the supplier to the position of a dispensable commodity, giving him little incentive to innovate and add value; his role is to provide the service at the lowest possible rate. This is hardly a basis for a mutually beneficial relationship. Not surprisingly, a study by consultants Morgan Chambers (Morris and Morgan, 2004) of over 150 companies that outsourced processes found that less than half of the outsourcers were delivering the innovation their clients wanted.

This disappointment has been exacerbated by the failure of many companies to reap the full scale of savings and returns they expected from offshore BPO. To understand why this has happened, you need to look at how the outsourcing market has evolved. As we all know, outsourcing isn't new. In fact, it started nearly 2000 years ago when the Romans subcontracted their tax collection. During the last century, however, it began to develop into a major market, initially with manufacturers outsourcing the production of basic components and then with the outsourcing of functions and business processes such as IT or finance and accounting. The business process outsourcing contracts were typically long-term contracts, delivered onshore, involving a mixture of simple activities with more complex processing and often including enhancement and management of the underlying IT systems. In such an environment, suppliers were able to invest significant funds in major process improvements, to deliver increased service levels and reduced costs. The recent emergence of offshore outsourcing has changed the focus with an explosion in the outsourcing of simple, repetitive tasks such as outbound calling and data entry. The problem is that with such a narrow process focus, the opportunity for adding value and delivering more than simple labour arbitrage is very limited.

To unlock the real value of offshore outsourcing, an approach which combines the traditional methods used for onshore BPO with the benefits of offshoring is needed. Our experience has shown that more complex processes such as underwriting, reconciliations and billing exceptions can be successfully delivered offshore. The recommended approach is therefore for clients to increase both the scope and complexity of the services that are to be relocated and to consider outsourcing the underlying IT systems. Equally critically, a more enlightened approach to the client-supplier relationship is required. Clients need to view it as a long-term strategic investment, with shared risks and rewards, not as a cost-driven, take-it-or-leave-it purchase. And like all strategic investments this requires a robust methodology for assessing the options, including the most appropriate form of outsourcing and the associated risks, and for managing the relationship to ensure it generates the maximum return.

Over the following pages the key issues that need to be considered to optimise the potential of offshore outsourcing are outlined. Although there isn't a one-size-fits-all solution, Xansa's experience, which spans a wide range of sectors from banking and insurance to utilities and consumer goods, has revealed that there are a number of common issues and pitfalls that all businesses face. Handled correctly and flexibly, the commercial returns can be substantial, far beyond the basic goal of cost reduction which should be taken as given.

Our work with a major international financial services firm gives a flavour of the value that can be achieved by offshoring complex processes, beyond simple labour arbitrage. Our role is to process 'chargebacks'[1] for a number of credit and debit card products, from our operations in India. This task is governed by rigorous regulations and involves staff liaising with a variety of parties, including the merchant acquirers (other banks), the cardholder and multiple internal departments of the issuer, and taking decisions about how best to complete the work.

The approach combines a highly qualified team in India that leverages Xansa's IT heritage to improve the process, with excellent operational management methods to deliver real added value to the client. For example, in the case where fraud is suspected, the team has a number of different options as to how best to maximise the monies that can be recovered for the card issuer. The team in India uses its judgement in conjunction with the VISA and Mastercard schemes rules to decide the best option to take.

Typically, a card issuer has a substantial sum of money tied up in provisions against write-offs as a result of fraud at any time. Previously, their backlogs of this work stood at 20 days. As a result of outsourcing and offshoring, these have now been eliminated. The team has also identified additional transactions that could be charged-back by reviewing the fraud filter rules, thus increasing total recoveries. And the high quality of judgement employed has improved the 'first-time-right' rate at which chargeback transactions 'stick' (the stick rate) from 70 per cent to 94 per cent.

Xansa's operational methods have increased the volume of work processed by 46 per cent, without enlarging the size of the team, and are enabling the client to increase their recoveries by 76 per cent. The net effect of offshoring this complicated and highly embedded process is a significant improvement to the client's bottom line in terms of tens of millions of pounds every year.

The purpose of this example is not to extol Xansa's expertise but to demonstrate that offshore outsourcing can dramatically improve the quality of the service, producing sizeable and measurable top- and bottom-line financial benefits. And it's these types of outputs, not purely the 'input costs', that should be uppermost in companies' minds when formulating, implementing and managing BPO strategies. However, it's not quite as easy to generate these improvements in service, revenue and profitability as some people would like companies to believe. The road to success is littered with stumbling blocks. The following sections describe how to recognise these to give a greater chance of unlocking BPO's full potential.

1 Treat BPO as a strategic business decision, with top-level sponsorship

The frenzy to jump on the offshore outsourcing bandwagon, often fuelled by pressures to reduce costs and companies' fears that they will fall behind their competitors, has led to many people responsible for procuring these services rushing into the field without thinking beyond the tempting carrot of quick, large savings. The bigger strategic issues can often be overlooked. Key questions, such as whether outsourcing a particular process is consistent with a business' overall strategy and, if it is, which route provides the most suitable balance of risk of rewards, are not addressed – oversights that can later come back to haunt a company. This, of course, assumes the BPO is given the green light by the board. In many of these cases, though, it is not approved, as others in the firm start questioning its strategic rationale and, rightly, block it. Not because it is necessarily wrong to outsource the process, but simply because the big picture issues have not been considered.

To compound this problem, it's common for visitors to India, the leading location for offshoring, to come back as evangelists. Such evangelists rightly extol the virtues of India, but all too often they also become insufficiently critical, leading to a failure to challenge vendors rigorously enough and an assumption that offshore outsourcing will be less problematic than it can be. Some evangelists are also swayed as much by the personal benefits of running an offshore outsource as the business rationale. It's an easy trap to fall into. The contrast between the grinding poverty of densely-populated cities such as Mumbai and the sleek, cutting-edge facilities operated by many suppliers in these regions is startling and leaves visitors with one unmistakable message: these regions have an abundant supply of low-cost, highly skilled labour.

However, while every project needs its evangelists, it's essential to take a long, dispassionate look at any outsourcing opportunity and not buckle to pressures to join the party without weighing all the options. And a critical first step in arriving at a balanced, commercially intelligent solution is to look strategically at your business processes as a whole. In particular, you need to identify the processes that are core to your competitive advantage and those that are not. Normally, only non-core activities are outsourced. But not all of these non-core processes will be outsourceable. Some, for example, might be too tightly integrated to core processes, making them difficult to separate and relocate. And when it comes to offshore outsourcing, there are further considerations – there may be legal or physical constraints, there might not be a suitable supplier or the costs of outsourcing might outweigh the benefits.

A further question to consider is 'what is the most effective way to outsource the processes that have been identified as eligible for outsourcing?' There are basically two options. You can either continue to exert 100 per cent control over the process and relocate it to an offshore in-house facility which is known as a 'captive' facility in the BPO lexicon, or you can hand over the process to a third party. The third party might manage the processes offshore or domestically, or a mix of the two. Or you can have a combination of captive and third party outsourcing solutions. Which route you choose will largely be driven by the degree of control that you feel you need to have over the process. This will be shaped by the risk profile of the processes (see next section), the trust you have in the suppliers available and other factors. Generally, the greater the need to control the process, the higher the likelihood that the process will be managed as a captive facility. Companies also sometimes choose the captive avenue as an opportunity to gain insights into a market prior to committing themselves more fully to the country.

One of the downsides with captives is that they tend to have higher costs than third party providers due to a variety of factors including high expatriate costs, over-specified infrastructures and high management salary costs. If the company is new to the country, it also faces a steep learning curve, slowing its ability to realise the commercial advantages of offshoring and increasing the risks. In addition, it might not be able to achieve the scale required to develop a successful captive. What you need to ask yourself is, 'If you were able to get the same savings and returns by outsourcing to a third party in your home country, would you still insist on keeping it in-house?' If not, then why does your sourcing decision change when the delivery location is remote? The answer often reveals more about a company's fear of the unknown than commercial logic.

While there are also potential difficulties with offshore third party suppliers, these are manageable and offset by many positives. Third party BPO suppliers specialising in key process areas for multiple clients are able to develop real economies of scale, reflected in lower costs, and the concentration of expertise needed to improve the quality of service. Needless to say, though, third party BPO suppliers are not *per se* superior. There are good, bad and indifferent suppliers, as there are in any market.

Whether you choose a captive or third party route, onshore or offshore, it's essential to develop a comprehensive outsourcing strategy, including a road map that defines what and how candidate processes should be outsourced, over what period and who will be responsible. These broad issues, which are explored below, will involve a variety of considerations, including strategic risk assessments, regulatory issues and the target supplier's capability. One of the most important factors, though – one that provides both the glue that holds the entire arrangement together and the fuel to propel it forward – is the individual or group of individuals who sponsor and champion the cause. It is essential to have a top-level executive, ideally a board member, behind the scheme. Without this, there will be insufficient commitment, resources and time allocated to the BPO decision and implementation. It will stagnate. Moreover, the involvement of an executive ensures that the right strategic and general business questions are asked, rather than simply the technical, procedural points. It also helps the two parties to spot and capitalise ways to enhance the service's commercial contribution. This is one of the great advantages of outsourcing: it creates opportunities to re-invent your processes and inject greater efficiency, as well as ways to improve revenue streams and service levels (see the boxed case study for an example of how Xansa helped a major utility do this).

2 Manage the risks, recognising that there is a trade-off between the risks and rewards

Although companies usually only outsource non-core processes, many of these processes can be critical and any disruption to them can have significant knock-on effects, undermining both the firm's ability to conduct its business and its brand reputation. Xansa, for example, manages a number of financial functions for a major player in the travel industry, with over ten million customers, including payments to its affiliated tour operators and hotels. Any failure to deliver these payments on time could jeopardise the travel company's relationship with these suppliers and its commercial health. Unfortunately, some companies are so focused on the cost side of the BPO equation that they either overlook these hazards or believe the cost savings outweigh the risks. While this belief might prove to be true, it is commercially cavalier to throw caution to the wind unless you have systematically evaluated your firm's vulnerability to the potential hazards of offshore outsourcing and the possible impacts on your business. Indeed, in many cases, companies may have a regulatory or legal responsibility to do so – as the issue of corporate governance continues to climb up the agenda so too will the question of risks.

There are seven broad categories of risks that have to be considered:

- **How will outsourcing the selected service affect your organisation's strategic direction?** What is your new business operating model? What business capabilities do you need to retain? What new capabilities do you need to attract?
- **How achievable is the outsourcing business case?** Are the numbers reliable, given the lack of cost and revenue benchmarks for these types of partnerships? How dependent is the business case on mutual cooperation between the supplier and various internal departments? How vital will the relationship with the supplier be? Does the supplier have the commitment to a long-term relationship, plus the resources to grow with you?
- **What is the risk of a disruption in the day-to-day delivery of the service?** How would this affect your business? Have you calculated its immediate financial impacts and long-term effects on your reputation?
- **What are the risks of moving the service to a new provider or location?** For example, how long do you expect the transition to take and what is the likelihood that you will hit your deadlines? If the transition is too rapid, requiring multiple transition teams, the risk of incomplete knowledge transfer and service failure increases. If it is stretched over too long a period, morale may plummet and staff could leave prior to completing transition, compromising the quality of your service.
- **Is the preferred supplier and its location in tune with your stakeholders' expectations?** How will staff and unions react to the deal? Is there a risk that your supplier's business practices or even location could alienate key customers, core shareholders and other stakeholders? The public backlash that Nike encountered by outsourcing its production to various South-East Asian countries is a classic example.
- **Will outsourcing compromise the security of your operations?** Consider the impact of entrusting commercially sensitive or customer confidential data to a third party. How is this risk changed if the third party is located overseas? What safeguards are in place to secure the integrity of this data? Are there any geopolitical risks?
- **How much experience do you have of selecting and managing these types of relationships?** Does your business have the management skills, linguistic ability and cultural insights to optimise this partnership? And

if you don't have this expertise in-house, how easy is it to recruit or train staff to a suitable level?

All of these risks must be methodically assessed. Inevitably, different companies will have different vulnerabilities. Heavily unionised businesses, for example, will score highly on the 'stakeholder' dimension, although it's worth noting that unions are increasingly receptive to the idea of BPO as many now recognise that it enables a company to concentrate on and grow its core business, safeguarding existing jobs and often generating enough additional employment to compensate for any in-house posts lost in outsourcing. In other companies, the main concern might be whether outsourcing will restrict its ability to divest an operating unit – an issue that also has clear strategic implications.

Irrespective of the nature of the vulnerability, nearly all the potential risks can be mitigated using a variety of 'levers'. For example, if a company is concerned about business continuity in the event of a problem at its supplier's location, it could adopt a multi-site or even a multi-supplier strategy. To overcome security worries, biometric recognition systems might be one option. Other solutions to risks can range from varying the onshore–offshore mix, to communication strategies to address stakeholder issues.

However, it's important to recognise that like an insurance policy, any risk mitigation has a cost. How high a price a company is prepared to pay will depend on the magnitude of the risk and the company's relative appetite for risk. It can also be influenced by the supplier. Several global suppliers who have established offshore operations in countries such as India and China play heavily on companies' insecurities and fear of loss control, offering them gold-plated 'Armageddon-proof' services. In some cases, this might be exactly what a firm needs. For others, it will be an unnecessary additional cost, eroding the savings. To reiterate a point made earlier, a cold rational look at the situation is recommended.

One of the mistakes that companies often make is to attempt to shift most of the risks and associated costs onto the supplier. This can have a number of unexpected counter-productive outcomes, including encouraging the supplier to cut corners in its service delivery in order to keep the contract profitable, therefore potentially magnifying rather than reducing the risks. In some instances, it can also be illogical. For example, a large regulated company that outsourced its monthly regulatory reports couldn't reasonably expect the supplier to pay the regulator's penalties if the reports were late: such fines are generally based on the profit of the client business and would probably bankrupt the smaller supplier, also leaving the client's business in a potentially precarious position. In many cases it is also possible for a client to include risk in the pricing of its services and products in a way that an outsourcer cannot – for example a bank covers its risk of default and payment errors in its interest charges and fees. An outsourcer delivering back-office processes for a bank cannot price for these risks in this way and therefore it is not appropriate for them to take liability for such risks.

There's also the less quantifiable issue of the tensions that these risk-cost pressures put on the relationship between the two parties, which can translate into a lower quality of service and reluctance by the supplier to invest. Examples are known of where a supplier has continually agreed to take more and more added risk either because he has a different view of the risk or because he didn't want to disappoint the client. This is often a direct result of cultural differences and can result in the client having the impression that the 'risk transfer' was reasonable and everything was safe and secure. In reality, the opposite might be the case. Recognising and managing this cultural dimension of a negotiation is vital, but often not taken into consideration.

The bottom line is that any outsourcing relationship needs to be treated as a business would treat a capital investment. It should evaluate the risks and ways to mitigate them, and where appropriate, share this responsibility equitably. It's not always easy to quantify the risks and understand what is appropriate but both parties are much more likely to arrive at a win-win solution if they work together and have an open, honest dialogue about the risks. Communication is the key, a point returned to later.

3   Assess candidate suppliers against a variety of value-added measures – not just cost

The obsession with costs in the BPO market has two major problems that can land companies in difficulties, over and above the lost opportunities to improve revenues and profitability by enhancing the quality of the service. First, it's hard to establish what a reasonable cost is as the offshore BPO market is still relatively immature and there are few reliable benchmarks or 'reference points'. This frequently results in a cycle where a client might request ever more detailed financial data. However, the responses received will typically be based upon different accounting policies and assumptions, raising more questions than they answer. If the client is not careful this can turn into a time-consuming and energy-draining process that not only delays the completion of the deal but also saps the company's commitment to the initiative. It is also a common symptom of a firm's fear that the offshore supplier is overcharging it. Sometimes this leads to the deal grinding to a halt, squandering the time invested in the transaction and potentially significant rewards if the supplier is, in reality, the best choice. Moreover, even if firms did have access to valid reference points, companies often have little idea of the true costs of their in-house processes, making comparisons difficult if not irrelevant.

The second problem with the 'cost-conscious mindset' is that costs can paint a highly misleading picture. In India, for example, a country with around one billion people and an annual average per capita income of just

$530 (World Bank, 2004), suppliers have no difficulty in finding low-cost labour. The question, of course, is what is the quality of the labour? What companies need to do when evaluating candidate suppliers is to adopt a 'multi-variate' approach that takes into account not just the costs but also the value and the risks. This will enable the firm to establish the supplier that provides the best value for money and is most closely aligned to the 'procurer's' strategic objectives. In this selection, clients should consider a range of suppliers including the offshore based IT and BPO pureplays such as Wipro and WNS in India, the global IT players such as Accenture and IBM, and specialist UK based businesses with major offshore capabilities such as Xansa and Vertex. Only once this process is completed should detailed negotiations commence with the optimum candidate. In short, the goal should be to find the supplier that matches your 'target operating model' – the model that supports your business' strategy – and not to find the cheapest solution and bend your organisation around the supplier.

Once the supplier is chosen, a broad range of service level agreements and other details will have to be finalised. Although it's important to have commonly agreed goals, it is equally vital not to be overly rigid and fixated on details. Circumstances will change and you need the flexibility to be able to adapt to these. An excessively contractual mindset can also undermine the relationship by reducing the supplier to the role of a commodity, a difficulty discussed earlier. Instead, companies should establish broad guiding principles that include specific, measurable targets, such as saving £5 million in the first year and improving customer satisfaction levels by 10 per cent by the second year and not be overly prescriptive about how these goals are achieved.

4   View the transition costs as a capital cost, not a service charge

Moving a service offshore is a hugely important stage in the project that requires careful planning, a robust methodology, appropriate human resources and that most painful of all resources to part with – money. Unfortunately, companies often fail to take the time to consider the transition in detail and underestimate the level of funding. This is partly due to historical precedence. To date, most services that have been offshored are so-called 'lift and drop' processes – simple tasks with defined interfaces that can relatively easily be taken from one location and dropped into another. For these types of processes, transition is typically no more than simple IT systems access and training to ensure familiarity with process documentation and basic rules. However, as discussed earlier, as firms look to extract more value from offshore outsourcing they will need to outsource increasingly complex processes. These processes are likely to be more deeply embedded in the organisation, touching on many other internal processes and relying on multiple IT systems. To relocate such processes without pain requires a highly robust methodology. Transitions of more complex processes will also require more care, more effort, and often more time and cost to ensure that insights and understanding of the client business – and how the process fits into it – are captured. This means not only having to earmark sufficient funds to cover these costs but, more significantly, viewing the transition as a long-term capital cost or investment, just as the relationship with the supplier should be seen, not simply as a one-off cost or service charge. But, as we saw earlier with the chargebacks example, great reward can come, if you have sufficient transition expertise, from migrating these more embedded but difficult to transition processes.

From a practical point of view, one of the best approaches is to agree on the detailed transition costs after the main on-going costs and other contractual elements have been broadly defined and the contract awarded. Do not allow the transition to become a bargaining chip in the overall cost negotiations – as the first practical step in offshore outsourcing, the transition is too important. Moreover, it is usually only after the contract has been awarded that the two parties will have the time to scrutinise the transition in sufficient detail. The speed of the relocation, which is mainly dictated by the scale, complexity and commercial sensitivity of the processes, as well as the company's appetite for risk, is equally critical. Questions that need to be addressed at the strategic planning stage include whether it should be phased to reduce the risks. If it is carried out too quickly, involving several transition teams covering the different processes, the risks increase dramatically. There is also the danger that you will be left with unoccupied in-house staff who previously managed the process. Take too long with the transition and in-house morale may plummet, staff will probably leave, and the company's quality of service and reputation will decline, with all the revenue implications this involves.

5   Build a long-term, mutually beneficial relationship with your supplier, based on sharing the risks and rewards

Only a small percentage of the success of outsourcing is down to having the right contract and the supplier living up to its conditions. The key to winning in this field is to build a strong, mutually beneficial relationship with the supplier. Agreeing on realistic goals is part of this. So, too, is good communication. Don't bombard each other with e-mails; talk over the phone. Face-to-face communication, notably via frequent visits to each other's sites, is also essential, not just to build the relationship but to enable you and your supplier to understand each others' businesses in more depth, including current issues, constraints and opportunities to make commercially fruitful improvements. And always be sensitive to the sometimes large cultural gulf between your region and theirs. In India, for instance, people are very keen not to disappoint and will often say 'yes' to a request to do something, which, in reality, will be a struggle to deliver. Or they might stay quiet about a problem or simply give you the answer they think you want to hear. All of this, of course, has the potential to elevate the risks and lead to significant difficulties unless this cultural issue is understood and catered for.

Above all, establish a commercial relationship which recognises that the partnership will grow and evolve over the years. Treat the contract as a flexible and constantly changing reference point shaped to reflect current business needs, not a straightjacket that restricts the relationship. And be prepared to share the risks and rewards. Introduce incentives into the relationship to create a win-win situation. These and other steps might cost a bit extra in terms of time and your financial commitment, but don't get hung up on the costs – the 'inputs'. Outsourcing is an investment and the returns can be very high, provided it is approached and managed properly. Seize the opportunity.

Case study
Tapping into the commercial advantages of BPO

Xansa's relationship with a leading utility illustrates both the complexity of the processes that can be fruitfully outsourced offshore and the improvements in the quality of service that can be generated.

Like many of Xansa's clients, the utility's goal wasn't simply to reduce the operating costs of its back-office activities but to use BPO as an opportunity to increase customer satisfaction, while maintaining its high regulatory and internal quality standards. The flexibility to scale up its back-office processes was also high on the company's agenda as much of this work is seasonal: bills are generated annually and customers tend to move house in the spring and the autumn, creating peaks of activity. In addition, the BPO solution had to support the company's stance on corporate social responsibility.

Initially, Xansa worked closely with the company using Xansa's domain knowledge to help the client shape its thinking about how BPO could be tailored to its business. Candidate processes were selected from the customer services function and focused on back-office processing as the client considered the customer experience and in particular the call centre to be a core activity which it did not want to outsource. Overall the utility's vision of the role BPO would play was an ambitious one with some two million transactions per year being identified for delivery by a BPO partner.

In developing its BPO plans, the utility was also conscious of the risks involved. Particular concerns were the highly unionised workforce and the potential reputational risks of offshoring. The workforce risks were addressed by working closely with the trade union through the planning and implementation stages. As a result of this, the client was able to redeploy staff into the call centre based in the UK as processes were offshored, incurring no direct job losses as a result of the programme. The reputational risks were partly mitigated by focusing on the corporate social responsibility of the supplier. A phased approach was also agreed on, to minimise the regulatory risks. By phasing the transition, the client not only managed its risks effectively but was also able to enjoy the planned benefits right from the start.

To test the feasibility of their business plan, as well as the capability of Xansa's Indian operation to rise to the challenge, they asked Xansa to pilot two types of processes. One of these involved complex processes to test the partner's ability to make the transition effectively and deliver quality improvements. The other involved customer-centric processes such as handling written customer correspondence.

One of the complex processes chosen for the pilot was billing exceptions, a multi-phase process that requires numerous internal handoffs with different departments, and judgement. 'Exceptions' are inaccurate customer bills that can be incorrect for any of 70 different reasons, for example if a property is unoccupied or its use has changed, making it a highly complex issue to resolve. Inaccurate bills like these have two cost implications. There is the increased overhead of dealing with the correspondence and phone calls, plus the impact of delayed bill payments on cash flow. As the pilot showed, Xansa was able to make significant processing improvements in resolving billing exceptions and, since it was awarded the contract, it has far exceeded the utility's targets, with 90 per cent of billing exceptions resolved within one day and 100 per cent within three days.

Equally impressive gains have been achieved in processing customer correspondence. Each day the utility receives over 1000 letters and has a regulatory obligation to respond within five days. Previously the process of replying was handled manually, in-house. Since this service has been transitioned to India, Xansa has from day one made use of imaging technology and streamlined working practices to process correspondence within four days, a 20 per cent improvement despite the added distance of India. Letters are now scanned and hosted at Xansa's UK operation but processed in India, where staff access the client's remote IT systems to initiate the production of the reply letters, which are printed in the client's print room and posted. This has raised the quality of the service to the client's customers, produced substantial savings and minimised the risk of regulatory non-compliance. In fact, the improvement in response times has helped the company enhance its regulatory rankings.

Xansa has also created operational auto-referrals on the client's systems to facilitate the redirection of out-of-scope work immediately to the correct unit within the company, rather than being sent by default to India. This has considerably reduced the amount of duplication of work and improved efficiency. Xansa has also developed a skill-based work allocation model with in-built quality monitoring, reporting and process improvement modules, leading to greater efficiency and management control. Some of the benefits of this innovation include online quality monitoring and feedback, as well as enhanced tracking and management of 'sales maximisation' revenues.

Following the pilot stages, the utility transitioned the remaining processes identified in the original plan. These included all remaining written correspondence, 'general actions' which includes the management of a number of complex issues that fall outside the remit of the call centre, and 'pending' which includes liaising with customers during the resolution of protracted issues.

Working together, Xansa and the utility have significantly reduced its direct costs and by improving the billing process have increased the cash flow. Integral to the success of the partnership has been a gainshare arrangement that ensures that both parties have the same imperatives.

Conclusion

The benefits of offshore outsourcing arrangements are clear and indisputable. However, in this chapter we have highlighted some of the less obvious issues and problems that exist when approaching offshoring. Many of these issues are hard to navigate as there isn't a convenient route map of the hazards that lie on the path to a successful offshore outsource: every company is different and will face different risks, opportunities and issues at different stages. However, by carefully working through the specifics of each client's situation, and applying some key guiding principles an appropriate outsourcing strategy can be developed and implemented. The key to success is to have a well-formulated plan that is led and shaped by the executive of the company and views BPO from a strategic perspective. This means moving beyond simple cost-cutting behaviour to adopting a long-term, win-win partnership with the selected supplier, with the carefully assessed risks and rewards shared equitably.

Note

1. A chargeback is a transaction returned because of non-compliance with the card associations' rules and regulations or because it was disputed by a cardholder.

Bibliography

V. Agrawal, D. Farrell and J.K. Remes, 'Offshoring and beyond', *The McKinsey Quarterly, 2003 Special Edition* (2003).

D.J. Hoch, 'Business Process Outsourcing – The Strategic Imperative', *FT NASSCOM Conference Paper* (2003), slide 19.

P. Morris and R. Morgan, 'The Performance of Outsourcing Providers in the UK Market', *Morgan Chambers* (2004), 23.

World Bank, World Development Indicators Database (2004).

Part IV

Achieving Business Transformation Through Outsourcing

7
BPO as Enterprise Partnership: The BAE-XChanging Transformation Strategy for HR Procurement

Mary Lacity, Leslie Willcocks and David Feeny

1 Introduction

By 2005, European business process outsourcing (BPO) is estimated as worth 72 billion Euros in revenues (2002 comparator: 43 billion). In semi-recessionary times from 2001, back-office activities and functions such as IT, Human Resource administration, procurement, finance and accounting, legal, energy management and real estate management have been obvious targets for efficiency, and even transformation, drives. But how to deliver on the very real promises outsourcing offers? In this chapter, we look at innovative, strategic approaches to this question, involving risk-reward contracting, the creation of a third entity joint owned by client and supplier, and the application of distinctive supplier core capabilities. The example we will focus on, drawn from BAE Systems' experiences and those of 'pure play' BPO supplier Xchanging, will be procurement.

Global business-to-business procurement expenditure was estimated to be $18 trillion in 2001 and rising thereafter by at least 10 per cent per annum.[1] We might think this market comprises primarily *direct spend* for companies' core materials. However:

- indirect procurement accounts for 60 per cent to 80 per cent of all purchasing transactions,[2]
- manufacturing, distribution, retail, financial and professional companies spend, on average, 40 per cent of their total revenue on indirect goods.[3]

These indirect goods include everyday items such as office supplies, travel services, furniture, car fleets and contract labour. Generally, companies do not manage indirect spend with anywhere near the rigour applied to direct spend, though, for example, a ten per cent reduction in procurement costs can result in a 50 per cent rise in profit margin.[4] The question becomes, how can a company corral its indirect spend to achieve such results? One possibility is to outsource part or all of the indirect procurement function. This chapter analyses how BAE Systems has been managing its indirect spend of over £900 million per year. Beginning with indirect spend controlled by HR, an estimated £80 million per year, BAE Systems sought to reduce spend through consolidating their buying power across 70 sites. Initially making inroads into this area, including taking a lot of costs already out of indirect spend, BAE Systems then created an enterprise partnership with a company called Xchanging in November of 2001. This jointly-owned enterprise, named Xchanging Procurement Services (XPS), is a 10-year deal, initially worth about £80 million per annum. XPS manages the entire supply chain for BAE Systems' UK subsidiaries in certain indirect spend categories such as car fleet, non-technical contract labour, recruitment, healthcare and training. During XPS's first years of operations, it had already delivered significant benefits to BAE Systems. But radical change is rarely painless. Throughout the case, we discuss the challenges that arose and how the partners coped with them. Specifically, the chapter:

- identifies competencies needed to transform indirect spend,
- discusses the pros and cons of five different transformation implementation options,
- assesses the enterprise partnership's ability to deliver the transformations espoused,
- profiles the ideal customer for the enterprise partnership model.

We now step back to the beginning of BAE Systems and Xchanging's enterprise partnership story.

2　BAE Systems: the customer context

British Aerospace was formed as a government owned enterprise in 1978, from a series of independent companies in the United Kingdom (UK) aerospace industry. It brought together businesses which included military aircraft, commercial aircraft (through its share holding in Airbus), Jetstream (commuter aircraft), Dynamics (missiles), and Royal Ordnance (weapons). Business units are in charge of their own profitability and support services, including indirect spend on items such as car leases and contract labour. The decentralised culture was required because each strategic business unit (SBU) operated under different production, marketing and legal environments.

In 1985, BAE went public under the Conservative Government's privatisation programme. BAE then embarked on a series of acquisitions, including the purchase from government of the Rover car group. In the early 1990s, BAE was confronted with loss of sales due to the end of the Cold War and economic recession. Dick Evans, Group CEO, sought to improve profitability by focusing on core competencies in aircraft, divesting non-core divisions and refinancing the company. BAE subsequently sold Rover, Corporate Jets, and Ballast Nedam. BAE reduced headcount by 21,000 employees. As a result, profitability increased to £230 million on £11 billion in sales in 1994. But from 1997 through to 1999, BAE's sales growth stagnated. Clearly, BAE needed to expand their global markets.

In January of 1999, British Aerospace and GEC proposed a merger between British Aerospace and GEC's Marconi Electronic Systems to create a global aerospace and defense company called BAE Systems. Investors were promised that the synergies from the merger would result in annual cost savings in excess of £275 million within three years of completion of the transaction. While BAE Systems would continue to invest in their core capabilities in military aircraft, weapon systems, nuclear submarines, and large commercial aircraft, all support functions were mandated to deliver significant cost savings.

In the area of human resource management, BAE's Group HR Director, Terry Morgan, was charged with delivering up to 40 per cent cost savings on an estimated annual HR spend of £25 million while maintaining the same level of service. Terry figured the only way to deliver the cost cuts was to centralise, standardise and downsize HR operations, which comprised over 700 HR staff in 70 locations. After an exhaustive decision process, Terry and his team decided that the best way to achieve shared services was through a 50/50 joint enterprise partnership with Xchanging, called Xchanging HR Services.[5] The deal, signed in February of 2001, was worth £25 million a year.

BAE Systems subsequently transferred their HR assets and 430 personnel to the enterprise partnership. The enterprise partnership, in turn, delivers HR services back to BAE Systems, now delivered via a web-enabled portal. As at 2004/5, BAE Systems was receiving guaranteed savings of 15 per cent and was sharing in any future profits from external customers to the venture.

As Xchanging took over BAE Systems' HR, it became clear that a large amount of indirect spend was buried in the 70 decentralised HR functions. BAE Systems, like many large companies, had used the HR department as a procurement catch-all for miscellaneous items such as health care, stationery, non-technical contract labour, training and recruiting. BAE were already addressing this issue when Xchanging came upon the scene and created a further alternative to deal with this disaggregated, indirect spend of approximately £80 million per year that actually dwarfed core HR spend.

The question became, how should BAE Systems manage the nearly £80 million in indirect spend that had previously been handled by their decentralised HR people? Clearly BAE Systems could achieve significant

Table 7.1   Competencies Needed to Transform Indirect Spend

---

1. Category Expertise:
  1.1   'Indirect' spend is a core capability
  1.2.   Full time experts devoted to indirect spend categories

2 Sourcing Methods:
  2.1   Ability to baseline indirect spend and costs
  2.2   Ability to decompose indirect spend & costs into commoditised units
  2.3   Ability to statistically analyse indirect spend and costs
  2.4   Ability to negotiate mutually favourable deals
  2.5   Ability to service deals, including controlling price and scope creep

3. Sourcing Tools:
  3.1   Ability to maintain correct supplier data
  3.2   Ability to create demand templates
  3.3   Ability to transform demand into RFPs
  3.5   Ability to facilitate user ordering, such as web portals
  3.6   Ability to facilitate auctions
  3.7   Ability to track and validate orders
  3.8   Ability to track and validate receipts
  3.9   Ability to track and pay invoices
  3.10 Ability to monitor service levels
  3.11 Ability to track and manage supplier complaints
  3.12 Ability to track and manage user complaints

4. Buying Power:
  4.1   Ability to aggregate spend across units within a company
  4.2   Ability to aggregate spend across companies

5. Supplier Appeal:
  5.1   Ability to offer large volumes
  5.2   Ability to offer long-term deals
  5.3   Ability to lower supplier transaction costs
  5.4   Ability to facilitate user orders
  5.5   Ability to pay supplier on time

6. Governance:
  6.1   Ability to align indirect spend agents' incentives with company interests
  6.2   Ability to reap cost-cutting rewards from indirect spend transformation
  6.3   Ability to keep demand variable (ie not having to commit to huge volumes
  for a long period of time to reap rewards)
  6.4   Ability to retain strategic decision making over procurement

---

savings if they could continue to develop key capabilities needed to transform indirect procurement spend. In fact, BAE Systems had already taken a lot of cost out of a number of categories of indirect spend before XPS came along. Commonly, the key capabilities for doing this would be recognised as those listed in Table 7.1.

3   Options for transforming indirect spend

In theory, BAE Systems, like all large organisations, had at least five viable options for developing further these transformative capabilities:

1. Do it yourself
2. Hire a consultant
3. Join a consortium exchange
4. Outsource to an e-procurement company
5. Create an enterprise partnership

For BAE Systems, the options were clearly biased towards the enterprise partnership choice, even though they had already made substantial inroads into improved management and cost cutting of indirect spend. This was because a lot of the spend was highly integrated with the Xchanging HR Services deal. However, the following discussion will guide readers through some of the pros and cons of alternative procurement implementation options.

Do It Yourself. Let us look at this as a general proposition. Of the six capabilities listed in Table 7.1, DIY generally would score highest on governance. In particular, the major benefit of DIY is that the savings are not shared with a third party. DIY would also enable a company to retain strategic decision making and to align the purchasing agents' incentives with company interests. But, the DIY option would often score lowest on developing and retaining category expertise. Frequently occurring impediments include:

- In-house purchasing agents lack interest in indirect spend categories.
- Attracting world-class experts in indirect spend is difficult because they will never have the same status or career satisfaction as direct spend agents.
- Developing in-house expertise takes too long.
- Senior management unwilling to make upfront investment required for transformation.

Purchasing consultants. Companies can also hire an outside purchasing consultant to manage a one-time, big-bang procurement project. The benefits of this option is that the consultants bring an infusion of expertise, methods and tools to indirect spend but some major risks of consultants include:

- High costs.
- Lack of accountability for and sustainability of results.

Consortium exchanges. The main advantage of a consortium is the ability to increase the customer's buying power by consolidating spend across many organisations. But, consortiums require a significant investment in enterprise development, including management and technology. Thus, the most powerful consortiums have typically been in direct spend categories. BAE Systems actually belongs to a consortium with Boeing, Lockheed-Martin, Rolls Royce and others for direct materials. While effective for core materials, there is no equivalent consortium for the breadth of indirect spend.

Outsource to e-procurement suppliers. The major advantage of e-procurement suppliers is that most have invested heavily in sourcing tools. The market, however, is still immature. Most dot.com start-ups are still light on category expertise:

Some have struggled or have indeed failed because they have no content. At the end of the day, what are you doing, you are applying tools into an existing one off volume/model.   John Doherty, Category Director, XPS

e-procurement suppliers also face the daunting task of developing a critical mass of suppliers and customers:

Start-up companies went into all sorts of problems because they went to the supplier and said, 'well give us a deal and we will get you some customers' and they said 'go away, you get us some customers and we will give you a deal.'   David Rich Jones, CEO, XPS

Enterprise partnership. The enterprise partnership model, as enacted by Xchanging, takes a customer's baseline indirect spend, transforms the spend using category expertise, spend aggregation, and better tools and methods to negotiate lower prices with suppliers and to improve both customer and supplier service. The savings are shared 50/50 between the customer and Xchanging.

According to Xchanging's executives, the enterprise partnership model is distinct from the other four options. Compared to the do-it-yourself and management consultants option, Xchanging claims that the enterprise partnership will yield better service and faster results. Figure 7.1 maps the timing and sustained value of the DIY, consulting and enterprise partnership options. Xchanging argues that DIY would require a 12 to 18 month project to redesign three categories of spend. Management consultants would require six to 12 months to redesign up to five categories of spend. The enterprise partnership can reengineer up to 10 categories of spend within four months.

Compared to purchasing consultants, the enterprise partnership's biggest distinction is accountability and sustainability of results. Xchanging makes

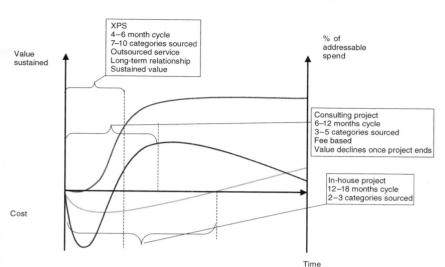

Figure 7.1   DIY, Management Consultants, and Enterprise Partnerships
Source: Copyright © Xchanging

money only if it can lower prices for the customer, thus incentives are highly aligned with this governance mechanism. Additionally:

> *I think for us, content is a big differentiator, I think expertise is a big differentiator because we are building specific expertise in a relatively narrow range of commodities rather than offering ourselves up as procurement consultants who can consult on anything. Although quite frankly, we could do that, but that is not our model. Our model is not a consultancy model.*   John Doherty, Category Director, XPS

Compared to the e-procurement dot.com, the enterprise model differs because of the focus on content and because technology is merely an enabler, not the solution in itself.

4   The XPS contract between BAE Systems and Xchanging

BAE Systems and Xchanging signed a 10-year contract for the enterprise partnership, XPS, on 01 November 2001 (see Table 7.2). The initial *scope of the contract* covered seven categories of indirect spend:

1. Fleets (estimated to be about £25 million per year)
2. Non-technical Contract Labour (~ £25 million per year)
3. Learning and Development (~ £25 million)

Table 7.2   BAE Systems-Xchanging's Contract Highlights

10-year partnership
Scope of contract entails seven categories of indirect spend
Xchanging is exclusive supplier on these seven baseline categories
Savings are shared 50/50 on baseline categories
Existing BAE Systems contracts were novated to Xchanging
BAE Systems gets 65 per cent of savings on categories added to the enterprise
beyond the seven baseline categories. BAE Systems gets 35 per cent of profits from
additional external customers
40 people to transfer at equivalent pay & benefits
BAE Systems spend is completely variable, they do not commit to minimum
volumes

---

4. Health Care (~ £5 million per year)
5. Permanent Recruitment (~ £2 million per year)
6. Remuneration & Benefits
7. Stationery

Xchanging has **exclusive procurement rights** in these categories. Thus, BAE Systems is obligated to purchase these items through Xchanging for the duration of the contract. BAE Systems can only go elsewhere if Xchanging fails. **Savings are shared 50/50 between BAE Systems and Xchanging** on the baseline spend in the seven categories. In addition, as Xchanging attracts external customers to XPS besides BAE Systems, Xchanging will share 35 per cent of the profits with BAE Systems:

We started off 50/50 but the more third party we actually bring in, we get 65 per cent of the shares and the more spend BAE Systems add in, they get 65 per cent of the share and when we moved on to negotiate the procurement contract, so we wanted a vehicle that would drive the right behaviours. David Rich Jones, CEO, XPS

The business plan calls for XPS to have revenues of £250 million by 2006. The estimated profits for the first five years of operation are as follows:

Year 1: £4.9 million
Year 2: £9 million
Year 3: £14 million
Year 4: £21 million
Year 5: £27 million

Out of the BAE Systems base of 100 indirect procurement people, 40 people were initially targeted for transfer from BAE Systems to the enterprise.

The governance of the contract entails **two important joint boards: the Management Board and the Service Review Board.** The Management Board's role is to oversee the relationship and to ensure success in terms of commercial benefit and delivery. The Service Review Board ensures that the service commitments are implemented and achieved. **Existing BAE Systems contracts were novated to Xchanging for ongoing management.** One example is the three-year contract BAE Systems had negotiated for non-engineering contract labour:

Let's take their non-engineering contract labour, which is a classic example, where BAE Systems did a strategic purchasing initiative in 1999, early 2000 which was concluded and contracts were signed in October/November 2000. As far as BAE Systems are concerned, they have done that job and they have done something that is non core to them. They dedicated some resources to it for six months, they did a deal for three years and then they will forget about it and come back in three years time. So they have passed that to us and said well you can have this, there is nothing left in it. John Doherty, Category Director, XPS

The enterprise partnership deal doesn't guarantee a certain amount of savings because the customer does not have to guarantee a certain amount of spend. One of the main advantages to BAE Systems is that they did not have to guarantee Xchanging that their indirect spend would remain around the £80 million-a-year mark. Instead, BAE Systems benefits from the complete flexibility of variable indirect spend:

We have a subtler model because people's requirements for these non-core categories that they are purchasing can fluctuate or can even disappear, particularly in the area of resourcing. John Doherty, Category Director, XPS

We will see that this last contracting clause proved to be potentially devastating to XPS because they were expecting at least £80 million for the seven categories of spend to make the economics work, when only £35 million was transferred initially.

Implementation: November 2001 to November 2002

The XPS contract went into effect 01 November 2001. The deal is structured so that XPS, at first, only earns a small administration fee. XPS does not earn real profits until they begin generating cost savings once they transact on the transferred spend. In order for spending to be transferred from BAE Systems to XPS, the baseline spend must be measured and approved, existing legal contracts must be novated, or new legal contracts must allow XPS to purchase on behalf of BAE Systems. XPS estimated that the initial benchmarking and approval activities would only take two months. Once the spend is transferred, then XPS can apply the competencies required for transformation:

category expertise, sourcing methods, sourcing tools, buying power, supplier appeal and overall governance. Like all major outsourcing endeavours, the transition period was much longer than anticipated by the parties. It sometimes took eight months to transfer a category of spend to XPS. Two factors caused major delays. The key learning point is that the parties did everything they could to resolve issues in the spirit of a partnership.

1. XPS had to coordinate and gain approval from a tremendous number of BAE Systems' managers. XPS had to visit up to 30 BAE Systems sites, converse with up to 50 people, and seek as many as 12 signatures from BAE Systems managers. Learning and Development was a particularly challenging benchmarking area because the spend was highly decentralised and distributed to over 1000 suppliers. Just gathering the existing data was a Herculean task and it took nearly six months to benchmark existing spend.

To complicate matters, many of the retained BAE Systems procurement managers were not fully informed of the contract, thus they did not place a high priority on meeting with XPS. Moreover:

> *It is a difficult thing to sell with some of our procurement people as well. It is almost like we are outsourcing it because you haven't done a good enough job, that could be the perception if you are not careful. That caused difficulty, also the XPS people learning and understanding the culture within BAE Systems.*
> Colin Webster, Supplier and Development Manager, BAE Systems

Because XPS would not earn a profit until the baselines were approved, it became increasingly aggressive in seeking BAE Systems' cooperation. This XPS 'task-master' approach caused friction early in the relationship. To remedy this problem, BAE Systems actually devoted more resources in terms of relationship managers to manage the XPS/BAE Systems interface. After the transition period, these liaisons transferred to XPS:

> *One of the things that we are clear about is, when we are outsourcing, we don't want to retain too much control and activity ourselves, otherwise why outsource it. Getting people to understand that, not that we have got sloping shoulders, and saying 'it is not our responsibility any more,' but if you have got an issue take it up with the appropriate person within XPS. If you can't get it resolved then come to me.* Colin Webster, Supplier and Development Manager, BAE Systems

2. The parties overestimated the amount of spend that would be transferred from the seven categories. Recall that the contract called for approximately £80 million spend to be transferred to XPS in seven categories (see above). By the middle of the year 2002, only £30 million in spend had been transferred in these categories. For example, the partners initially thought that £25 million in learning and development was going to be transferred, but the actual number was only about 30 per cent of the estimate. This underestimation threatened XPS' ability to meet their projected profitability targets. BAE Systems and Xchanging's executives held many strategic planning sessions to address the shortfall. The partners agreed that it was in both of their interests to transfer over the intended critical mass of spend to XPS. This would be achieved by adding eight more categories of spend, bringing the XPS controlled spend to nearly £100 million by year end 2002. Some of the new categories included:

1. Travel (approximately £40 million)
2. Printing (£3 million)
3. Office furniture (£2 million)
4. Computer consumables (£1.3 million)
5. Mobile Phones

Of course, procuring 15 smaller categories rather than seven large ones has increased XPS' transaction and administration costs:

> *The complexity and the cost of taking on these small categories is almost as great as the big ones. They still need twelve signatures, they are still taking four to six months.*   David Rich Jones, CEO, XPS

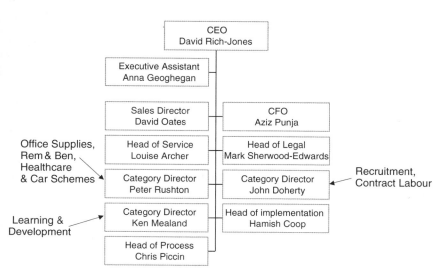

Figure 7.2 XPS Organisational Chart
Source: Copyright © Xchanging

The second effect is that XPS has less negotiating leverage with suppliers since the value of the deals is smaller. But the good news is that both parties have reduced the benchmarking cycle times significantly. As new categories of spend are added to scope, XPS is able to benchmark within a few months rather than eight months. And despite the added transaction and administration costs, XPS has been able to earn margins on all categories of spend, ranging from a low of five per cent to a high of 45 per cent, depending on the category.

The remainder of the story focuses on how XPS unleashes its six competencies – category expertise, methods, tools, buying power, supplier relationships and governance – to achieve such margins. We begin by looking at the XPS organisation.

The XPS Organisation. XPS is set up to be an independent enterprise with P&L responsibility. XPS senior management includes the CEO, CFO, Head of Service, Head of Process, Head of Legal, Sales Director, Head of Implementation and three Category Directors (see Figure 7.2). These Category Directors, prominently placed within the organisational hierarchy, serve the leadership role for the first major competency: category expertise.

Competency 1: Obtaining category expertise

At the start of the venture, Xchanging already had sourcing experts in senior management positions. For example, Xchanging's first Sourcing Practice Director, David Rich-Jones, had previously removed 40 per cent of spend from a £100 million procurement budget and added 25 per cent profits to a global building products company. Other Xchanging employees with careers in procurement include John Doherty, who delivered £54 million in savings as a senior category manager with two years at one prior site. The initial idea was that such leadership would be used to motivate, mentor and empower the 40 targeted BAE Systems employees. But when XPS went live in November 2001, only eight of the targeted 40 people transferred from BAE Systems. BAE Systems could not transfer more people because there simply weren't enough experts in indirect spend and BAE Systems wanted to retain some of those precious few experts on-site.

Xchanging was forced immediately to recruit category experts. Attracting top purchasing talent requires considerable expense in terms of salaries and incentives. To supplement these, Xchanging hired nearly 30 people and trained them to become full time category experts:

What we find is a procurement professional who thinks strategically and with our competency can understand that market place, not because he is an expert in it and he comes from that market place, but because he has the right mindset.   John Doherty, Category Director, XPS

Table 7.3   Category Expertise Assessment

Transformative Capabilities	Do-It-Yourself	Enterprise Partnership
1.1 'Indirect' spend is a core capability	LOW	HIGH
1.2. Full time experts devoted to indirect spend categories	LOW/ MED	HIGH

Xchanging partners these new hires with existing category experts. It actually views this as a better model than hiring only existing category experts:

We want to put the expert alongside a very bright, strategic thinker because the expert in our view is the solution and the problem. They will tell you very articulately why you can't do something, but if you turn that positively, they can help you actually do it.   David Richard Jones, CEO, XPS

Finding 1: For BAE Systems, the enterprise partnership model was a better way to access category expertise than do-it-yourself. As highlighted in Table 7.3, the investment in expertise and training was something BAE Systems could not see as a major priority, though inroads into indirect procurement management were still rapidly being made just before the deal setting up XPS. Thus, one of the first benefits of the XPS partnership was the development of significant category expertise. In addition, XPS has suffused its experts in the fast-paced, team-oriented Xchanging culture:

In terms of people, well there wasn't a team. So we have gone from two people to thirty-five since November 1ˢᵗ and the application of the competencies to be able to build a team. One of the compliments paid by somebody who came into it was, 'you wouldn't believe this team has only been together for such a short period and some of them had only been in the business three weeks.' So spending that time through that competency has been very important.   David Rich Jones, CEO, XPS

Competency 2: Applying sourcing excellence methods

Xchanging has several methods for reducing a customer's costs and increasing their service levels. Three representative examples:

Strategic method: portfolio management. XPS focuses on the indirect spend categories that will reap the greatest rewards. XPS assesses a customer's entire spend portfolio and targets different methods to maximise effective sourcing. Figure 7.3 provides a high-level view of the strategic portfolio analysis. Along the X-axis, XPS partners assess the level of customer business impact, including the level of spend, percentage of total spend, price volatility, impact on profitability and relationship of product to the customer's core

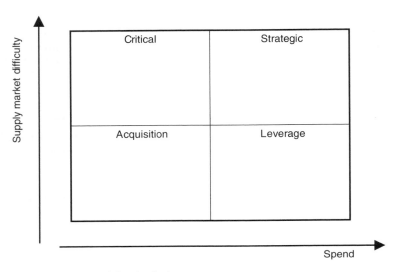

Figure 7.3   XPS Portfolio Analysis
Source: Copyright © Xchanging

business. Along the Y-axis, XPS partners assess the level of supplier risk and complexity, including the level of supplier concentration, threat of substitution, threat of new supplier entrants, buyer leverage, supplier market share, time sensitivity and technical risk. Considering both these dimensions, four strategies for managing spend emerge:

Strategic: As the most difficult and important categories, spending is managed through strategic alliances with key suppliers, focusing on close integration between the supplier and customer.

Critical: In these categories, the customer has less leverage because the spend is smaller and the supplier environment is complex. The strategies include developing critical relationships, engaging in long-term contracts, engineering out – and, as one participant put it – 'at times, groveling'.

Acquisition: The customer business impact is low and supplier environment is not complex. The strategies here focus on reducing transaction costs including automation, delegation and simplification.

Leverage: In these categories, the customer has the advantage. The sourcing strategies include adding competitors and negotiating multiple short-term contracts to procure lowest prices.

Tactical method: baselining and unitising category spend. We have addressed the political issues of baselining but not the actual method itself. Obviously, the parties need a precise baseline to later calculate and distribute the savings XPS generates. But the real power of baselining is the decomposition of indirect spend to its component parts so XPS can negotiate better deals on these unbundled goods and services (see Figure 7.4).

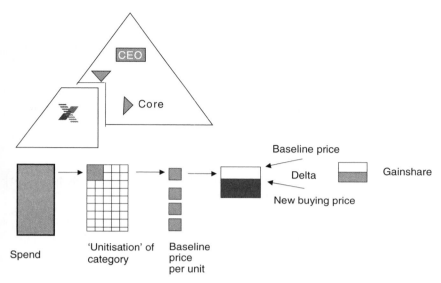

Figure 7.4   Xchanging's Methodology for Indirect Spend Cost Analysis
Source: Copyright © Xchanging

To illustrate the method and benefits of unitisation, three categories of indirect spend will serve as examples: contract labour, car fleets and recruitment.

Contract labour. Nearly 80 per cent of BAE Systems labour contracts were already fixed. BAE Systems did not expect additional savings from these, although Xchanging was able to extract some modest savings.

At BAE Systems, temporary staff are paid by temp agencies. The temp agencies bill the customer a bundled price which includes the temporary staff pay, employment tax and temp agency mark-ups. This latter quantity represented up to 80 per cent of the price in some cases. At BAE Systems, there are thousands of temp workers from different agencies. Xchanging, for the first time, analysed spend across the entire category of contract labour. Xchanging decomposed agency bills into their component parts.

By year end 2002, XPS had worked with BAE Systems to reduce 350 job titles down to four job classes with just 16 job titles overall. The four job classes are industrial workers, secretarial and administration workers, finance professionals, and support professionals. Within each job class, four skill levels based on experience are defined. Contract rates are now based on averages, which standardises bill rates for BAE Systems. The real power of 'unitising' prices and aggregating volumes across agencies will be flexed when existing contracts expire.

In the interim, however, this method of aggregating and standardising requires communicating overall effects with decentralised budget holders. Because some budget holders will incur higher rates in the short term, they need to understand that in the aggregate, BAE Systems' total contract labour rates were constant:

If you look at the budget holder on an individual site, you could end up paying more than you did previously. That doesn't help the budget holder who pays more, and we had some difficulty there. Colin Webster, Supplier and Development Manager, BAE Systems.

Within six months of the existence of XPS, Xchanging was able to reduce an additional five per cent from existing contracts and took another 10 per cent out within the year. Once existing labour contracts expire, Xchanging is then in a better position to obtain better deals on behalf of BAE Systems.

Car fleets. Car fleet provides another example of the benefits of baselining and unitising. Prior to Xchanging, BAE Systems managed car leases in the typical manner:

How would their procurement department go about buying fleet? They would tender it to multiple lease companies quite, frankly, and say, here are our requirements, you, you, you and you, tender for that please. The suppliers will all apply the same model and you will get three prices which are remarkably similar. John Doherty, Category Director, XPS

XPS decomposed the costs of car leasing into its component parts depicted in Figures 7.5 and 7.6. XPS then asks suppliers to bid on these sub units, such as car purchase price, maintenance price, roadside recovery price, financing prices, etc:

We went to the manufacturers separately and said no, no we don't want you to provide your standard list price, we will negotiate a price with you which we will take to you and apply your financing costs to service maintenance and repair. John Doherty, Category Director, XPS

As of Summer 2002, Xchanging has managed the fifth largest car fleet in the UK, in excess of 10,000 vehicles.

Recruitment. The recruiting category was estimated to be worth about £2 million a year. In reality, only £1 million was transferred to XPS. Despite the shortfall, XPS was able to generate significant savings by reducing the number of suppliers from 100 to 15. Besides reducing the transaction costs by limiting the number of suppliers, XPS was able to negotiate much better deals because the 15 suppliers now had significantly larger deals. But when XPS centralised recruitment, there

Example of 'Un-bundling'

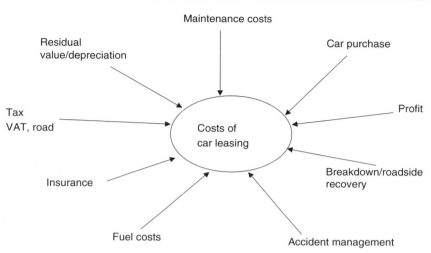

Key cost elements of car leasing

Figure 7.5   Xchanging's Methodology for Indirect Spend Cost Analysis for Car Fleet
Source: Copyright © Xchanging, 2002

Cost analysis

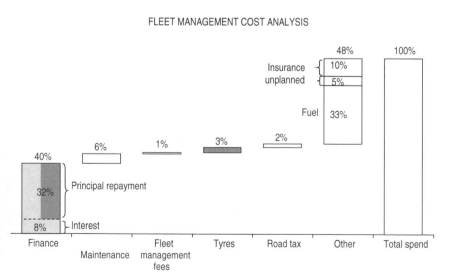

Figure 7.6   Xchanging's Methodology for Indirect Spend Cost Analysis for Car Fleet
Source: Copyright © Xchanging, 2002

was significant resistance from the BAE Systems SBUs. However, the BAE Systems' users were delighted with the savings as well as the improved processes for recruiting:

> *Recently in Recruitment, I had one of the businesses saying what an excellent job Xchanging did, helped them with some difficult recruitment that needed to be done. They really praised them.* Colin Webster, Supplier and Development Manager, BAE Systems
> *I think the benefits that they are driving out, the signs are very good, so we have got a level of confidence that some of the benefits built into the original business model will be achieved.* Jim Robinson, Procurement Director, BAE Systems

Operational method: enact models. Xchanging designed processes for contract enactment so stakeholders could easily make orders, receive goods or services, verify invoices and make payments. Rather than a 'one size fits all' model, Xchanging developed three enactment models: (1) transactional (2) a mid-level and (3) thick. These enactment models aim to minimise transaction costs by matching the most efficient process to the attributes of the category of spend.

Transactional model. For commodity types of indirect spend, such as stationery, Xchanging uses a transactional model in which the users place orders directly with suppliers from their desktop portal (see Figure 7.7 below). The supplier delivers goods and invoices directly to the users. The users pay the supplier and the supplier pays Xchanging a commission. This model was deemed the most efficient way to facilitate customer-supplier interactions and to distribute the gain shares.

As an illustrative example, suppose 15 different SBUs within BAE Systems had previously spent, on average, £100 per unit of stationery

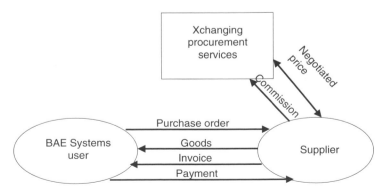

Figure 7.7 Xchanging's Transaction Model for Commodity Products

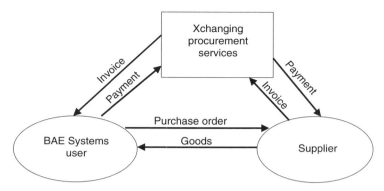

Figure 7.8   Mid-level Model

with 30 different suppliers. The idea is that Xchanging will aggregate the spend from the 15 SBUs and renegotiate with one or two select suppliers. Suppose Xchanging is able to negotiate a price of £80 per unit of stationery. The £20 savings would be equally split between BAE Systems and Xchanging. The supplier would send the stationery and an invoice for £90 to the BAE Systems user. Thus, the 10 per cent savings would be directly evident to the user. The supplier, in turn, would send a £10 commission to Xchanging.

Xchanging also designed this model to avoid upsetting users in years to come. An alternative design would have been that the supplier invoice the user for £80 and Xchanging could invoice the user for £10. The financial results would be the same but the users over time may question why they are paying Xchanging.

Mid-level model. For more complex types of indirect spend such as car fleets, Xchanging uses a mid-level model (see Figure 7.8 above). As an illustrative example, suppose 15 different SBUs within BAE Systems had previously spent, on average, £1000 per car lease per period with thirty different suppliers. The idea is that Xchanging will aggregate the spend from the 15 SBUs and renegotiate with one or two select suppliers. Suppose Xchanging is able to negotiate a price of £800 per unit. The £200 savings would be equally split between BAE Systems and Xchanging.

In this scenario, the BAE Systems user would again send the order directly to the selected supplier, and the supplier would deliver the car directly to the user. Xchanging would invoice the user for £900, thus the 10 per cent savings would be directly delivered to the user. The supplier would invoice Xchanging for the agreed upon price of £800, thus Xchanging would generate a £100 revenue.

Thick model. For very complex services, such as contract labour, Xchanging designed the thick model. This model will also be used to aggregate

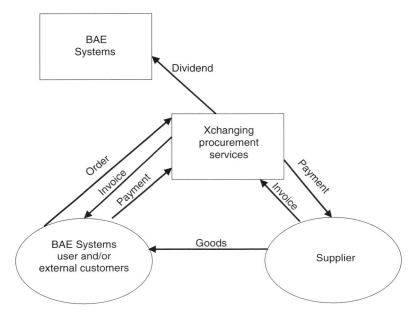

Figure 7.9   Thick Model

buying power beyond BAE Systems as other external customers sign with XPS (see Figure 7.9 above).

As an illustrative example, suppose 15 different SBUs within BAE Systems had previously spent, on average, £2000 per week for a certain type of non-technical contract worker. Once again, Xchanging will aggregate the spend from the 15 SBUs and renegotiate with one or two select suppliers. Suppose Xchanging is able to negotiate a price of £1600. The £400 savings would be equally split between BAE Systems and Xchanging.

In this scenario, the BAE Systems user and external clients would send the purchase order to Xchanging. Xchanging would aggregate the orders and negotiate a favourable deal with suppliers. Xchanging would invoice users and external customers for £2000 and pay suppliers £1600. BAE Systems would then receive a £200 dividend at the end of the specified time period.

Finding 2: For BAE Systems, the enterprise partnership model was a better way to improve sourcing methods than do-it-yourself. As the previous examples illustrate, there is ample evidence that Xchanging scores high on all transformative capabilities concerning methods (see Table 7.4). Indeed, Xchanging itself views its methods as one of the two key differentiators in the market:

Two things, we can deliver service and procurement through service definition in a way that others wont and secondly, outsourcing will fail without adequate

Table 7.4   Sourcing Methods Assessment

Transformative Capabilities	Do-It-Yourself	Enterprise Partnership
2.1 Ability to baseline indirect spend and costs	MED	HIGH
2.2 Ability to decompose indirect spend & costs into commoditised units	LOW	HIGH
2.3 Ability to statistically analyse indirect spend and costs	LOW	HIGH
2.4 Ability to negotiate mutually favourable deals	MED	HIGH
2.5 Ability to service deals, including controlling price and scope creep	MED	HIGH

base-lining and we are experts in base-lining and those two elements are what they have latched on to as our differentiators, which is quite interesting.
David Richard Jones, CEO, XPS

Competency 3: Delivering sourcing excellence tools

Xchanging committed to invest over £7 million in new technology over the first five years. Technology is another one of Xchanging's major transformation capabilities. At XPS, the major technologies implemented in the first year were the *Sourcing Workroom* to help procurement managers define, benchmark, research, analyse, negotiate and manage categories of spend, and the *Sourcing Portal* which enables users to order resources direct from their desktops.

XPS' Sourcing Workroom is a web-based online repository of methods and supply market knowledge. Figure 7.10 is a screen capture of the homepage, illustrating the links to the market interfaces, base-lining tools, supplier management tools, strategic sourcing plan, consortium engine, analytical tools and supplier market data.

David Rich Jones describes how the Sourcing Workroom is used:

> *We have a trading platform which allows us to operate the thin or the thick model depending on what we put into it and whether we just do the accounts payable or take the ordering requirements…the software supports data capture, analysis and strategic thinking templates. There is hard data capture because otherwise it's quite a tedious task of actually going round and discovering these things, it takes time. And then it is the analysis of it and it's then the strategic thinking templates that say once you have got an analysis and unitization of it, you can then say how am I going to take this to the market.*

In addition to the Workroom, XPS launched their first version of the sourcing portal on 30 June, 2002. This enables users dispersed throughout

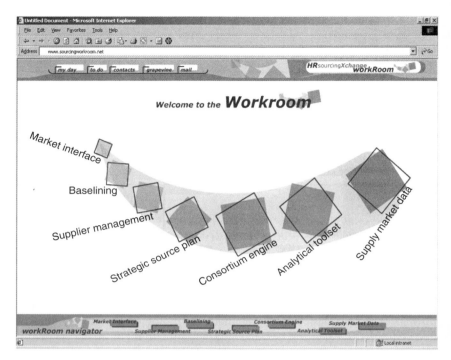

Figure 7.10   XPS Sourcing Workroom
Source: Copyright © Xchanging

BAE Systems to directly request resources from their desktop. For example, users now use the sourcing portal for recruiting:

> *We built a web-based portal, which people within BAE Systems can use for things like Recruitment. They can post a requirement from a portal. So they have been doing that investment, they are building the technology there. They have put into place a Call Centre as well, Help Desk and Call Centre and monitored that performance of it etc. They have done quite a lot.*   Colin Webster, Supplier and Development Manager, BAE Systems

The Sourcing Portal is seen as a key enabler of scalability in that Xchanging can easily replicate the technology to woo other customers:

> *Instead of going to a new customer and having a number of business develop-ment meetings, instead of going into a big bank and actually saying we will buy your contract labour for you, we actually go in and say we will apply our technology. So on every desk we will put the capability for you to order your contract labour under a portal called Xchanging Procurement Services, come*

Table 7.5 Sourcing Tools Assessment

Transformative Capabilities	Do-It-Yourself	Enterprise Partnership
3.1 Ability to maintain correct supplier data	LOW	HIGH
3.2 Ability to create demand templates	LOW	HIGH
3.3 Ability to transform demand into RFPs	MEDIUM	HIGH
3.5 Ability to facilitate user ordering, such as web portals	LOW	HIGH
3.6 Ability to facilitate auctions	HIGH	HIGH
3.7 Ability to track and validate orders	MEDIUM	HIGH
3.8 Ability to track and validate receipts	MEDIUM	HIGH
3.9 Ability to track and pay invoices	LOW	HIGH
3.10 Ability to monitor service levels	LOW	HIGH
3.11 Ability to track and manage supplier complaints	LOW	HIGH
3.12. Ability to track and manage user complaints	MEDIUM	HIGH

back to us and you get the benefit of our behind the scenes aggregation. Hugely powerful and we are beginning to realise that where the category is broad enough, such as resourcing and professional services, it will warrant the expenditure on the technology to actually be able to go in and sell that. David Rich Jones, CEO, XPS

Finding 3: For BAE Systems, the enterprise partnership model was a better way to implement better sourcing tools than do-it-yourself. As a back-office function, clearly BAE Systems would not want to invest £7 million in new technology to support indirect spend procurement. Because Xchanging will be able to leverage the investment over many customers, Xchanging is willing to make an investment that a back-office function would not. Table 7.5 clearly gives high marks to Xchanging's technical capabilities.

Competency 4: Increasing buying power

The two main ways to increase buying power are (1) to aggregate spend *within* a company and (2) to aggregate spend *across* companies. Xchanging has increased BAE Systems' buying power on both these dimensions.

Concerning the first dimension, the enterprise partnership model immediately created a centralised procurement function for indirect spend. Some participants estimate that as much as £400 of the £900 million indirect spend will eventually be consolidated and transferred over to XPS. To ensure this increased buying power potential from consolidation, BAE Systems had to guarantee Xchanging exclusive procurement rights. However, XPS and BAE Systems senior executives realistically know that bullying the few offenders will alienate users.

Table 7.6   Improved Buying Power Assessment

Transformative Capabilities	Do-It-Yourself	Enterprise Partnership
4.1 Ability to aggregate spend across units within a company	MED	HIGH
4.2 Ability to aggregate spend across companies	LOW	HIGH

Concerning the ability to aggregate spend across companies, XPS already has other external customers such as Heywood Williams for car fleet services and Lloyd's. In total, XPS controls in excess of £100 million in yearly spend beyond BAE Systems and the amount is still growing.

Finding 4: BAE Systems, the enterprise partnership model was a better way to increase buying power than do-it-yourself. The previous discussion certainly provides compelling evidence that Xchanging was much better positioned to consolidate buying power within BAE Systems as well consolidating buying power across companies (see Table 7.6 above).

Competency 5: Supplier relationships

The ability to attract and retain good supplier relationships is a capability required for indirect procurement transformation. After all, what good are the experts, methods and tools if they cannot be leveraged to negotiate lower prices? The key here is to offer significant benefits to suppliers by offering larger volumes, long-term deals, lower supplier transaction costs, facilitation of user orders, and prompt supplier payment. At the beginning of the venture, XPS managers were frustrated because they were not allowed to directly talk to BAE Systems suppliers. This impediment was eventually overcome as soon as the legal contracts were novated over to Xchanging. Once XPS had control of a category spend, they were able to effectively develop supplier relationships. Suppliers were very interested in working with Xchanging because of their exclusive procurement rights:

Yes, BAE Systems can't decide that they can go with someone else now or competitively put you against someone else. That's very, very powerful for us as a launch pad because it means that when we talk to the car manufacturers or leasing companies or the contract labor, we are here for ten years so you get a better deal with them one way or another, they know we won't go away in a year.   David Rich Jones, CEO, XPS

Offering suppliers long-term deals also fosters good relationships:

And the ten year exclusive works for suppliers because they think, 'well hang on a minute, if I want to deal with BAE and I have to deal with you but

Table 7.7 Supplier Appeal Assessment

Transformative Capabilities	Do-It-Yourself	Enterprise Partnership
5.1 Ability to offer larger volumes	MED	HIGH
5.2 Ability to offer long-term deals	MED	MED
5.3 Ability to lower supplier transaction costs	LOW	HIGH
5.4 Ability to facilitate user orders	LOW/MED	HIGH
5.5 Ability to pay supplier on time	LOW/MED	HIGH

I know you have got a ten year deal, a ten year contract, so if I keep you on the side then I should be OK.' John Doherty, Category Director, XPS

In some instances, Xchanging helped existing suppliers. For example, Xchanging discovered instances where suppliers were not being paid – to the tune of £12 million in one case. Xchanging analysed the problem and discovered that the sheer size of BAE Systems was causing invoices to get lost in the decentralised organisation. With the enterprise partnership, suppliers have one interface, easier user ordering through web-enabled portals, and timely and accurate payments.

Overall, participants agree that there are mixed reactions from suppliers, but overall the enterprise partnership has benefited them:

Yes the suppliers like it. There are two perspectives on it – they feel threatened by it and they are often unsure whether to be extremely pleased by it or threatened by it...Others would be positive because they are getting more focus and attention. For others, the downside is that they are having to give a better margin, but others are quite excited about what extra business we could bring them. David Rich Jones, CEO, XPS

Finding 5: For BAE Systems, the enterprise partnership model was a better way to attract good suppliers than do-it-yourself. Table 7.7 compares the supplier capabilities of the DIY and enterprise partnership options. Concerning the ability to offer suppliers larger volumes, we have already noted instances where Xchanging offers suppliers bigger deals through the consolidation of spend, but they also offer bigger deals by reducing the number of suppliers. In the case of recruitment, Xchanging reduced the suppliers from 100 to 15, leaving a very attractive package for the retained 15 suppliers. Concerning long-term deals, there is always a delicate balance to signing longer term deals to get better prices and signing a short-term contract to limiting the supplier's power. Neither the DIY or enterprise partnership options have an obvious advantage here, but Xchanging does note that the exclusive procurement rights for 10 years does foster good supplier relationships.

Concerning the last three competencies, the enterprise partnership clearly is a better option than DIY. In indirect spend categories, BAE Systems had signed contracts with hundreds of suppliers because spend was all decentralised. Thus, suppliers never dealt with a united customer interface, but had to manouevre through the BAE Systems bureaucracy to find the right people to invoice for payment. BAE Systems were addressing this issue when the opportunity of the XPS deal came along.

Competency 6: Governance

Many of the governance issues have been addressed in the context of the other competencies. Most importantly, we believe, is that the governance model of the enterprise partnership aligns incentives much more powerfully than a traditional outsourcing or consultancy model. In particular, XPS only generates a profit when they deliver the cost savings, thus they are highly motivated and accountable for results. To temper this highly aligned incentive for shared finances, the parties also included governance mechanisms to protect and even improve service levels. In particular, the joint Service Review Board has been an effective mechanism in this regard.

But we note that the enterprise partnership does not perfectly align incentives, as BAE Systems was motivated to reduce costs prior to transferring spend to XPS. This way, BAE Systems could reap benefits of the savings they could achieve on their own. XPS was subsequently handed a smaller piece of the pie:

What we are finding, in fact, in a lot of the categories BAE Systems have taken a lot of the cost out. For example in stationery they have already taken 20% out before we have got to it, in contract labour, they had halved the margin that the contract labour suppliers were getting before we got to it. Recruitment they didn't but in a lot of the categories they had taken it out, so it is tough.
David Rich Jones, CEO, XPS

From the customer perspective, the enterprise partnership offered the best of both worlds by extracting the easy savings themselves and passing

Table 7.8 Governance Assessment

Transformative Capabilities	Do-It-Yourself	Enterprise Partnership
6.1 Ability to align indirect spend agents' incentives with company interests	HIGH	HIGH
6.2 Ability to reap cost-cutting rewards from indirect spend transformation	HIGH	MED
6.3 Ability to keep demand variable	MED	HIGH
6.4 Ability to retain strategic decision making over indirect procurement	HIGH	MED

the more difficult challenges over to the supplier. From the supplier perspective, gross deviations from their assumptions can truly hinder their ability to deliver their business plans. Clearly, the parties have to find fair ways to adapt to extreme changes in assumptions.

Finding 6: For BAE Systems, the governance capabilities would have been higher with DIY, but the enterprise partnership model was designed to retain as much governance advantage as possible.

Conclusion: Lessons on enterprise partnership

In conclusion, our preliminary assessment of the Enterprise Partnership Model is that it is a very viable option for transforming indirect spend. The model is most suited for customers with the following profile:

- Category spend is managed by multiple, decentralised budget holders, allowing the opportunity for significant savings from spend aggregation.
- The customer has a large back-office spend of at least £25 million per year in a few high volume categories, making the deal large enough to attract a competent external supplier
- The customer's category procurement spend is such that further opportunities for significant savings and service improvement from better management are available.
- The customer's centralised procurement is not interested in indirect spend because they have more exciting challenges in core spend.
- The customer does not have the inclination or resources to carrol other customers to create a stronger buying power on their own.
- The customer's organisation would resist centralising and standardising themselves due to internal political resistance, unwillingness of senior management to make the required upfront investment, or lack of skills and experience of existing staff to make the transformation.

This profile of back-office complexity, dispersion and relative neglect can be seen as typical within companies which have grown to be large global corporations. *It arises because the customer organisation simply and purposefully wants to focus on core parts of their business.* But in order for an enterprise partnership to work, the customer and supplier must be willing to truly act in the spirit and trust of a partnership. The BAE Systems/ Xchanging transition offers some powerful lessons for customers:

1. **The customer must be willing to aggressively communicate and disseminate the meaning of the partnership to all budget holders and users in the customer organisation.**

I know everybody says it but the communication one is a big one. We didn't do those as well as we should have done. Colin Webster, Supplier and Development Manager, BAE Systems

Large deals get negotiated by top management, but contracts are enacted in a large user community – potentially to all employees of the customer company. These decentralised users must understand the overall effects of the partnership or else they only see how a miniscule portion of the deal affects their budgets.

2. The customer must be willing to help the partner traverse through the political and bureaucratic terrain of the customer organisation. As a corollary to the previous lesson, it is not just a matter of educating the user community, but actively managing the interface. The important thing was that once the parties recognised this lapse in communication and coordination, they devoted more people to manage the XPS/BAE Systems interfaces. These additional people will help to foster the relationship during the transition, but will likely be moved to XPS once the user community has fully adapted to the new way of sourcing.

3. The customer must be willing to adapt flexibly to discoveries during due diligence. Transitions are difficult. The main activities during the transition included the immense legal work to novate existing supplier contracts and the base-lining of current spend. The biggest testimony to the partnership was the way the parties adapted to the discovery that only £35 million was transferred in the seven contractual categories of spend. Both parties found a way to inject the partnership with a critical mass of spend by adding eight additional categories. A more distant customer-supplier relationship, such as a traditional fee-for-service deal, would not likely foster such adaptability.

4. The customer and supplier align objectives with the enterprise partnership contract, but the parties must realise there is no such thing as an instant partnership.

I am one of these people that really like to live something, to understand it myself rather then somebody telling me 'this is something you must do.' So certainly for the first couple of months I was challenging XBS about what they were doing. Although they sounded a little bit difficult at times it was only so I could understand, from my point of view, why we were doing exactly what we were doing in the way that we were doing it. I guess over the last six months I have become comfortable with that – it sits well with me as an individual. Colin Webster, Supplier and Development Manager, BAE Systems

Trust is not instantaneous, but evolves over time. We have consistently found in all of our research that the largest trust-building factor is operational delivery. Clearly, as XPS delivered the cost savings and improved service levels, the trust levels of the parties increased. Further evidence of the trust is found in both parties as BAE Systems plans to transfer more indirect spend categories to the partnership. But XPS will

still need more business from BAE if it is to achieve ever more payoffs management of coordinated purchasing and economies of scale.

Notes

1. see www.bizreport.com for estimates on global B2B spend in both traditional and electronic commerce.
2. Neef, Dale, e-Procurement, Prentice Hall, New York, 2001, p. 25.
3. Ibid.
4. Fisher, Andrew, 'It's a Small World After All: Understanding E-Procurement,' *The Financial Times*, Winter 2000, p. 6.
5. For details on the HR deal, please see the OXIIM working paper, 'The Enterprise Partnership as Vehicle for Transforming Back Office to Front Office: The Story of BAE Systems and Xchanging's Human Resource Transformation.' by Mary Lacity, David Feeny, Leslie Willcocks. Templeton College, Oxford website: www.templeton.ox.ac.uk.

8
Sustainable Transformation. Where IT Outsourcing Falls Short and BPO Must Deliver
Mike Friend

IT outsourcing has often been used to deliver one of two key objectives; the transfer of the management of costly legacy systems to a third party and/ or their replacement and management by a third party provider. With organisations increasingly questioning the value add that IT contributes to the business and seeking justification for the large investments made in IT, greater emphasis has been placed in recent years on returns on investment and business value. This subtle shift has led to organisations questioning not just what cost savings might be achieved through IT outsourcing but whether the business processes that the IT supports are in fact adequate to meet both current and future market conditions.

The scale of this shift can be measured by the speed with which the IT outsourcers have repositioned themselves to meet this new demand and the sudden proliferation of business process outsourcing (BPO) service providers. Now, instead of just outsourcing their IT, organisations are outsourcing their human resource, finance and accounting, customer care, and procurement functions. And this trend is apparent both across industries, and the public and private sector.

BPO is, however, a far more complex sourcing engagement than IT outsourcing – with service level agreements (SLA's) being tied to a range of businesses as opposed to IT metrics that are not always easily quantified – such as customer satisfaction. The attempts to measure the business value of the outsourced process also requires a recognition that as an organisation's business environment changes, so too should the processes that support it. Sustainable transformation over the term of the outsourced contract is therefore a vital component of the agreement if the customer is not to feel imprisoned in a competitive and contractual straight-jacket. How are service providers engaging with their customers to achieve sustainable transformation through BPO and how are they measuring these cost and service delivery gains?

This chapter will focus on how service providers are delivering on the promises of 'sustainable transformation' through BPO and how the service delivery gains are actually being measured.

1   The IT outsourcing evolution

IT outsourcing, which includes network and desktop outsourcing, applications management, application service providers (ASP) and data centre and systems outsourcing is the largest and fastest growing of the IT services markets. Increasingly used as a means of returning part of the cost of IT investments back to the organisation – in the form of cost savings for reinvestment in other business critical areas – IT outsourcing has also spawned a language of its own to help market the adaptability of the services provided; utility, on-demand, agile, dynamic, transformational. According to research consultancy IDC, Worldwide spending on outsourcing services reached over $133.5 billion in 2003 and is expected to surpass $198.8 billion by 2008.[1] In Europe (see Figure 8.1 below), outsourcing spending in 2003 was $44.5 billion and is forecast to grow to $66.5 billion by 2008, representing a five-year growth of 8.4 per cent.[2]

Such a huge market was not created overnight and to achieve this scale of spending, it is also clear that successful outsourcing contracts have so

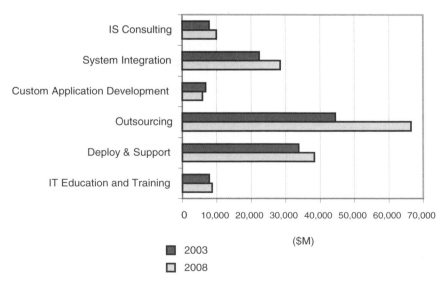

Figure 8.1   Western European IT Services Viewed by Engagement Type, 2003 and 2008 ($m)
Source: IDC, 2004

far, far outweighed the bad press generated by unhappy client outsourcing experiences.

And yet by the early 1990s, a new wave of outsourcing engagements were being discussed, which sought to address the problem of aligning IT more closely with the business processes they were intended to support. To achieve this, IT could not be outsourced in isolation but had to be viewed in terms of the relationship between individuals working in the front or back-office, the business processes and the technology.

The outsourcing relationship, therefore, moved from one of cost cutting and system management to maximising the efficiency of the business processes, understanding the relationship between the processes themselves, corporate performance and profitability.

This new sourcing relationship became known as business process outsourcing, which harnessed the service provider's expertise in integrating its change management (people), process management and technology capabilities (see Figure 8.2 below). BPO also required the marriage of two largely disparate cultures and disciplines, 'blue-collar' outsourcing and 'white-collar' consulting. Whilst outsourcing sought to derive value through the commoditisation of its services, using technology and largely low-skilled tasks to drive down transaction costs, the consulting capabilities of the service provider would be leveraged in short project cycles to deliver real value add, using the highly paid skills and intellectual property at its disposal to audit, benchmark and re-engineer the client's business processes.

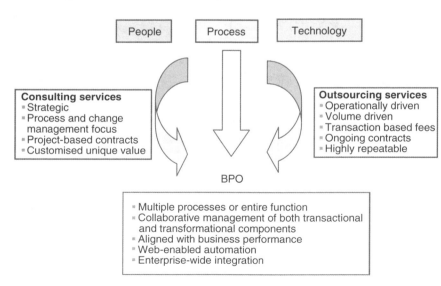

Figure 8.2 The Marriage of People, Process and Technology
Source: IDC, 2004

2 Performance measurement

The added complexity of a BPO style outsourcing relationship has led, in turn, to more intricate contractual and financing structures, plus service level agreements and key performance indicators tied to an ever expanding range of productivity, efficiency, loyalty and satisfaction metrics. In customer care BPO, these performance management indicators (PMI's) range from call handling, call response times and call escalation to client acquisition or retention. In Human Resources BPO, these include payroll error rates and off-cycle runs, timeliness of print and dispatch, time to hire, training days delivered, benefits and enrolment cycles. In Finance and Accounting BPO, it may include days sales outstanding, order to cash administration. In Procurement, it may be related to supply chain management, direct and indirect spend administration. The application of technology in achieving defined PMI's varies from business process to business process, as does the emphasis placed on the need to re-engineer the processes and re-skill the employees.

To counterbalance the risks associated with these sometimes lengthy outsourcing contracts, incentives for over performance, penalties for underperformance and gain/share clauses are also invariably built in.

3 Delivering sustainable transformation through BPO

The European BPO marketplace represents a large and diversified market with processing and IT intensive business functions handling customer care, procurement and extended supply chain management as well as back-office processes such as HR and finance and accounting, attracting the bulk of BPO spend. In addition, a strong industry specific BPO service industry has also emerged to tackle business processes such as billing (in telecoms), social benefits management (in government), TV licensing (in media), cheque processing (in banking), ticketing (in transport) and claims administration (in insurance).

The growth rates in each of these segments have been high, reflecting the relative untapped immaturity of the BPO market as a whole. At 11.4 per cent, the combined IT outsourcing and BPO market in Europe is forecast to grow at nearly twice the rate of IT Consulting and System Integration in 2006[3] (see Figure 8.3), and will likely remain the growth engine of the IT Services industry for some time to come.

Whilst not beholden to technology, innovation in the business process outsourcing market has, however, been driven in the last few years by, amongst other things, open systems, EAI tools, Web technologies and the wide array of both enterprise ERP as well as process specific applications. These have led organisations as well as service providers to assess the level of process integration and automation that can be achieved and the impact

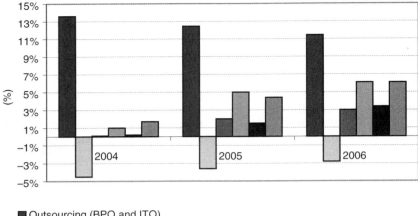

■ Outsourcing (BPO and ITO)

☐ CAD

■ Deployment and Support

☐ IT Consulting

■ IT Education and Training

☐ System Integration

Figure 8.3 Comparison of Growth Rates, Western European Outsourcing (ITO and BPO) and IT Services Viewed by Engagement Type, 2004–06 (%)
Source: IDC, 2004

this might have on organisational efficiency and productivity. The net impact of this assessment has been a growing conviction that the scale of cost savings and business related productivity gains are in some cases vast – big enough to generate a healthy operating margin for the service provider, certainly big enough to attract the interest of customers in a commercial proposition.

However, unlike the majority of IT outsourcing contracts – where benefits are largely associated with IT specific metrics such as network availability, bandwidth and processing power – BPO contracts are measured by a range of hard (cost-related) and soft (performance or customer satisfaction) related business metrics. Whilst the former may be achieved by measuring the difference between past service delivery costs with future costs, the latter is often far harder to quantify and often potentially more beneficial. Listed below (see Table 8.1) are examples of some of the benefits that have been generated by BPO contracts that have reached operational stability – divided into those that are easy to identify and measure like cost savings and the less tangible benefits of BPO relating to service improvement.

Table 8.1 More Than Just Cost Savings: The Benefits of BPO

Contract Signed	Service Provider	Client	Industry	Cost Savings	Service Improvements
Dec-01	Accenture	MOL	Oil & Gas	40 per cent cost savings over the six years of the contract, generating annual savings of HUF1 billion (€ 3.9 million)	Improved the cost and quality of MOL's accounting operations – managed core operations more flexibly – absorbed acquisitions rapidly – customer satisfaction measured and improved through feedback and feed-forward.
Oct-01	Xchanging	BAe Systems	Defence	33 per cent productivity improvement – £500,000 recruitment cost savings	Centralisation of 30 different processes for remuneration and benefits – Peer reviews completed in three weeks rather than three months – launch of customer-service centre in Preston – defined HR service specification and associated service metrics
Jun-01	HBS	Middlesbrough Council	Local Government	£20 million in cost savings over 10 years for investment in front-line services, 71 new jobs created	Establishment of a single contact centre to deliver improvements to the Councils front line services, including housing benefits and council tax. These services would be extended across all the council's customer facing reception areas, leisure centres and libraries.
May-01	Xchanging	Lloyd's Claims Office	Insurance	£2 million productivity improvement – a further 28 per cent (£1.51 million) reduction in contract IT costs and £1.5 million reduction in facilities management costs also achieved in year 1.	Insurance processing services benchmarked and process performance measured – 'e-repository' service launched

Table 8.1   More Than Just Cost Savings. The Benefits of BPO – *continued*

Contract Signed	Service Provider	Client	Industry	Cost Savings	Service Improvements
Dec-00	EDS	Abbey National	Retail Banking	15 per cent cost reduction in mortgage and loan processing operations	'Service efficiency improved by 10 to 15 per cent with 98 per cent of service-level targets met by service provider. Loan processing operations consolidated in one operational site, enabling Abbey's customers to benefit from a seamless, proactive, and personalised service.'
Dec-99	Exult	BP	Oil & Gas	>15 per cent cost savings in in-scope administrative HR services	Measured Service delivery by process area – User satisfaction now tracked by process area per cent BP HR focus shifting to discretionary activity
Nov-96	EDS/PwC	BBC	Media	50 per cent productivity improvement	18 financial processes reengineered with SAP R/3
Dec-90	Accenture	BP	Oil & Gas	>50 per cent reduction in Finance and Accounting service costs. Contract since renewed again in '94 and '99.	Standardised technology – Improved forecasting of financial performance, joint venture accounting, preparation of management information, preparation of group and statutory accounts, and the processing and payment of 15,000 invoices per month. Streamlined F&A enabled and accelerated BP post-merger growth

Source: IDC, 2004

The motivation to outsource business processes changes from one organisation to the next. Often, the critical factors include the need to respond to changes to the global competitive landscape in which the organisation operates, industry dynamics such as deregulation or consolidation, and to customer buying behaviour. Cost savings in such circumstances are just part of an overriding objective which is to achieve an organisational structure capable of meeting both current and future challenges.

Under these conditions, outsourcing can only be deemed to be effective if the service provided delivers sustained transformation over the full term of the contract. Naturally enough, this value added service requires ongoing investment in the re-engineering of business processes and the enabling technologies, and achieving these aims places a huge emphasis on partnership and an intimate understanding of both the customer and the industry in which the customer operates.

Since 'relationship' and 'partnership' are often overused words in the vocabulary of commercial organisations, it is easy to overlook those examples of sustainable transformation that exist which help to demonstrate the radical changes to the client organisation that can be achieved through BPO.

3.1 The oil and gas industry

One of the best examples and one of the most revolutionary in its time was Accenture's work with BP in 1991 which went far beyond any previous consulting engagements, moving from an initial discussion concerning the consolidation of offices to the taking over by Accenture of BP's entire North Sea finance and accounting function.

BP had built its exploration and support activities in the North Sea in a market where the price of oil was $25 per barrel. In the period from 1980 to 1991, BP's production costs had tripled. The sudden drop in the oil price to around $10 per barrel in the mid to late 1980s (hard to believe in the current $50 per barrel economy) made North Sea oil even more expensive, undercutting the viability of BP's production. The cost structure of the business needed to change dramatically and quickly.

The solution, when all the details had finally been hammered out, saw the transfer in July 1991 of some 320 BP staff from six different locations to Accenture's new centre in Aberdeen. While BP retained control of financial policy, Accenture assumed responsibility for all other accounting functions, including forecasting of financial performance, joint venture accounting, preparation of management information, preparation of group and statutory accounts, and the processing and payment of 15,000 invoices per month.

For the BP business which since 1991 has almost doubled in size in the North Sea, the Accenture Finance and Accounting outsourcing service has achieved a better than 50 per cent reduction in costs on a real basis, with workflow, technology, productivity and efficiency savings across the board helping BP to compete not just in terms of cost per barrel but also to move strategically to acquire large interests in the North American market. This record of achievement was marked by contract renewals in 1994 and again in 1999, and has attracted a host of other oil clients to the shared-service centre, including Talisman UK, Conoco UK and Britannia Operator.

BP currently outsources $1 billion of business process related costs each year to its network of third party providers. In 1996, BP outsourced additional Finance and Accounting related activities to PricewaterhouseCoopers (since acquired by IBM). IBM now provides finance and accounting services for BP's European refining and marketing business units as well as F&A activities for BP's US upstream business. BP's European upstream and US refining and marketing are now outsourced to Accenture. The competition between these two service providers has proved beneficial to BP, with neither service provider wishing to fall behind the other in the delivery of cost savings and thereby ensuring that both IBM and Accenture strive to achieve further innovation in the delivery of best practice F&A services.

3.2 The insurance industry

Lloyd's of London and International Underwriting Association (IUA) were faced with similar challenges in the insurance industry. Between them, Lloyd's of London and the IUA settled more than £20 billion of claims each year within a network of some 250 companies.

In response to the growing competitive threat posed by international markets, Lloyd's of London and the IUA jointly launched a major programme of reform in 1999. The focus of this initiative in particular was to address the inefficiencies and costs of the back-office processes that supported the London insurance markets' ability to issue policies, collect premiums, pay brokers' commissions and settle claims.

The London insurance market had traditionally been served by two processing centres operating at arm's length from each other, each issuing a separate policy in respect of their shares of the same risk and, as a result, creating a considerable amount of unnecessary duplication and inefficiency. In addition, Lloyds had previously negotiated IT outsourcing contracts which were to represent 40 per cent of the total cost base. To dramatically reduce the overall business costs and the inflexibility posed by these seven year IT contracts, alternative strategies needed to be explored for managing the supplier base more effectively.

Backed by Lloyds' CEO, Nick Prettejohn, and IUA Chairman, Tim Carroll, the London insurance market set out to find a service provider who could tackle the emerging challenges of the global insurance industry.

The choice of Xchanging by the IUA and Lloyd's from several companies that had offered themselves as potential service providers was, in large part, due to the Joint Venture concept underpinning the creation of Xchanging Ins-sure services (XIS); the guarantee of service fees fixed in line with inflation and the commitment to ongoing investment in the business processes and technology. Whilst Xchanging would have operational and investment responsibility for the new company and provide market participants with a full range of insurance processing services, the IUA and Lloyd's would retain a say in the strategy of the enterprise via the board of XIS.

A number of alternative strategies had been assessed and then rejected:

- In-house approach. This approach was rejected because the necessary changes required levels of management attention and investment that did not exist at the time and would take significant time and resources to build up. A previous attempt at applying in-house management expertise to indirect procurement had still left significant room for further improvement.
- Management Consultancy. This route it was felt would represent high up-front costs to achieve one-step rather than sustainable change. There were also concerns about the accountability for, and ownership of, outcomes and about lack of skills and knowledge transfer.
- Fee-for-Service Outsourcing. Whilst this approach was recognised as a credible alternative, with the added advantage for the client of full up-front commitment to reduced cost levels, a roadmap did not seem to exist dealing with the mid to latter stages of the contract lifecycle and the inevitable changing business priorities as well as incentives of both client and provider.

On 1st May 2001, XIS was formed to manage and commercialise the combined back-office operations of Lloyd's of London (which had been served by the Lloyd's Policy Signing Office, or LPSO, in Chatham and the members of the IUA, served by the London Processing Centre or LPC in Folkestone).

XIS now employs 500 people and on behalf of Lloyds and IUA sends 1.3 million electronic transaction advices a year electronically as well as checking Lloyd's insurance policies for regulatory compliance.

As well as serving the market as a whole, for which it has developed an electronic document repository, XIS has helped to make the London Insurance market an attractive one for start-up companies. By offering virtual back-office services that have helped brokers and underwriters (including Axis, Ascot and PRI) to get up and running in as little as four months, XIS has helped to make the market more appealing to these types of company, and attract new capital to the London market

The XIS business was tasked with an objective of saving 16 full time jobs in the first year. In fact the first wave of process work identified a headcount reduction of 84 people – equivalent to a £2 million annual saving in a £7 million cost base. Transactional costs, which have risen as the market has consolidated, and the resulting economies of scale have diminished, have not only been contained as the market reform plan required, but they have actually decreased. The duplication of checking and data entry at the back-offices of the Lloyd's and Companies' markets, operated in Chatham and Folkestone respectively, were identified early on as a significant source of cost and inefficiency. Since signing the contract in 2001, the number of processes have been reduced from 22 to three, speeding up workflow and also resulting in cost savings of £2 million per annum.

By leveraging the obligations of the supplier under the terms of the existing IT outsourcing contract (to benchmark and deliver best practice based cost-effective service), XIS were also able to negotiate an agreed £1.51 million (28%) reduction on £5.4 million of IT service-related costs by attacking variable costs like customer liaison charges and inflationary clauses. Lloyd's, and the companies market as represented by the IUA, have been able to share in the proceeds of the joint venture according to the ownership model (50 per cent owned by Xchanging and 25 per cent each by Lloyd's and the IUA). To date, XIS has paid a £3.4 million ($5.45 million) dividend to the market. The dividend payment equates to a nine per cent reduction in transactional costs over 2001.

3.3   The aerospace industry

Sonaca's decision to partner with IBM in the mid-1990s provides a copybook example of sourcing evolution and the benefits to be gained from leveraging the industry, business process and outsourcing expertise of a service provider.

Sonaca SA, headquartered in Belgium, employs 2000 staff. Ranked the 91st largest aerospace company in the world, with locations in Belgium, US, Brazil and Canada, its main activities are focussed on the development, manufacture, assembly and test of wing leading edge and main landing gear fuselage panels for Dassault, Embraer and Airbus, for whom Sonaca is the sole source supplier.

In the mid-1990s rising costs of fuel and declining passenger numbers resulted in a significant slump in the airline and related aerospace manufacturing industries. In 1995, Sonaca generated revenues of €62 million and a loss of €24 million.

The immediate response required the slashing of costs from the business in order to stabilise the business as a going concern and these aims were largely achieved at the expense of the workforce, which fell from 1150 to 975 by the end of 1996. However, Sonaca recognised that its business model was fundamentally flawed and uncompetitive and could only succeed in a strong growing airline industry. With no guarantee of growth in the near future, Sonaca chose to partner with IBM to look at ways in which it could re-organise, adapt, re-engineer its business processes and manage the whole transformation.

Beginning with a series of projects looking at aligning the business competencies with customer buying behaviour, Sonaca's business processes, workflows, manufacturing and assembly capabilities were re-engineered and mapped to enabling technologies and a new ERP system. The productivity gains achieved and resulting cost savings enabled Sonaca to compete once again for new business and grow revenues between 1996 and 2001 from €77.98 million to €259.33 million (a 27 per cent compound annual growth rate) and operating income at 99 per cent CAGR.

The importance of this series of projects was driven home by the events of September 2001 and the SARS outbreak of March 2003 which precipitated a catastrophic slump in passenger numbers. The bankruptcies and record losses experienced by the airline industry in this period exceeded all previous experience and led to a fundamental shift in the dominance of the traditional domestic carriers. With low-cost airlines emerging as the only major purchasers of new fleets and therefore able to demand and receive significant reductions in the cost of airplanes, Airbus and Boeing in turn put huge pressure on their suppliers such as Sonaca to reduce their costs still further.

Since 2001, the cascading impact of price pressure has led IBM and Sonaca to leverage new business models to help sustain the continuous cycle of change required to remain a global competitive company. Front- and back-office business process outsourcing and component business modelling, where the components of each product and service are broken down and rebuilt within the organisation, are now the cornerstone of a strategy to deliver increased growth, an ongoing reduction of €30 million in the cost base and Sonaca's evolution as a truly networked organisation.

The importance of this strategy to Sonaca is borne out by the results of the European airline industry which suggest that recovery is still some way off; the Association of European Airlines which counts 31 members, announced a combined loss of $2.4 billion in 2003, the fifth consecutive year of losses. Since exchange rates alone have the potential of adding a further 20 per cent to the cost base of the European aerospace manufacturing industry in 2006 (when many contracts hedging against a drop in the value of the dollar expire), the need to deliver this change rapidly is critical.

4 The future conflict between the aims of IT outsourcing and BPO

Service providers with a foot in both the IT outsourcing and the BPO camp are having to carefully position the value propositions of these offerings against each other. Arguments made that IT has proved too expensive and has failed to deliver key strategic benefits to business may ring true but are also often an over simplification of the facts. As a justification for the move to a BPO model (which invariably also requires additional investment in IT) this argument is also not necessarily in the interests of the service provider (ergo why should the customer invest in more IT to support business processes, if IT has supposedly failed to deliver business benefits in the past?).

The proliferation of and the many advances made in business process management applications has, however, made the argument for a move to the emerging BPO model a more attractive and convincing one. Infrastructure outsourcing at the enterprise level, whether for desktop, network, communications, database, mainframe or server has its place in the sourcing strategies of every organisation since the application of these technologies is broad and largely non-process specific.

Organisations are, however, recognising that many operational and productivity efficiencies remain untapped in the business processes themselves. The failure of these processes to support the business (whether managing the supply chain, handling customer enquiries, matching billing and accounts receivables etc) can hamstring the organisations ability to respond to a changing market in which customer choice and customer churn are on the increase. Whatever the route taken by the customer, whether IT outsourcing or BPO, the signing of outsourcing contracts which fail to take into account the need for sustainable transformation, will likely see both customer and service provider ill-served in the long term.

Notes

1. Source: IDC, Worldwide Services 2004–2008 Forecast and Analysis: A Market in Transition, IDC #31344, May 2004.
2. Source: IDC, Western European IT Services Market Forecast: 2003–2008, IDC #Q03L, April 2004.
3. Source: IDC, Forecast and Analysis of the Western European BPO Market, 2003–2008, IDC # BP02L, May 2004. Western European IT Services Market Forecast: 2003–2008, IDC #Q03L, April 2004.

Bibliography

Market data quoted in the above article has previously been published in the following IDC reports:
- Forecast and Analysis of the Western European BPO Market, 2003–2008 (IDC# BP02L, May 2004)
- Worldwide Services 2004–2008 Forecast and Analysis: A Market in Transition (IDC#31344, May 2004)
- Western European IT Services Market Forecast: 2003–2008 (IDC#Q03L, April 2004)

Part V

Managing the Outsourcing Relationship

9
How to Manage the Outsourcing Relationship

Graham Beck

1   Introduction

The increasing adoption of outsourcing solutions over the last twenty or so years has brought new dimensions and associated pressures to the management of businesses. The customer and supplier interaction is well understood and experienced – isn't outsourcing just an extension of this? If this gross over-simplification were true, why are there so many examples of failed or problematic outsourcing solutions?

No two outsourcing deals are the same, but more importantly the one aspect of any deal that has failed to gain sufficient credibility is the nature of the relationship between the customer and the supplier. The mere mention of outsourcing being a business relationship usually provides either a degree of casual amusement or a polite but, soon forgotten acknowledgement from the majority of senior customer management. Experiences over the past two decades have left supplier management equally sceptical.

There may be some light at the end of the tunnel. In a recent survey of customers experienced in the use of outsourcing,[1] PA Consulting Group found that in response to the statement:

The problems in outsourcing relationships are mainly the responsibility of the supplier

Eighty per cent of customers disagreed! The implication is that customers are at least beginning to recognise that they have an important part to play in the whole process.

The link between the fundamentals of the deal and their influence on an outsourcing relationship is explored later in this chapter. The aim is to debunk the concept of a business relationship as a soft, intangible issue and show just how influential it is on making the outsourcing deal a success or not.

2   Assuming the appropriate psychological posture

Look deeply into most first-generation outsourcing contracts and you are likely to find eloquent terms and ideals about an 'intent to work in a partnering fashion', 'with close cooperation', 'for mutual benefit' and other such token statements. All represent meaningless window dressing designed to reinforce an organisation's perception of itself. They appear to say the right things but actually add nothing practical or deliverable to the arrangements.

In the same contracts, one is just as likely to find punitive measures, inappropriate risk apportionment, large liabilities and never ending breach clauses. This is, essentially, all of the weaponry required to go to war, which is just as well, because such 'hard-nosed' unbalanced deals usually lead to a swift breakdown. In such instances, commercially savvy suppliers will have loaded their price with appropriate insurance and/or negotiated such tight constraints on the deliverables that if the customer sneezes out of place, they end up paying more under the ubiquitous change control provisions in the contract.

For either party, the adoption of an adversarial approach usually results.

2.1   How the seeds of war are sown

Generally speaking, outsourcing deals usually represent a significant and sizeable commercial event. Therefore, there is likely to be executive management awareness or even partial engagement in the deal. As such, the deal is often shaped in a political climate where laurels can be won, reputations can be made, enhanced or destroyed and egos can be massaged. This climate owes its potency to the one aspect of the deal that always receives the highest profile, creates the most excitement and is seen as sorting out the men from the boys: the negotiation. Many see this from the simple viewpoint of winning and losing. There appears to be a fundamental lack of recognition that the basis of developing and sustaining a successful business solution is directly aligned with the development and sustainability of a business relationship.

By comparison, the opposition, more accurately described as the suppliers, are characterised as a collection of sharp commercial practitioners and cannot therefore be trusted. Their role in life is seen as maximising private sector profits in the shortest possible time. Customer satisfaction, customer relationships and cooperative working are all perceived by the customer community as sacrificial lambs when it comes to the pursuit of profit.

These impressions may be extreme but serve to highlight the psychological influence that can be exerted at a crucial time of building the relationship: during negotiation.

2.2   Why the seeds germinate

The cost of securing an outsourcing deal can be significant. The elapsed timescales to design, procure and negotiate a typical IT outsourcing arrangement usually fall between nine and 15 months. The corresponding drain and impact on a customer organisation's capacity and capability should not be, but usually is, underestimated. It is, therefore, not surprising that most customers wish to get the exercise over and done with as fast as possible. It is not unusual for target and deadline dates to be set that bear no relation to the practicalities of life. An existing contract renewal or exit provision is a common driver of deadlines; this can only be considered commercially sensible if the scope of work and associated timescales to procure alternative arrangements have been evaluated and factored into planning. Another common driver is the message or diktat from 'on high'. If the CEO wants it done by a certain date, then the command becomes law. This stance may have some of its origins in a macho culture, but is more likely to be tied to a business need, such as change or cost, or both. With some senior managers reluctant to 'advise' their CEOs, the CEO's word will generally become law.

Through the combination of racing to get things done and setting impractical deadlines, momentum is gathered towards the inevitable war. The certain result is that the risk profile of the whole procurement is elevated considerably, because:

a) the customer will be unable to accurately articulate what they wish to procure; and
b) the customer will not have prepared or marshalled the plethora of information necessary to support and evaluate the procurement.

The consequence of this approach is that the customer may 'back-fill' with the use of consultants' and lawyers' time, which, from a cost effective stance, is far from best use of their outsourcing competencies. How effective the consultants and lawyers are in recovering this situation will determine how much insurance suppliers will need to factor into their proposals and terms.

The flawed deal that provides the motivation to ultimately go to war is already taking shape. The suppliers are loading their price, and further protecting themselves through restrictive contract terms because of the risk involved.

2.3 The inevitable flowering of the seeds of war

Taking the worse case scenario that combines implausible deadlines, poorly defined requirements, risk management pricing together with generous measures of testosterone leads to an outcome with which no one is satisfied. This will require either repair or separation sooner rather than later. Even scaling back from the worse case, it is hard to see the basis of a sustainable business relationship when outsourcing is approached in such a Dickensian fashion.

In terms of relationships there is a strong parallel between outsourcing and matrimony. Many outsourcing deals aspire to long-term arrangements; five, seven and 10-year deals are commonplace, with a variety of extension provisions up to 20 years being lodged. For such deals to stand any chance of being successful, fundamental consideration of the business relationship is needed, before the deal is even cast. Equally there has to be recognition that, like any relationship, it will evolve as it matures through the experiences gained, both good and bad.

The term of the deal is not the sole governing factor within a relationship – far from it. The rapidly changing face of business has fuelled the appetite for outsourcing as organisations increasingly see this as an opportunity to focus on core business activities or enable their business change strategy. Either way, the dependency on the outsourcing supplier is increasing to the point where it is inextricably linked with the performance and related success of the customer business. This dependency, over longer timescales, means that the need for a well-defined and managed business relationship with outsourcing supplier has become an imperative. Returning to the matrimonial theme, the time-honoured adage: 'Marry in haste and repent at leisure' would become 'Marry in haste and the likely divorce will be painful, disruptive and costly'!

In many instances, a customer may need to engage the outsourcing supplier to help define and implement the business change, adding more weight to the case for consciously developing the appropriate business relationship from the outset. Business change within all market sectors during recent years has provided many outsourcing suppliers with greater business opportunity and a genuine case to add value to their services. Such work takes the supplier to the heart of the customer organisation and its business issues. The need to get things right in such potentially sensitive areas makes the need for a sound business relationship a primary factor when mitigating risk on such deals.

Like it or not, outsourcing has become an accepted business solution, irrespective of the scope or role afforded it and, by implication, its impact on customer business performance is likely to increase. The need to make it work and work well is therefore fundamental.

3   How to avoid going to war

Learning from the problems observed and experienced in the market, it is not so much a case of applying 'golden rules' as adopting and fostering the appropriate mentality when constructing the deal. The pragmatic way for any customer to test their planned approach is to focus upon the following areas, before moving down the outsourcing route.

1) Do you understand the reasoning and rationale behind the decision to outsource? Is it sustainable?

2) Do you know what the quantified and un-quantified business benefits are and who is responsible for their delivery?
3) Do you know what success looks like and how you would measure it?
4) Do you know what the risks are to your business in pursuing an outsourced solution?
5) Do you know the strengths and weaknesses of your company and what you need to do to supplement them in order to manage an outsourcing relationship successfully?
6) Do you recognise the organisational cultural aspects that your company both responds to, or is repelled by?

If and when you can determine the answers to all of these aspects, you will be in a position to formulate the type of business relationship you need to underpin your outsourcing solution. By implication you therefore have to sell these requirements to the market place as part of the initial market engagement.

All of these aspects will become an integral part of the evaluation process of the supplier, and the supplier will equally test for comparable sincerity of intent by the customer throughout proceedings.

3.1 Lawyers – think value, not just cost

It is a highly prudent practice to engage the customer's legal representatives, (preferably third party firms with a proven expertise in the outsourcing market place), in the formulation of the ideal business relationship. This has a number of direct benefits:-

1) The lawyers usually have considerable practical experience of what does or does not work with regard to business relationship aspirations
2) The basis of the required business relationship informs the nature of the contract to be drawn up
3) The basis of the business relationship will directly influence both the controls and measures to be incorporated in the contract and how these should be used
4) The lawyers usually ensure that a realistic and pragmatic business relationship is developed, given that they are responsible for incorporating its essence within the contract
5) This early involvement avoids the legal team having to second guess the customers' requirements and intentions when asked to draft a contract from a 'standing start', usually late on in the proceedings.

There is a natural tendency for customers to be very cautious about 'burning' legal fees and this usually translates into minimising the involvement of the legal team as far as possible. This usually ends up as a false economy due to the time spent by lawyers drafting and redrafting their interpretation of the customer's requirements, having been kept in the dark until the latest possible moment. The customer will also experience comparable wasted effort through the need to reiterate requirements. The problem is further compounded by the timing constraints imposed by the late introduction of the lawyers, which puts artificial pressure on everyone involved at a stage of the procurement that is usually close to the target deadline.

Certain law firms have responded to this problem by offering fixed price arrangements for the pre-procurement phase, in order to prepare both the customer and the groundwork more thoroughly. Some law firms, experienced in outsourcing, are considering the adoption of radically new approaches to the market in terms of segmentation of the outsourcing life cycle, which is aligned to variable pricing.

3.2   Why governance is fundamental to success

Another aspect that will influence the business relationship is the contract mechanics. These fall into both strategic and tactical categories. The single most consistent factor evident in the failure of first generation outsourcing contracts is the lack of, or ill-defined, strategic requirement for corporate governance. There are two primary dimensions to governance:-

1) The definition of the agreed rules by which both parties will operate the contract, incorporating areas such responsibility and authority for ongoing procurement and supply, service management provisions, quality management, contract change, escalation and arbitration arrangements, and so on
2) Nomination of the various formal bodies' forums or committees and their respective roles and responsibilities in managing the contract and the business relationship itself.

Even when governance provisions are made in the contract, they are prone to failure. This is due to the lack of customer management time being invested at the appropriate level to provide authority and sponsorship to the business relationship and overall management of the contract. Suppliers will take a strong lead from the degree of customer management sponsorship invested in the deal and its ongoing commitment as specified within the governance arrangements. It is the supplier's benchmark to determine if customers are 'walking the talk' in terms of their approach to the proposed business relationship.

The tactical aspects of the contract mechanics usually manifest themselves through the measures and related reward and penalty terms. The presence and potential application of these aspects serve as drivers to behaviour; they are not an end in themselves. It is, therefore, imperative to link these behavioural drivers to the desired outcomes and business benefits, identified at the outset. Although this may be appear to be an obvious statement, experience has shown that this alignment is often missed, usually due to the failure to apply measures to the aspects of supply that either directly or indirectly affect the business benefits sought. The natural consequence of this misalignment is to drive inappropriate behaviours within the supplier organisation, resulting in disaffection by the customer and a souring of the business relationship all round.

3.3   Why the take-up of outsourcing is increasing

Competitive market pressures will continue to provide the stimulus for the use of outsourcing. This is because a realisation has dawned that this business solution cannot only 'fix' a problem, but in mature business hands it can be applied to derive numerous benefits. Its application to consciously free up retained core skills can enable an organisation to focus upon business imperatives without the need to import resources that are initially alien to the host business practice and culture.

Outsourcing will also enable organisations to become more agile in responding to the need to bring products and services to market in shorter timescales as new entrant competitors change the market paradigm. On a parallel course, the experience of customers is becoming an increasingly sensitive issue as modern business processes bring organisations into closer proximity with the customers they are serving. As such, the performance perspective of a business will increasingly focus upon the success of their interaction with customers.

Outsourcing is already seen as a vehicle by which particular skills and expertise can be both temporarily and permanently imported to enhance the ability of the existing organisation. This is especially attractive when particular expertise is required for specific events or periods of time within a business, such as designing and implementing change programmes.

Looking beyond the orthodox business drivers to adopt forms of outsourcing, it can be argued that the increasing cost pressures of direct employment may stimulate greater consideration of shared or split resourcing; outsourcing suppliers are ideally placed to offer this option.

Similarly, the well-publicised lack of certain skills and expertise available within the UK economy is being used to balance the debate regarding the economic case for considering immigration. The origins of outsourcing were partially born out of the lack of IT staff and expertise during the 1980s and beyond. Are we about to witness an expansion of this way of working?

Irrespective of which of these drivers takes precedence, it is apparent that greater use of outsourcing will be made during the immediate future, arguably to a point where it becomes a 'business norm'. As a consequence, we will see the development of increased capabilities and expertise within businesses to successfully procure and manage such solutions. To date, the track record of businesses in this respect has not been that impressive and there are some danger signals that need to be heeded.

Outsourcing is on a roll, therefore organisational skills and capabilities necessary to successfully procure and manage such solutions will need to become core competencies.

The scope of deals is likely to become much wider and more diverse; the commercial arrangements that support them will become more closely aligned to customer business outcomes. The sophistication of contractual rewards and penalties will develop to reflect the impact performance will have on a business's bottom line and/or its customers' experience. The pace of business change will create greater uncertainty, thereby, increasing risk for both parties. The pace of technological development will only be limited by the market's ability to absorb and adopt it, which will directly influence the nature of business change.

All of these aspects strengthen the need for greater and more formal engagement by customers in determining and developing the business relationship on which they need to base their outsourcing solutions. The degree of potential impact that an outsourcing solution may have on business performance is set to increase significantly. It will require something more substantive than 'a will to work together' and a set of contractual clauses to sustain organisations in their relationships.

4 Conclusion

The growth of outsourcing over the last two decades has witnessed the development of supporting commercial arrangements on something of a laggard time basis. Customer aspirations with regard to benefit achievement through outsourcing have, by and large, failed to fully materialise. Although the reasons for this are varied, experience has shown that one of the fundamental areas of weakness has been the lack of thought and engagement between the customer and supplier in defining and developing a business relationship. From an external perspective, it seems logical that two companies entering into business arrangements likely to last a number of years will work out how they will best work together. Moving straight to contractual terms as a means of managing the ongoing and often long-term relationship is akin to baking a cake with only half of the ingredients. It won't taste very good and it will quickly go stale.

As previously stated, the breadth and scope of outsourcing is continuing to widen as both businesses and suppliers are driven to become even more innovative in order to stay competitive. No two deals are the same ar e motives behind the deals are probably even more diverse. Therefore, the ness relationship required to successfully underpin each deal is likely to i varied. There never has been a 'one size fits all' solution, but success is n likely if management recognises and delivers on three key aspects:

1) the need to pre-determine the basis of the business relationship sough

2) ensuring that the measures placed in the contract drive the appropriate behaviours to support the business relationship,

3) ensuring that the formal governance arrangements for the contract are complementary to and support the monitoring and review of the planned business relationship.

Within these principles there is room for any style of business relationship, including the 'be tough, treat them mean and keep them keen' version. Macho tactics have their place, provided that they support and drive a business relationship that delivers the right outcomes for both parties. In 2004 it is hard to conceive of such a mutually productive relationship emanating from macho tactics, but as in so many walks of life, never say never!

Recognition that a business relationship has everything to do with being mutually successful, commercially savvy and refusing to accept second best is half the battle with many traditional senior managers. The 'pink and fluffy' assertions made about business relationships belong in the ark. Being aggressive and being seen to be tough may be self gratifying but hardly a substitute for being successful and seeing your supplier share in that success. It's as much a mind set switch as it is a discipline born out of business maturity.

Note

1. *Outsourcing: Mindset Switch – moving from cost control to benefits realisation*, *PA Consulting Group, 2002.*

10
Designing Successful Outsourcing Relationships – Selected Techniques from a Lifecycle Perspective
Sara Cullen

1 Introduction

There has now been over a decade of information technology outsourcing (ITO) research producing a considerable volume of thoughts, theories and propositions regarding outsourcing. A search on Amazon.com will typically yield over 200 titles and Hui and Beath (2001) uncovered 143 papers and books on IT sourcing in major academic journals and the like.

It appears, with the preponderance of literature, that academia is feeling comfortable with its understanding of what drives organisations to outsource and a general belief of the maturity of the outsourcing processes undertaken by the purchasing organisation. 'With an abundance of recent literature supporting best practices and critical factors in IT outsourcing, there is a firm knowledge base of when, what and how IT outsourcing should be approached,' (Shuen, 2002). Now the focus has turned to what makes an outsourcing deal more successful than others.

Some have proposed that 'selective' outsourcing is more likely to be successful than 'total' outsourcing, the latter being where 80 per cent or more of the annual IT budget is outsourced to a single supplier (Lacity and Willcocks, 2001 and Sambamurthy et al., 2001). Others have recognised the importance of the client/supplier relationship in outsourcing deals (Kern and Willcocks, 2001; Goles; 2001; Alborz, 2004). It is the latter topic, relationships, that is the topic of this paper.

This paper addresses the nature of the business-to-business, or organisational outsourcing relationship between the client and the supplier entities. It recognises the importance of relationships and describes the power versus trust-based orientations that can be displayed. It then presents the outsourcing lifecycle that was derived from 100 cases over the last decade, highlighting selected techniques used by these cases to design successful outsourcing relationships.

2 Issues

2.1 Importance of the relationship

There is no question that ITO knowledge has come a long way from the dominant transaction cost economic perspectives in the early 1990s (Ang and Beath, 1993; Ang and Straub, 1998; Domberger, 1998) to the relationship focus we are seeing today (Kern and Willcocks, 2001; Goles, 2001). Nonetheless, the introduction of the importance of the parties' relationship into the ITO literature lags behind that of the sociological and legal academic community (for example, Macaulay, 1963; Macneil, 1978).

Contract academia has recognised that it is not the contract, or contract law, that is worth studying, but relational theories of behaviour (Vincent-Jones 2000; Stinchcombe and Heimer, 1985; Campbell, 1997; Collins, 1996). Law and economic rationality has been marginalised by the recognition of the complexity of relationship behaviour (Collins, 1999). Accordingly, academic contract lawyers, drawing on other disciplines such as economics and philosophy, are arguing that classic contract doctrine is outmoded and should be replaced with a more relational theory (Campbell, 1997). Fundamentally, the contract is acknowledged to play an important part in developing behavioural norms within and between the parties, but it is the actual practice itself that forms the total contracting behaviour. The relationship is the crux of the deal.

In fact, a study by Oxford and Melbourne Universities of 235 Australian client organisations credited good relationships as the third most important factor just behind the supplier delivering to expectations and good contract management by both parties (Cullen et al., 2001). In that study, a good contract, per se, was not mentioned, although good relationship management techniques were – such as flexible working arrangements, the ability to change, and open, frequent, and effective communication.

2.2 Nature of relationships

Recognised in Figure 10.1, the contract is an important, but superficial driver of day-to-day behaviour. The deep behaviour drivers are the underlying values and attitudes held by the individual parties and the people involved in the agreement (Cullen and Willcocks, 2003).

The underlying, or deep, drivers of behaviour are underpinned by the orientations of communication, conflict resolution, relationship, strategic and values. These determine whether the relationship will exhibit more power-based or more trust-based characteristics as shown in Figure 10.2 (Cullen and Willcocks, 2003). In most cases, the client will want a balance between the two extremes of a completely power-based relationship and one based solely on trust. Extremes of either are rarely adequate for either party.

Further support for the power and trust relationship attributes comes from Deakin and Wilkinson (1998). Trust and power are alternative means

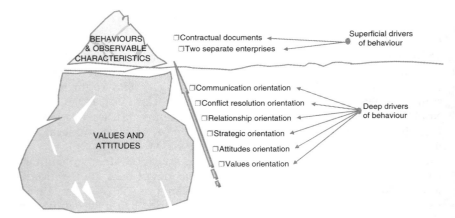

Figure 10.1   Underlying Drivers of Behaviour
Source: Cullen and Willcocks (2003)

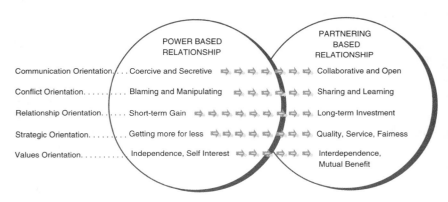

Figure 10.2   Power vs. Trust Relationships
Source: Cullen and Willcocks (2003)

of minimising risk and securing cooperation. Power is the negative threat of sanctions that might be applied to gain compliance. However, power is regarded as an inferior substitute for trust due to the higher transaction costs involved with monitoring and imposing sanctions. Therefore, relations capable of generating trust stand to gain an important competitive advantage over those that do not.

3   A lifecycle perspective

The relationship is an amorphous, ambiguous, but all-encompassing critical success factor of the overall outsourcing initiative. Nonetheless, there continues to be an almost ideological belief that outsourcing represents a relatively simple transaction involving services that are easily handed over to a supplier, and inherent benefits will follow. However, outsourcing is neither simple nor a transaction – it is a complex strategy for managing the delivery of services. Like all management strategies, the key to success lies in how that strategy is planned, implemented and managed – hence, the introduction of the lifecycle perspective.

3.1 The outsourcing lifecycle

All outsourcing initiatives go through a lifecycle. Various authors have proposed a number of different lifecycles with different degrees of comprehensiveness (Hui and Beath, 2001; Lacity and Willcocks, 2001; Hurley and Costa, 2001; Klepper and Jones, 1998; Kern and Willcocks, 2001).

Cullen and Willcocks (2003) have put forward a comprehensive lifecycle comprised of three phases and eight key building blocks (Figure 10.3 and Figure 10.4). This lifecycle was developed through the hindsight and experiences of 100 cases occurring between 1994 and 2003 across the Asia-Pacific

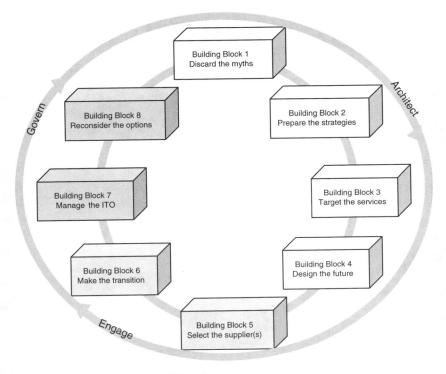

Figure 10.3 The Outsourcing Lifecycle
Source: Cullen and Willcocks (2003)

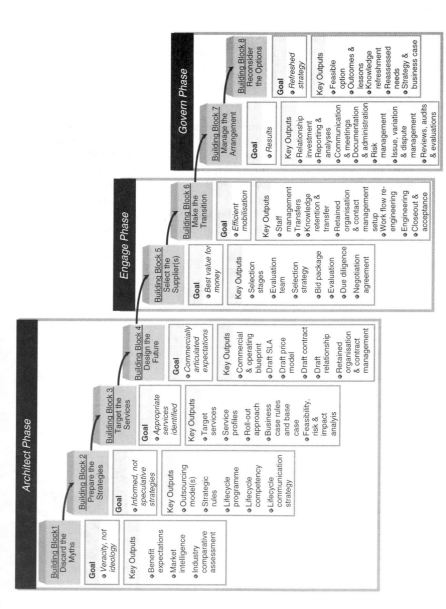

Figure 10.4 Lifecycle Building Blocks
Source: Cullen and Willcocks (2003)

Table 10.1 Highlighted Techniques in the Chapter

Building Block:	Relationship Technique Highlighted:
1 – Acumen	• investigate relationships that have worked (or not) and why
2 – Strategies	• craft the type of relationship best suited to the envisioned deal
3 – Target	• profile the services, in particular the stakeholder profile
4 – Design	• articulate desired behaviors through a relationship charter/code of conduct
5 – Selection	• choose a supplier that has demonstrated the desired relation ship
6 – Transition	• define clear and comprehensive transition roles
7 – Manage	• instate continuous improvement through relationship health checks
8 – Reconsider	• incorporate lessons via a relationship SWOT near the contract end

region. The author was directly involved with these organisations as a consultant or as an independent reviewer.

This lifecycle represents only the activities of one party – the client. It does not represent the supplier's activities. Undoubtedly, there is a need for both. Nevertheless, the need for a client model is evident from Cullen et al. (2001), which found that 60 per cent of clients attributed their own lack of experience as one of the most significant problems encountered – more than the other 14 typical problems identified. It is this lack of experience that the lifecycle aims to counter. It provides a comprehensive process that clients can consider tailoring to their individual context and constraints.

This paper uses the lifecycle to highlight techniques for clients to design the relationship they desire. A particular focus is given to the design of sustainable relationships and the issues and practices regarding such design. In doing so, the relationship is one that has been carefully planned and calculated.

There are a number of relationship techniques that have emerged from the annals of good practice in the last two decades of outsourcing. This paper highlights a few of those that have been replicated numerous times to superior effect (Table 10.1).

These are discussed in the remainder of this paper, including case vignettes where the technique occurred (or did not occur) and what happened as a result.

3.2 Building block 1: gather acumen

The purpose of this building block is to replace ideological concepts with realistic expectations appropriate to the client's circumstances and the outsourcing markets in which it may procure services. These investigative activities answer the question: *What are our theories and beliefs about outsourcing and how do they compare to what others have experienced?*

It is very important not to believe everything one is told about outsourcing. As Loh and Venkatraman (1992) discovered in their landmark paper on the adoption of ITO, outsourcing is a highly imitative behaviour where organisations attempt to duplicate the superficially observed success of others beginning with the widely publicised Eastman-Kodak outsourcing decision in July 1989.

This imitative client behaviour correlates to the concept of *institutional isomorphism* (DiMaggio and Powell, 1983), 'When organizational technologies are poorly understood, when goals are ambiguous, or the environment creates uncertainty…organizations tend to model themselves after similar organizations…they perceive to be more successful.' Institutional isomorphism is the reduction of uncertainty by imitating the behaviour of other organisations. Envious organisations then attempt to duplicate the *imperfectly* observed success. For example, Kodak's estimated cost savings are commonly quoted. What is not often mentioned are the five studies it performed, each between six to nine months in duration, before the outsourcing decision was made.[1] However, as Loh and Venkatraman exposed, it was the outsourcing that was imitated, not the precursor studies.

Accordingly, any organisation considering outsourcing may not have a safe general set of assumptions from which to make outsourcing decisions. It is therefore important to go out and test those assumptions with experts, other organisations and the market before embarking on the outsourcing journey.

One state government did this assumption testing to good effect. As part of formulating their outsourcing strategy, they investigated peer organisations in the commercial and public sectors regarding the commercial relationships they had in practice, identifying what worked and did not. In doing so, the government achieved a significant learning breakthrough. The management team had previously not attributed any importance to the transition and, in particular, the client's role in the transition. But it found so many instances of transition mishaps and underestimating the role the client played, that it recognised it needed a dedicated transition team and needed to include the transition plan as part of the tender. This was not only critical to a smooth transition but also critical to relationship formation because it set a precedent for the ongoing operational relationship to follow. As one organisation that was investigated stated, 'begin how you intend to continue'.

Compare the previous investigation and learning example to a joint venture (JV) between a global IT company and a European telecommunications company. The telco was advised by its consultants to form a service delivery JV, as it 'was the best way to ensure compatible goals'. So, it did. While it had formed other JVs in the past, to enter new markets, this was the first in which the JV would be providing services back to the company. It did not investigate how equity/service JV relationships work in practice and did not set up any form of retained competencies, contract management or even JV oversight. It was quite surprised to discover that the supplier would sell resources to the JV at inflated prices to make a profit rather than wait to split the profit from the potential distribution of JV dividends. It later put in a contract management team and an independent JV oversight board, but this was nearly two years after the JV had been operating – after significant cost escalation and inadequate service. The fatal untested assumption, in this case, was that a JV vehicle would inherently result in mutually beneficial behaviours, not in opportunism.

3.3 Building block 2: prepare the strategies

The purpose of this building block is to conduct the planning that enables objective and knowledgeable decisions to be made throughout the lifecycle. These concept articulation activities answer the question: *Is outsourcing right for us, in what form, and what do we need to do to make it work?*

This building block is crucial to the effective navigation of the entire outsourcing lifecycle. It defines the vision regarding the use of outsourcing within the client as well as setting up outsourcing as a programme identifying the right skills at the right time, and developing the communications framework. Strategy sets the parameters for what subsequently will happen. It is important to get this right. Wrong strategies create inflexibilities that are difficult and expensive to shift.

When formulating the relationship strategy, one must first look at the underlying business intent of the deal. Kern and Willcocks (2001) have proposed a useful model to differentiate the types of relationships that result from the intersection of strategic and capability intent. In their model, clients seek degrees of operational efficiency versus business value with regard to the intent of the deal (vertical axis in Figure 10.5) and seek degrees of resource accessibility versus unique leadership with regard to the capabilities sought from the supplier (horizontal axis in Figure 10.5).

Organisations that do not think about different ways of modelling the desired relationship, like that proposed by Kern and Willcocks above (as well as other models), end up with unarticulated expectations. Implied, but never expressed or agreed, expectations are very difficult to achieve indeed.

The IT help desk of a law enforcement agency was outsourced to a contract labour supplier (body shop) as a means of introducing organisational change in an attempt to promote new professional ways of working. Effectively, the client's management believed that once their 'traditional workers' observed the contractor's highly educated, motivated staff in professional attire, they would model themselves accordingly. It was expected that the workers would upgrade their act – dress better, come in earlier and stay later, as a matter of course. Since this was a foregone conclusion, there was no need to sign anything other than an 'operational service' contract, no need to put in any relationship strategies to enable this change or even a need for a culture change

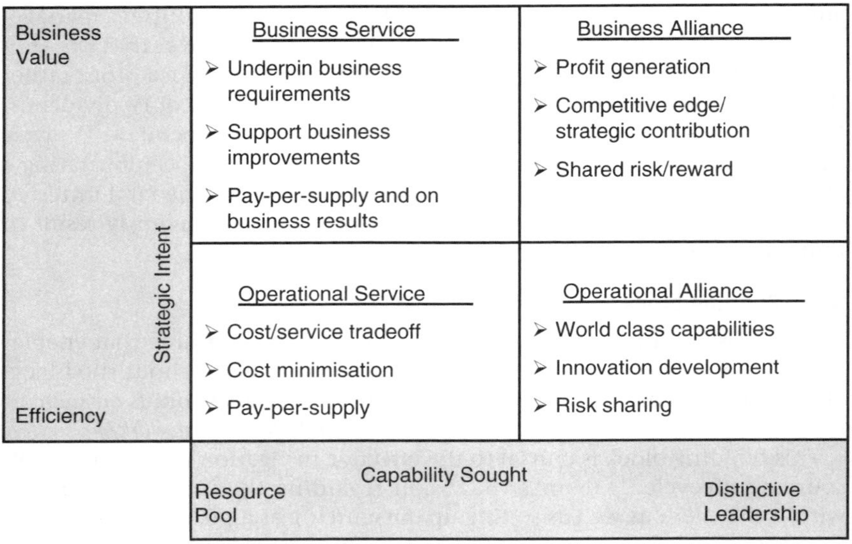

Business Value		Business Service	Business Alliance
	Strategic Intent	<ins>Business Service</ins> ➢ Underpin business requirements ➢ Support business improvements ➢ Pay-per-supply and on business results	<ins>Business Alliance</ins> ➢ Profit generation ➢ Competitive edge/ strategic contribution ➢ Shared risk/reward
Efficiency		<ins>Operational Service</ins> ➢ Cost/service tradeoff ➢ Cost minimisation ➢ Pay-per-supply	<ins>Operational Alliance</ins> ➢ World class capabilities ➢ Innovation development ➢ Risk sharing
		Resource Pool	Capability Sought	Distinctive Leadership

Figure 10.5 Business Intent Model
Source: Kern and Willcocks (2001)

programme. Within months of the supplier's staff coming onsite, a two-culture 'us against them' environment quickly formed. The supplier's staff were ridiculed and anyone caught emulating them was quickly put in their place.

Compare this with an educational institution that looked at outsourcing as a strategy to get organisational change and planned that strategy with care. It did not assume cultural innovation was a guaranteed benefit naturally occurring from outsourcing. Management was preparing a whole-of-IT outsourcing contract but wanted more that just an operations contract. It believed the supplier would be well-placed to introduce innovation and re-engineering sorely needed into a business that has not had the return on investment from IT. Accordingly, it knew it needed more than the 'standard agreement' for this to occur – akin to an operational alliance. It evaluated different re-engineering approaches to determine the one best suited. It designed detailed evaluation criteria and 'real life' scenarios that the bidders were to respond to. It tested various models with the industry (different payment and risk/reward schemes) until it had a model that it believed would work. The model chosen recognised that the supplier should be paid to generate ideas and business cases first. After the business cases were accepted or rejected, then remunerated for implementing them (but with some 'skin in the game'). Within the first year, it had received more innovation ideas than it had ever generated internally. The actual number of innovations implemented remained less than had been hoped, as the client had very entrenched ways of operating and was change-resistant. Nonetheless, management believed the introduction of the ideas and supporting business cases, alone, provided substantial benefits in unfreezing current mindsets on how and why technology was under-employed to move the organisation from a change-resistant mentality to a change-embracing one. Thus, the desired relationship, that of the supplier delivering operational services as well as being a vital change agent, was successful.

3.4 Building block 3: target the services

The purpose of this building block is to determine which activities are appropriate for outsourcing and to fully understand the nature and extent of each service that is being considered for outsourcing. The analyses activities answer the question: *What services should we investigate for outsourcing, for what reasons, and what is the current state, or 'snapshot', of the targeted services?*

A detailed understanding of the current state of the target services is essential if one is to approach the market knowledgeably. This is invaluable information not only for one's own piece of mind, but also when dealing with the supplier's pitch on service delivery. Being fact-based is vital; this enables the client to sit down and analyse with the supplier, rather than having to negotiate in an ill-informed way. The recommended profiles are made up of the components detailed in Table 10.2.

Of particular importance to the design of an effective relationship is the 6th profile – the stakeholder profile. This profile identifies who cares about the service and what they care about – the people with whom the supplier is likely to require some form of relationship. This is best demonstrated with an example.

A government agency responsible for the management of owned and leased property wanted to conduct a BPO initiative. It knew that any supplier would have difficulty in managing the various stakeholders that made up the organisation, and understanding what all the disparate needs were. Senior management wanted assurance of best practice and quality service, value for money and assurance that the government's best interests were represented. The finance department wanted accurate and timely financial data delivered in formats compatible with the various financial systems used. The IT department wanted data compat-ibility, accurate and timely updates, and a secure environment. Tenants wanted timely response and resolution. The special projects group wanted expert recommendations. The policy group wanted assurance that policy was complied with, information on areas in which the supplier was having difficulties, and recommendations for policy changes. The third party subcontractors wanted timely payments for services rendered,

Table 10.2   Profiles

Type of Profile	Components
1. Service	• Service Environment • Current and future service requirements • Volume, trend and load data (i.e. # users, transactions, desktops, calls, etc) • Performance criteria, service levels, measurement methods • Customer satisfaction indices
2. Baseline Costs	• Costs at current service levels and loads • Estimated costs at required or future service levels • Future capital expenditure programme
3. Balance Sheet	• Assets (including intellectual property) – type, quantity, location • Liabilities
4. Staffing	• Organisation chart(s) • Job descriptions • Staff numbers and full time equivalents • Remuneration • Accrued and contingent liabilities

5. Commercial Relationships	• For each current contract, licence, lease, agreement, etc
	  – Scope
	  – Value
	  – Inception and end dates
	  – Assignment, novation and termination options

6. Stakeholder	• Internal (i.e. users, management, departments) • External (i.e. end customers, other suppliers, affiliated organisations, media)
7. Governance	• Management • Administration • Control • Reporting • Systems • Risks and mitigation

fair assessment and feedback, and information to facilitate service performance. The agency prepared individual stakeholder profiles and facilitated the bidders in meeting the stakeholders to better understand their requirements. Each bid came up with innovative solutions in stakeholder management and the final agreement with the winning supplier had Key Performance Indicators (KPIs) reflecting all the stakeholder needs, not just the standard industry metrics.

Contrast this to another agency within the same government that also went to market with a BPO initiative. In this instance, no stakeholder profiles were provided nor were potential bidders allowed to meet any stakeholders to make their own determinations. Of an initial five-supplier race, two experienced suppliers refused to participate further after being shortlisted and one was not invited. That left two – the incumbent and a new entrant into the market who had no previous experience delivering outsourcing services, only in implementing the enabling software. Because the new entrant was prevented from conducting any meaningful needs analysis, they over-engineered the software solution and under-engineered the relationship component (under-resourced the account management team and customer care centre). The client stayed with the incumbent, who offered a much more resource intensive service with an elementary system. The new entrant departed that particular public sector market and the three other bidders refused to bid against incumbents to the agency, as the second time bidders were prevented from establishing the core understanding necessary to begin the basics of successful service delivery and relationships understanding the customer.

3.5 Building block 4: design the future

The purpose of this building block is to envision and detail the outsourcing arrangement as well as how it will be operationalised. These defining activities answer the following question: *What is the most appropriate outsourcing arrangement and how will we plan to manage it?*

This building block builds on the previous blocks to convert the desired arrangement into a commercially sound framework. This precedes the selection process because, logically, accepting a bid for an ill-defined product is unsound practice. It covers the detailed design of the arrangement and the desired relationship is part of that design. Determining who the client is going to live with and depend upon for many years is akin to an arranged marriage, albeit one in which the client has sole discretion.

Mature outsourcing clients have adopted a form of agreement called a 'Relationship Values Charter' or a 'Code of Conduct' that describes and agrees to the behaviour to be demonstrated during the course of the relationship. Modeling the desired behaviours at this stage is invaluable as it significantly contributes to the selection of the supplier who best demonstrates it 'lives' these values. Getting the right value and culture between the parties has proven to be one of the most difficult aspects of an outsourcing agreement (Cullen et al., 2001).

A relationship values charter agreed between a communications manufacturer and its Tier 1 IT infrastructure supplier is provided below in Figure 10.6. This charter was designed during building block 4 and was used in the remainder of the lifecycle – in building block 5 to draft the relationship-related questions in the request for tender and to guide customer reference checking, and in building block 7 to evaluate the relationship on a bi-annual basis. As a result, the client selected a supplier who had demonstrated the behaviour with other clients and the parties had a mechanism for gauging the degree to which the behaviour was exhibited in their deal.

- **Service** – We do not desire to apply penalties. The Services will be of a consistent high standard, comparable to market standards, and customers will be delighted.

- **Financial** – We will achieve our financial goals:
  - Client – reduce cost over time and have competitive pricing at all times
  - Contractor – reasonable profits

- **Communication** – We will communicate frequently, openly and honestly with each other.

- **Meet Needs** – We will be both proactive and reactive to each other's needs.

- **Creative Solutions** – We will constantly search for better ways of doing things.

- **Conflict** – We recognise conflict as natural and will focus on solving the problem, not apportioning blame. We will resolve conflict at the lowest level.

- **Fairness** – We will be fair to all parties.

- **Time** – We will provide each other time and management focus.

- **External Relations** – We will project a united front and will not discuss sensitive issues outside of the relationship.

- **Industry Model** – Our relationship will be seen as an industry model.

- **Enjoyment** – We enjoy working together and respect one another.

- **Added Value** – We will both derive more value from our relationship than just the exchange of money for services.

- **Work Seamlessly** – The services value chain will appear seamless.

- **Technology Leadership** – We both wish to have recognised technology leadership

Figure 10.6   Example Behaviours in a Relationship Values Charter

Clients who do not specify the behaviours they seek must work with the behaviours they get, as well as the behaviours the client itself exhibits.

In one case, the spiralling adversarial behaviour initially occurred from the client. A property company and a supplier agreed to an 'outsourcing alliance' – a partnering style of relationship. All worked very well together during negotiation and while planning the transition. Then, on the first day of the contract, the supplier walked into the client's office asking where the relationship manager would be accommodated (expecting an office next to the director in the spirit of 'partnering'). The director was quite surprised – he had expected the supplier's staff to be offsite and he certainly was not going to provide free office accommodation. Reluctantly, the director gave the supplier an office in the basement. The supplier was wounded by what it thought was an overt gesture normally found in a 'master-slave' relationship. Rather than discuss expectations of partnering behaviours, the supplier went on the defensive stating that 'if that's how they're going to treat us, fine.' The supplier instructed his staff to perform only to the letter of the contract and rely on the client's instructions as opposed to introducing the potential innovation ideas that were enthusiastically thrown about during negotiation. The client then interpreted this behaviour exhibited by the supplier 'typical: say anything to get the deal, then run it the way they like' and the adversarial relationship began.

3.6 Building block 5: engage

The purpose of this building block is to plan the competitive process and select the best value for money supplier(s). These evaluation activities answer the following question: *How should we approach the market, manage the process and obtain the best value for money?*

A competitive process is the most common selection technique and most clients employ a tender to select their ITO suppliers. Such an approach provides pressure on suppliers to deliver best value for money against their industry peers, exposes the organisation to a variety of capabilities and potential solutions, and allows an informed selection decision to evolve and mature.

Where the bid price is the sole criterion, the evaluation process is relatively straightforward. However, where 'value for money' is the key criterion, the tender evaluation becomes more complex. Value is often intangible and subject to the perceptions of the valuer, thus each organisation must develop a way of assessing the value each supplier and their bid offers in terms of unquantifiable attributes.

Service delivery is often the foremost criteria, as it should be. It is the number one factor for successful outsourcing (Cullen et al., 2001). However, deals that were more successful had the supplier exhibiting a far greater range of skills (Figure 10.7).

Clients who assess potential suppliers in this holistic manner have achieved faster and more sustainable results than those who have not. Particularly relevant to a successful relationship are the 'customer awareness skills'.

A state government department responsible for providing sport and recreational services to the community had all of these supplier capabilities with relative equal weight within its evaluation criteria. It was particularly interested in working with suppliers who had shared values with regard to the department's passion and reason for, 'community participation in sport and recreation'. It also had very specific needs with regard to staffing, as the suppliers chosen would be directly representing the department within the community. Furthermore, the demonstrated ability to operate a successful and sustainable business while demonstrating partnering behaviours and implementing continuous innovation was critical. Based on the portfolio of criteria, it chose three

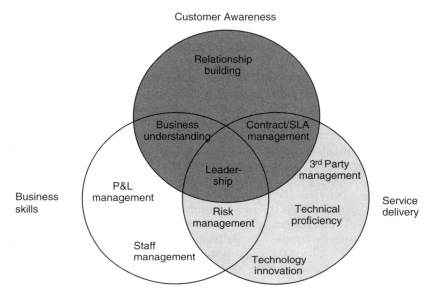

Figure 10.7   Required Supplier Capabilities
Source: Kern and Willcocks (2001)

suppliers in different regions. Each exceeded KPI targets in the first year –
KPIs that were considered stretch targets that the department was not
able to achieve under insourcing. Furthermore, each supplier reinvested
the KPI bonus in the service operations, although it was not required
under the contract. This then enabled the service providers to beat the
KPIs again and again.

Contrast this to a telecommunications client that selected a newly
formed consortium to deliver a wide range of services. The qualitative
criteria revolved around technical proficiency only. No single party had all
the core technical competencies, thus a consortium of three best-of-breed
suppliers was the winning bid. Within the first few months of operations,
the client realised that the contract would be unworkable. These parties
had never worked together before and every meeting required a representative of each consortium member to be there. In addition, no decision
could be reached without achieving time-consuming tri-supplier consensus. The client had only assessed technical proficiency of the bidders; it had
never assessed the business skills of the consortium as a business entity and
their customer governance and account management strategies. It lived
with this situation through the initial three year term and then went to
market for a sole supplier.

3.7 Building block 6: transition

The purpose of this building block is to develop and efficiently execute the transition strategy with minimal disruption to normal operations. These mobilisation activities answer the question: *How do we ensure a smooth transition – what needs to be done, by whom and when to ensure the deal is operationalised quickly, fully, and without disruption to normal operations?*

The transition process often officially begins at contract commencement and ends on a specified date or by the signing of a transition acceptance form. Irrespective of the official start and end dates, the transition actually begins much earlier and ends much later; or, if not managed properly, may not end at all. Accordingly, it is critical that both parties begin planning for the transition as soon as it believes outsourcing may go ahead.

A good jump out of the starting gate will pave the way for a smooth process thereafter. One key to the jump is to have clearly defined roles regarding the transition. The client organisation will typically have the following transition roles (Figure 10.8), for which a counterpart (or counterparts) exist with the supplier.

The relationship prior to transition is akin to a courtship and this is where the honeymoon starts and ends. Those that recognise that this is a resource-intensive period for both parties and plan a bi-party programme are in a much better position to have a successful 'marriage'.

A federal government department conducted its first BPO initiative as part of a whole-of-government mandate. The supplier was awarded a contract to begin in October and had planned a three week transition period. However, the client made all but three staff redundant in June (to meet financial year-end headcount goals). This caused a number of problems. First, no regular work was done for three months, which created a huge backlog and disgruntled customers. Second, information and data was left at different stages of completion and much information was not available at all. The supplier tried throughout the contract to cleanse inaccurate and incomplete client data. Third, no staff were available to assist with the transition. It was well known in the industry as a 'total disaster' for the first six months. The client, in this case, had assumed no responsibility for any contribution to the relationship or its operations. It eventually cost more and the quality of services expected was not provided.

Contrast this to a global mining company that ensured the parties worked efficiently and effectively from the start. It had multiple transition teams, a detailed transition programme, numerous transition planning workshops and test runs with the supplier. The parties were able to perform a 48-hour weekend transition – moving assets to the supplier's facility, connecting the network and getting all applications up and running. On Monday morning, it was business as usual.

Transition Roles	Description
Steering Committee or Joint Reference Panel	1. guide the project and provide strategic input to the implementation process 2. facilitate timely decision-making and resolve issues escalated from the transition team 3. monitor the quality of key deliverables 4. provide a forum for communicating progress and achievement of project milestones
Transition Programme Leader	5. manage all the transition activities across all the divisions to ensure consistency 6. report to the steering committee
Transition Project Team Leaders	7. manage the transition for a specific service, geography or customer group
Human Resource (HR) Representative(s)	8. provide HR specific advice 9. coordinate the HR initiatives and services to staff 10. assist in setting up the retained organisation
Business Representative(s)	11. provide business unit specific advice 12. coordinate business unit transition activities 13. liaise with business unit line management 14. test and accept the business unit's data migration and functioning
Technical Representative(s)	15. provide technical advice 16. coordinate technical transition activities 17. liaise with supplier's technicians and system integrators 18. test and accept technical migration, configuration and operational functioning
Business Process Representative(s), if applicable	19. provide business process advice 20. coordinate business process transition activities 21. liaise with the supplier's business process re-engineering team and service set-up team 22. test and accept business process migration, configuration and functioning
Communications Representative(s)	23. provide communication and change leadership advice 24. develop communications messages and media 25. liaise with supplier's communications representative 26. manage the feedback loop
Administration Resource	27. coordinate logistical support 28. create and manage control files

Figure 10.8   Client Transition Roles

3.8   Building block 7: manage

The purpose of this building block is to efficiently and effectively manage the outsourcing arrangement. These management activities answer the question: *What needs to be in place or occur to ensure the arrangement works now and in the future?*

When implementing such a new way of operating that outsourcing represents, it is inevitable that the type of work, or how that work is accomplished, will need to change. The old ways of doing things will no longer be appropriate under an outsourcing arrangement. New work flows, communications, paper flows and sign offs are required. New relationships will need to be quickly formed, and people accustomed to a certain way of operating will need to operate in a completely different manner.

Whether the relationship exhibits more power-based characteristics or more trust-based characteristics as explained earlier, long-term success will be dependent upon how the relationship is managed. The best governing documents (contract, SLA, etc) become merely weapons in a poorly functioning relationship – to be used against the other party rather than to guide successful outcomes. A successful relationship requires the investment of time and effort at all levels of both parties, where many times, the journey is more important than the destination. It is an investment well worth making to establish fundamental understandings and insights into the other party, establish key interpersonal relationships in order to overcome inevitable hurdles, and establish shared as well as discrete values.

Given the importance of the relationship, a 'health check' diagnostic used in practice has been provided to assist determining whether an outsourcing relationship is exhibiting healthy vital signs (Figure 10.9).

Relationship evaluations should not be a one off event, as the following company had learnt.

A telecommunication company made a large investment in relationship during the bidding and negotiation process. They had conducted a similar relationship diagnostic as part of the transition acceptance and both parties scored reasonably well. However, the contract management function was not involved in the earlier stages of evaluation, negotiation, or transition. The client's contract managers, when they were handed the deal to run day-to-day, were traditionally adversarial and stayed that way – disputing all claims for out-of-scope work, disputing all bonus claims, disallowing any requests for excusable delays, etc. Accordingly, the supplier quickly changed tactics and set up its defences. This included not performing work until a variation was signed off (a very long process in the telco), refusing to scale up KPIs that were being achieved with little effort and reporting only the minimum information that was explicitly defined in the contract, not the plethora of information available in the system (unless the client paid handsomely).

An electric utility in a nearby country had none of those problems. They evaluated the relationship every quarter, and had an improvement agenda to focus on the key gaps. In fact, the relationship was deemed so unusually superior that an independent consultant was brought in when a new general manager took over at the client. This was to verify that it was, in fact, arms-length (no collusion, etc) and good governance was in place.

Category	Diagnostic Questions
Behaviours exhibited	1. Do both parties display ethical behaviour? 2. Is there an 'us' vs. 'them' mentality? 3. Are both parties proactive? 4. Does either party blame the other when problems arise? 5. Does either party misrepresent the relationship to others? 6. Do the parties give each other recognition when it is due? 7. Are there key individuals who dislike each other?
Perceptions of the parties regarding one another	8. Do both parties respect one another? 9. Do both parties think the other party is a good listener? 10. Do both parties believe the relationship is a role model for the industry? 11. Do both parties use the relationship as an example of good practice within their respective organisations? 12. Are both parties reliable? 13. Are there unfulfilled promises by either party? 14. Does either party think the other party is not pulling their weight or living up to their accountabilities? 15. Do the parties think of the other party as trustworthy? 16. Does either party display the NIH (not invented here) syndrome (i.e. 'it's not our problem, it's their problem')? 17. Do both parties understand each other's business, underlying drivers and motivations, and politics?
Investment in the relationship	18. Are both parties investing management time and effort? 19. Are there solid relationships at all appropriate levels? 20. Does each party get the management attention it needs from the other? 21. Is the client organisation an enthusiastic customer reference site for the supplier?
Communication	22. Is there regular communication? 23. Is there regular feedback? 24. Do the parties provide early warning to each other? 25. Do the parties suggest improvements to one another?
Relationship processes	26. Are there clear protocols between the parties? 27. Does each party assess the satisfaction of the other party? 28. Do the parties plan together? 29. If the contract has financial rewards for superior performance, have such awards been applied? 30. If the contract has financial consequences for poor performance, has such recourse needed to be continually applied? 31. Do the parties continuously seek better ways of doing things?

Figure 10.9   Relationship Health Check Diagnostics

Nothing unseemly was found. Only minor 'tweaking' of process transparency (forms and signoffs) was recommended, stating 'the commercial relationship and behaviours exhibited were what parties everywhere aspire to'.

3.9   Building block 8: reconsider

The purpose of this building block is to evaluate options prior to the end of the contract and strategies for moving to the selected option. These investigative and strategy-formulating activities answer the question: *How should we prepare for the end of the contract, ensure all our options are feasible, and improve the next generation sourcing?*

Typical options, for any or all of the scope of work, include renewal, renegotiation, retender, return to inhouse and discontinue service. In practice, all options take place. Some services are backsourced, some eliminated, some the incumbent supplier provides, and some a new supplier provides. To what extent this occurs varies widely.

To be able to evaluate the best options going forward and to determine a new set of expectations, the client will need to undergo the same series of activities conducted in the Architect Phase, but now armed with the benefit of hindsight and experience. Most clients, who have been through at least one outsourcing cycle can approach these assessments in a different manner from a first generation client because of the knowledge and hindsight gained from the first wave of outsourcing – thus, focusing on 'surgical strikes' throughout the building blocks. Nonetheless, there is one new assessment of particular relevance to the potential future relationship under any option – the prior generation outsourcing SWOT (Strengths, Weaknesses, Opportunities, and Threats) assessment. This analysis is designed to determine:

- strengths – to be retained
- weaknesses – to be corrected
- opportunities – to be taken
- threats to be eliminated or mitigated

While the SWOT assesses all aspects of the past arrangement, moving forward, including the contract/Service Level Agreement (SLA), supplier characteristics, scope of services, the contract management function, the retained organisation, etc – it also pays particular attention to the relationship aspects.

A federal government department went to retender and selected a supplier who was well below the incumbent bid. The incumbent had been quite flexible in its approach, allowing the client to exceed capacity restrictions without extra charges, allowing scope creep in certain areas but maintaining the same fixed price, etc. The new supplier was well-known in the market as a vigorous 'out of scope' hunter, typically bidding low, then aggressively making profits from minimalist interpretations of scope and charging for additional work. Relationship SWOT assessment and redesign was not even considered in the redesign work as it was assumed that all suppliers behave the same. The client behaved as it did with the incumbent and quickly learnt that the new game was different and all about managing scope and cost escalation.

Contrast this to a utility company that had conducted a detailed SWOT of the incumbent contract relationships. It believed this was particularly necessary, as it had amalgamated three geographic regions comprising five contracts into two regions. It was planning on conducting a tender for one region and backsourcing the other region, to a wholly-owned subsidiary, to regain the operational competence it had lost from nearly 15 years of outsourcing (this was the third generation). The contract management function was concerned that having a related entity as a supplier would throw out the very successful governance and relationship management processes that had evolved. Based on the SWOT, the key areas of strength were a comprehensive and 'reader-friendly' contract, diligent contract management, monthly detailed performance review, retaining of inhouse operation of core operational systems and benchmarking between the parties. Weaknesses were a fixed price contract when the client needed to be able to chop and change services (changed to a fixed-price base-load, with interchangeable service units, and volume discounts for work above that). The company signed substantially the same agreement with the subsidiary as it did with the independent supplier and put in the same governance. After some initial politicking, the subsidiary 'fell into line as an arms-length provider' and was soon delivering the market equivalent standard of service.

4 Conclusion

Even though the legal academia recognised the importance of the relationship 20 years ago, it has only recently received attention in the IT outsourcing literature. Of course, anyone who has been managing outsourcing deals knows that the relationship is a critical factor in a well-performing agreement and differentiates one deal from another.

Relationship management is a key element that leads to outsourcing success (or otherwise). The techniques presented here are just a few of the commercial solutions that have been put into practice. These techniques are not easy for those that have let relationships happen rather than proactively design and select relationships that are fit for purpose. However, such techniques have elevated the deal beyond the traditional, more adversarial relationships that can often transpire when relationships are poorly designed and left unmanaged. In these, one party, and often both parties, become victims of a dysfunctional relationship rather than participants in a performing one.

At the end of the day, outsourcing will be more successful if it is viewed as a strategy, not as a transaction. Accordingly, the relationship is part of that strategy – not an inadvertent consequence of executing a contract. Through proactive effort, the client organisation can be very well placed to ensure successful outcomes and have interparty relationships that are operating in an effective manner.

Note

1. *Industry Week*, June 1, 1992 Vol. 24, No. 11, pp. 42–44.

References

A. Stinchcombe and C. Heimer, *Organizational Theory and Project Management: Administrative Uncertainty in Norwegian Offshore Oil*, Oxford University Press, Oxford (1985).

D. Campbell, 'Socio-legal Analysis of Contracting' in P. Thomas (ed.) *Sociolegal Studies*, Dartmouth Publishing Co Ltd 1996, England (1997).

H. Collins, 'Competing Norms of Contractual Behavior', in D. Campbell and P. Vincent-Jones (eds) *Contract and Economic Organization: Sociolegal Initiatives*, Dartmouth Publishing Co Ltd 1996, England (1996).

H. Collins, *Regulating Contracts*, Oxford University Press, Oxford (1999).

I. Macneil, 'Contracts: Adjustments of long-term economic relations under classical, neoclassical, and relational contract law', *Northwestern University Law Review*, LCCII (1978) 854–906.

J. Shuen, 'Critical Success and Failure Factors in Outsourcing of IT', Working Paper, University of Melbourne (2002).

L. Loh and N. Venkatraman, 'Diffusion of Information Technology Outsourcing Influence Sources and the Kodak Effect', *Information Systems Research* (1992) 334–358.

M. Hurley and C. Costa, *The blurring boundary of the organization: Outsourcing comes of age*, KPMG Consulting Australia (2001).

M. Lacity and L. Willcocks, *Global Information Technology Outsourcing: Search for Business Advantage*, Wiley, Chichester (2001)

P. DiMaggio and W. Powell, 'The iron cage revisited: Institutional isomorphism and collective rationality in organizational fields', *American Sociological Review*, 48 (April 1983), 147–160.

P.P. Hui and C.M. Beath, 'The IT Sourcing Process: A Framework for Research', Working Paper, University of Texas at Austin (2002).

P. Vincent-Jones, 'Contractual Governance: Institutional and Organizational Analysis', *Oxford Journal of Legal Studies*, Vol. 20, No. 3 (2000) 317–351.

R. Klepper, 'The Management of Partnering Development in IS Outsourcing', *Journal of Information Technology*, 10, 4, (1995) 249–258.

R. Klepper and W.O. Jones, *Outsourcing Information Technology Systems & Services*, Prentice Hall (1998).

S. Alborz, 'Impact of Configuration on IT Outsourcing Relationships', Working Paper, University of Melbourne (2004).

S. Cullen, P. Seddon and L. Willcocks, *IT Outsourcing Practices in Australia*, Deloitte Touche Tohmatsu, Sydney (2001).

S. Cullen and L. Willcocks, *Intelligent IT Outsourcing: Eight Building Blocks to Success*, Elsevier, Oxford (2003).

S. Deakin and F. Wilkinson, 'Contract Law and the Economics of Interorganizational Trust' in C. Land and R. Bachman (eds), *Trust within and between Organizations: Conceptual Issues and Empirical Applications* (1998).

S. Domberger, *The Contracting Organization: A Strategic Guide to Outsourcing*. Oxford University Press, Oxford (1998).

S. Macaulay, 'Non Contractual Relations in Business: A Preliminary Study', *American Sociological Review*, XXVIII (1963) 55–67.

T. Goles, The Impact of the Client-Vendor Relationship on Information Systems Outsourcing Success. Unpublished Ph.D. Thesis, University of Houston (2001).

T. Kern and L. Willcocks, *The Relationship Advantage: Information Technologies, Sourcing and Management*. Oxford University Press, Oxford (2001)

V. Sambamurthy, D.W. Straub and R.T. Watson, 'Information Technology Managing in the Digital Era', in Dickson, G.W. and G. DeSanctis (eds) *Information Technology and the Future Enterprise, New Models for Managers*, Prentice Hall, New Jersey (2001)

Part VI

The Legal Foundations

11

The Outsourcing Contract: Structure and Tactics

Peter Brudenall

1 Introduction

All too often, the parties to an outsourcing arrangement realise soon after the commencement of the relationship that they have, unintentionally, not been following the contract, or that the contract fails to address specific issues. While there may be any number of reasons why this has happened, typically they involve the parties not taking the time to fully articulate in sufficient detail the key obligations of each party. Not spending enough time establishing the scope of services to be performed is perhaps the most common problem. The pressure to finalise the deal can often result in a lack of attention to what is most important to ensuring a successful outsourcing relationship. In such cases, the parties will often need to renegotiate the contract or, in a worst case scenario where the relationship has broken down, the customer may need to start the process again.

If your company is considering an outsourcing arrangement, the contract, and its various schedules and attachments, will form an essential 'user's manual' to the business relationship that you will develop. However, great care needs to be taken in getting the fundamentals right. A well drafted and thought-out contract will capture the financial and operational elements of the parties' relationship. Adhering to a clear, considered and even-handed contract will provide discipline to the parties' conduct throughout their relationship, and also provide a framework for dealing with situations that were perhaps unforeseeable when the contract was being negotiated.

This chapter will attempt to set out, in plain English, the issues that should be considered – both in developing the contractual structure and then in negotiating the contract – and provide a basis for ensuring that your strategy reflects best practice.

2 Deal structure

All outsourcing deals are governed by the framework set out in the base terms and conditions, together with the schedules attached to the terms and conditions. The structure of the terms and conditions will often be determined by the scope of the transaction. In an international arrangement, for example, a company seeking to centralise decision-making and strategic direction might consider entering into a 'master' agreement with specific site or service agreements attached. The master agreement would set out the general terms and conditions that are then applied to all site or service agreements entered into under the master agreement. Alternatively, and more typically, the terms and conditions could be structured as a standalone document. This tends to be less complex than a master agreement and most applicable to those outsourcing transactions that do not involve the roll-out of international sites or a phased services transfer.

Similarly, because of evolving enterprise requirements and industry changes, it is vital that a long-term, large-scale outsourcing agreement be able to accommodate continuous change. Provisions allowing for the contract to evolve over time will need to be carefully considered and drafted if the parties are to avoid the need for renegotiation.

Fundamental to any consideration of the overall structure for the terms and conditions is the development of the contract schedules. The schedules set out the detailed information regarding the operational responsibilities of the parties, the services to be performed, how the relationship should be managed, and the process of managing changes to the relationship or scope of work. A company looking to outsource some, or all, of a particular function should first determine the scope of the services that would be transferred to a service provider. Defining and documenting the services to be outsourced can often be time-consuming and extremely difficult – particularly where these services are not centralised in one function within the company. This is why many companies engage consultants to manage this part of the process.

However, as difficult as determining the scope of services may be, companies that develop this material early in the process are likely to benefit from a more efficient procurement process.

3   The tendering process

Ensuring the contract is given primary consideration by both vendor and customer is one of the essential ways of managing risk. As a general rule, the earlier a draft contract can be considered by the potential vendors, the better. Certainly, customers should consider including either a draft contract or, if that is not possible, contractual principles or 'heads of terms' within the tender documentation. Potential vendors should then be requested to indicate their compliance with such terms or principles in their response. This will ensure a level contractual playing field, and will also indicate to the customer whether there may be any pricing implications from the use of certain terms. It should also save time during negotiations if the vendor's position on key principles is known.

However, if draft terms and conditions are included with the Request for Proposal (RFP), the customer should keep in mind the following:

(a) it is important that terms be 'reasonable' to elicit 'sensible' bids. This is particularly important where a customer is hoping to gain indicative pricing from the vendor. There is little point including overly one-sided terms if it leads vendors to pricing in a significant level of risk, resulting in distorted pricing.
(b) if it is too early to be specific about certain terms, the customer should at least set out the contractual principles to be adopted. As with describing the required services in the tender documentation, the customer must be careful so as not to give too little information for the vendors to go on, and being so precise that initiative and alternative views are stifled. It should be remembered that the vendor may well have excellent ideas as to how the services can be provided, so being too prescriptive is often as unhelpful as not providing enough information.
(c) As suggested above, the tender documentation must make it clear that the vendors must respond to the draft terms by either accepting them or raising all major issues in the response. The customer should use the element of competition to its advantage.

As stated above, such an approach will increase the speed of negotiating the contract, and lessen the risk of major contractual points being raised at a later stage.

3.1 Transferring assets

Where physical assets, such as computer hardware, are owned outright, there will most likely be a sale of those assets. In such an event, the assets should be properly identified in the contract and any tax implications considered.

Where the assets are subject to a finance lease, matters may be more complex. It would be usual for such a lease to contain prohibitions on parting with possession of the assets and on assignment of the lease itself. It may well be that even if the asset is to remain in its current location, the fact that it will be operated by the employees of the vendor will be sufficient to constitute a breach of its terms. This can seem an odd position, given that those same people were probably employees of the customer immediately prior to the outsourcing.

The customer must review any finance leases and obtain any necessary consents from the finance house involved so as to avoid breaching the terms. The issue of consents in respect of third party contracts will be considered in more detail below.

3.2 Third party contracts

Many other forms of contracts with third parties will be relevant to an outsourcing, if they are important to the function which is being transferred. These will include contracts for the supply of goods such as consumables and services such as maintenance. In some cases, contracts will need to be transferred over to the vendor.

One particular area of concern will be in relation to software licences. These will almost inevitably contain similar prohibitions to finance leases. This means that the customer will be in breach, either if it assigns the licences, or even if it simply allows the vendor to operate the software on its behalf. By using the software in such circumstances, the vendor will be infringing the copyright of the licensor and will also be liable. Given the fact that the customer is in the best position to obtain any necessary consents, the vendor will probably expect an indemnity from the customer in respect of such a liability. The customer is then in a very awkward situation. Whilst the software vendor is unlikely to either terminate the licence or sue, it will simply charge for giving the vendor consent to use the software. This could be expensive and it is vital that the customer is aware of that price as early as possible in the process.

The key is for the customer to carry out a due diligence exercise on its own software licences and, if possible, to seek all the relevant consents in plenty of time before the commencement date. This enables the customer to isolate the problem licences while there is still time to negotiate a reasonable consent fee. The customer should not, however, underestimate the task. It is a process that may take some time; from experience even locating copies of the licences can be a challenge! The more time the customer gives itself to manage this process, the better and, ideally, it should begin at the outset of the tendering procedure.

3.3 Transfer of employees

One of the most critical aspects of an outsourcing to get right is the handling of the employees in the department to be transferred. In Europe, this issue is regulated by the Acquired Rights Directive (ARD) and implemented locally in the laws of member states (in the UK, known as 'TUPE'). While the ARD itself cannot be contracted out of, the customer and vendor are free to re-allocate cost amongst themselves for the consequences of the ARD (including re-allocating the cost of meeting transferring claims). One of the major commercial issues is the cost of redundancies of surplus employees at the end of the agreement, as the vendor will wish the customer to bear this cost (whether or not the employees are deemed to have transferred to the customer by virtue of the ARD). But the ARD is but one of several issues that needs to be addressed in relation to employees. Pensions, employment terms and conditions, and benefits also need to be addressed.

In general, if ARD applies to an outsourcing transaction, all employees caught by the regulations will transfer automatically with the undertaking to the vendor. All employees transferred under ARD will retain the same terms and conditions of employment which they enjoyed with the former employer, the customer. If ARD does not apply, there is no automatic transfer of the employees, and the customer will continue to be responsible for them and any accrued liabilities in respect of their employment, including redundancy payments.

Specific advice will need to be sought for each country in which there may be employees who could be affected by the outsourcing.

4   The contract terms

Once the process of selecting the vendor and negotiating the terms of the transfer of the function to that vendor have been completed, the longer term relationship is then governed by the contract. This agreement is likely to be in place for as long as 10 years and has two main functions:

(a)   to set out clearly the parties' obligations to each other from day one; and
(b)   to allow the parties to evolve the service provision over time and to end the relationship rationally.

The aim must be to prepare a contract which balances them so as to best serve the commercial needs of both parties.

Developing this further, the key points the contract should address are as follows:

4.1   Describing the services

One of the most repeated questions asked by customers is 'every time that we want the service provider to perform new work, we receive an additional invoice for fees. Is this right?' Confusion as to whether a particular service is included within the scope of work being performed by the vendor is one of the major causes of disputes, and why contracts are re-negotiated. To avoid this, the description of services within the contract should be clear enough to avoid later questions over what services are in scope under the contract and what constitutes a change to be addressed by extra fees. This can often take a lot of work and discussion between the parties, and requires careful drafting and a thorough legal review. Vendors taking over a service need to understand what the customer (or service provider) was previously doing, at what level of performance and at what cost. There needs, therefore, to be a clear service description, a clear statement of customer responsibilities and a clear delineation between the two. As stated above, all too often this is ignored.

Firstly, both parties should be careful to avoid problems with pricing and scope of services – or, as it's more commonly described, 'scope creep'. In most circumstances, the vendor will charge a base price for services and use separate adjustments and fees for additional services, such as per-project consulting. Thus, early in negotiations, the parties need to openly discuss the scope of services, especially if the vendor plans to negotiate subcontracts.

4.2 Controlling quality

Failure to provide services to the standards set out in the descriptions will be a breach of contract entitling the customer to sue for damages. However, unless the customer is also prepared to terminate the agreement, it is unlikely to want to damage the ongoing relationship by resorting to litigation. The contract should therefore set out less contentious alternatives to make sure there is recourse for the customer should service provision be inadequate. The usual method is to link service levels to pre-determined credits against charges ('service credits'). Such credits should be an automatic remedy, and not limit the customer to other remedies. In other words, it should not be an exclusive remedy for a failure to miss a service level.

Increasingly, both customers and vendors are approaching the issue of service credits in a more considered manner. Contracts now often include service credits that are defined clearly and configured relative to the monthly fees. Current regimes for service credits range from 10 per cent to 20 per cent for failure to meet key service levels. It goes without saying that it is critical to set service levels and associated service credit regimes as part of the initial contract as it is much harder to negotiate into the contract.

It should be remembered that service credits are not a perfect solution to non-performance, and have to be engineered with care in conjunction with other mechanisms (such as reporting requirements and escalation) designed to identify and mitigate poor performance. Beyond service credits there may be other levels of remedies, including the payment of more substantial damages, ending with total or partial termination.

4.3 Controlling change

A key risk in any outsourcing is the extent to which there may be changes during the life of the contract in terms of business contexts and strategies, the technology itself and developments in the IT services market in relation to supplier capabilities, labour supply and pricing. It is inconceivable that the customer's IT and telecoms requirements will remain static and therefore the agreement must incorporate a mechanism for managing change. The contract should contain an appropriate mechanism for the negotiation, agreement and implementation of these changes. It should address whether the supplier can charge for changes, and, if so, on what basis. Most importantly, the change mechanism should be designed to fit the needs of the people who will use it (that is, the project teams).

4.4 Controlling prices

The customer will also expect to see a mechanism for controlling price increases over the life of the agreement. As technology improves, the services should be provided more efficiently so this must also be reflected in the charges.

4.5 Dispute management

This breaks down into two areas:

(a) Preventing disputes: In addition to the strategic reviews mentioned above, the agreement should provide for regular liaison meetings and exchange of information. This will be dealt with in the governance arrangements and is a useful means for both parties to gain early visibility of potential problems.

(b) Resolving disputes: the contract should set out the basic mechanisms for internal escalation of disputes and their further referral to alternative dispute resolution or the courts. As a breakdown in the customer/vendor relationship is likely to be very damaging to both parties, serious thought should be given to the merits of alternative dispute resolution.

4.6 Regulation

The parties must address regulatory requirements, including the requirements of international law, such as intellectual property laws and other country-specific legislation such as labour laws. Foreign labour laws could greatly complicate a customer's plan to transfer its employees to the vendor and expert advice must always be sought in such circumstances.

Similarly, legislation enacted under the European Commission's Data Privacy Directive could prohibit the transfer of personal data to non-EU countries unless certain additional notice, consent and security requirements are satisfied.

Outsourcings in the financial services sector are usually subject to supervision by a regulator (in the UK, the Financial Services Authority). A proper balance needs to be struck between customer and vendor regarding who bears the cost of changes to the outsourced service required as a result of changes in regulation. The customer will also have to make sure that its regulatory responsibilities are reflected by 'back to back' arrangements in the agreement (such as audit rights and restrictions on subcontracting).

4.7 Management and corporate governance

An established body of market research on outsourcing shows that one factor that is consistently absent in failed outsourcings is a proper management and governance structure. It is now accepted that the long-term success of an outsourcing project depends, in large part, on the customer's management of both its internal organisation and the vendor. Gartner Research suggests that a customer should spend between three per cent (a best practice goal) and 12 per cent of the value of the outsourcing contract on managing the relationship (Gartner, 2004).

Accordingly, the terms and conditions should establish the management teams of both parties, including each party's central point of contact for matters relating to the project and the membership, and responsibilities of an overall contract management committee.

With respect to the vendor's team, the customer should require that certain 'key' personnel of the vendor be in place prior to the execution of the contract. These key personnel would then be familiar with the project, as well as the customer's personnel and culture. In order to provide the company with a certain amount of stability and consistency in the management of the project, the contract should include terms restricting the vendor's reassignment or replacement of the key personnel.

Many vendors will look to subcontractors for the performance or provision of a portion of the outsourced services. Accordingly, the customer should require the vendor to submit, for the customer's approval, the identities of any subcontractors and the services such subcontractors would provide. If approval of all subcontractors would be too burdensome for the customer, the contract could specify that only those subcontracts for certain 'core' services or in excess of a particular amount require the customer's approval.

The customer's management of the vendor should include review of the vendor's performance against objective measurement criteria. The contract between the company and the vendor should include terms relating to the vendor's performance, such as service levels and credits for failures to meet the service levels. Accordingly, including a benchmarking clause with defined criteria is crucial for any outsourcing contract and has become the trend among customers.

However, the criteria established must be realistic and must serve both parties. For example, any operation can achieve a 'lowest-cost' status if end-user satisfaction is reduced or risks are taken by not having appropriate maintenance coverage or business recovery standards. Ultimately, such an approach could jeopardise a business and an outsourcing relationship. Maintaining or improving the relationship should be the primary goal of a benchmark.

The outsourcing contract should specify when this benchmarking may occur, what entities and services should be included in the benchmarking pool and what remedies are available to the company in the event the benchmarking results in a finding that the vendor's services or pricing, or the service levels achieved by the vendor, are not on par with those available in the marketplace.

A company may also wish to track the vendor's performance through customer satisfaction surveys, in which end-users of the outsourced services rate the vendor, the quality of the services provided and the interfaces between the end-users and the vendor. Finally, the issue of corporate governance needs to be specifically addressed in the contract: a jointly appointed management committee, an independent chair, a dispute resolution mechanism, an escalation procedure, joint participation in continuous improvement and other classic 'signatures' of good corporate governance should be designed for the deal.

4.8 Liability

One of the most contentious issues in an outsourcing is the allocation of liability between the customer and vendor. The vendor will want the degree of liability it takes on to reflect the reward it is receiving, while the customer will wish to transfer risk to the vendor. Issues such as liability for data loss or corruption can be major issues for a vendor. Creative solutions are sometimes called for. For example, can the vendor accept liability because it has insurance for that kind of loss? Can liability for delay be quantified in advance by way of liquidated damages? For such issues, it is preferable to discuss them with your external advisors before committing to them within the agreement.

4.9 Termination

Both parties, particularly the customer, should give some thought to the circumstances in which the contract can be brought to an end. The most obvious time is at the expiry of a fixed term arrangement. However, it is usually difficult for an outsourcing arrangement to 'drop dead' on a particular date so fixed term contracts are rare. More usually, the parties can bring the contract to an end on the service of notice after the initial term, otherwise the contact rolls on. Where there is a long-term contract (e.g. 10 years), the customer may wish to have the option to terminate earlier, albeit on payment of a termination fee.

The typical triggers for termination are considered in section 5.

4.10 Exit strategy

Whilst setting up an outsourcing is a complex task, it is equally true that bringing one to an end is also very complex, involving the unwinding of the original transaction. However, there are additional complications:

(a) The assets and staff originally transferred will have changed over time. The equipment, software and people which the customer may need to take from the outgoing vendor will therefore be different from those with which the customer was familiar.

(b) The customer is likely to be unable to take service provision back in-house and is therefore likely to want to transfer the services to a new vendor.

In addition, employment regulations may well apply to the change of service, so that the staff of the outgoing vendor employed in service provision at the time of transfer would automatically become the employees of the new vendor.

The agreement therefore needs to anticipate and specify the rights which the customer may require on expiry or termination of the outsourcing.

5   Re-tendering and changing vendors

Once the parties have decided to terminate their arrangements, the outsourcing contract itself should provide clear timelines and designation of costs and responsibilities between the parties to enable them to plan and execute a disengagement from each other as quickly and cleanly as possible.

The consequences of not addressing at the outset how the parties are to manage the end of the relationship can be severe. From the customer's point of view, it can find itself trapped with an unsatisfactory vendor with no real ability to do anything except renew the contract. From the vendor's perspective, a messy 'divorce' could mean bad publicity, so handling the end of a contract smoothly and professionally should be a high priority.

The aim of this section is to highlight the issues involved in this critical stage in the history of an outsourcing transaction.

5.1   Recognising what needs to be done

There are three main scenarios that the parties to an existing outsourcing relationship can find themselves in:

(a) The contract is approaching its end and the customer wants to re-tender to decide whether to renew the contract or change vendors.
(b) The contract is being terminated at its end with a change of vendors or the taking of services back in-house.
(c) The contract is being terminated for breach, with a consequent change of vendors or the taking of services back in-house.

In each case, the contract should set out adequately what the parties' rights and obligations will be.

5.2   Re-tendering

Assuming that neither party is in breach and even if the customer is satisfied with the services, it is likely that the customer will want to go through a re-tendering process even if the aim is only to renegotiate the existing contract. If the customer allows an existing contract to roll on, it is unlikely to benefit from the competitive edge offered by other potential vendors, in terms of quality and range of service and price. To do this, the customer first has to make sure that it allows itself sufficient time. Given that from start to finish the original outsourcing is likely to have taken a number of months, the customer should ideally start thinking about the re-tendering 12 months before the contract expires or can be brought to an end by notice.

If there is to be a meaningful re-tendering exercise, the customer will want to issue an RFP to a number of potential vendors. In order to elicit sensible bids, this RFP will need to contain basic information about the assets and services which the potential new vendor will inherit. To understand the issues involved, the customer has to look back to the original outsourcing and go through the same analysis of the relevant assets, people and services, bearing in mind that all these assets are now in the hands of the sitting vendor.

5.3 What does the customer need to know?

The customer will need to be able to give any potential new vendor information about:

- Physical assets

Potential new vendors need to know what equipment is being used in the provision of services, what state they are in and what can be transferred at what cost.

- Contracts with third party vendors

Particularly in relation to software, maintenance or other critical services, again, the new vendor will want to know what these are and whether they can be transferred to it, and, if so, at what cost in terms of consent fees.

- Staff

In Europe, the Acquired Rights Directive can apply to the change of vendors and the effect can be to transfer the relevant employees of the sitting vendor to the new one. Potential new vendors need to know whether TUPE will apply and, if so, exactly who will transfer and on what terms.

- Services

In order to set out in the RFP what the customer wants, it needs to know what it currently receives. This means that the customer must have accessible information both as to the nature of the current services and also the levels to which they have been provided and any problems with that service provision.

- Access to information and cooperation

Potential new vendors will also want to know what general level of access to information, key personnel, premises and other material they will have and what obligations the existing vendor will have to cooperate in the handover of services.

5.4 Termination and transfer of vendors

There are two scenarios here: the contract is being terminated for breach or one party has exercised a right to terminate at the end of the agreed term. The latter is relatively straightforward – so it is termination for other reasons which requires further consideration.

5.5 Termination for breach

The first issue is to assess what rights of termination the contract should contain.

From the customer's point of view, the triggers for termination could include:

(a) breach of a material obligation of the vendor. What is 'material' may not always be clear and the contract may include a non-exhaustive list of breaches which would be treated as being material, for example, where a particular service is performed particularly badly over a period of time. Where a breach is capable of being corrected, it is normal to specify a reasonable period during which the vendor must remedy the breach;
(b) if the vendor is in financial difficulties – it is often useful for an obligation to be inserted in the contract requiring the vendor to notify the customer when something occurs that may significantly affect the vendor's financial position, thus giving the customer an early warning of problems in this area;
(c) convenience: if the contract is for a long fixed duration, then the contract may allow the customer the right to break it at certain points, usually subject to the payment of a fee (often called a 'break charge') giving the vendor compensation for failing to see out the term; and
(d) change of control: if the ownership of the vendor is of importance to the customer (and it usually is), the contract may specify that the customer has a right to terminate the contract if the ownership changes. Similarly, if the vendor disposes of business interests or assets such that the customer loses confidence in its long-term commitment to the contract, the customer may also have a right to terminate.

The vendor will also want the right to terminate for the customer's breach or insolvency, however it should be recognised that the only serious breach a customer can generally commit is to fail to pay.

5.6 Following termination

Irrespective of the cause of termination, whether by expiry or on breach by either party, both the customer and the vendor will want to see an orderly transfer of service provision. This involves considering what is in effect a reversal of the original transfer, although the services and relevant assets will have changed and there is also the likelihood that the service will be transferred to a new vendor rather than be taken back in-house. The rights which should be considered are:

(a) information: as noted in connection with re-tendering, the customer will need information about how the current services are being provided, who is providing them and who is using what assets and contracts;
(b) contracts: the customer will want to be able to compel the vendor to assign relevant third party contracts either to the customer or to a new vendor, including any important software licences;
(c) hardware and other physical assets: the customer may need the option to purchase necessary equipment being used by the vendor and will also want to set out the basis of valuing that equipment; and
(d) intellectual property: where the vendor uses its own software in the provision of the services which cannot be obtained in the market place, the customer may require a licence for it or the new vendor to use the software, at least on a temporary basis. Where this is the existing vendor's proprietary software, this may be a sensitive point.

The customer may also want the right to solicit key staff members, irrespective of the TUPE situation, and, in extreme circumstances, a right to enter the vendor's premises to take back relevant equipment and information.

6 Conclusion

When companies are trying to build a 'win-win' scenario where the customer is happy with the quality and cost of the services and the vendor makes a profit, it is vital that the legal issues not be allowed to get in the way. Contract documentation should enable the relationship to work, rather than acting as a straightjacket.

Perhaps more than any other commercial transaction, outsourcing requires careful preparation and measured consideration of the legal issues. The computer maxim 'garbage in – garbage out' is an apt one. Both customer and vendor should be prepared to fully address the legal and commercial side of their negotiations and to invest the time and effort it takes to properly debate and agree upon all of the key issues of the deal – preferably before the contract is signed!

The reward should be a contract that reflects both parties' business needs and thereby enhance the chances of achieving a strong, long-term relationship.

Bibliography

Gartner, 2004, *Best Practices and Trends in Outsourcing*, http://www4.gartner.com/4_decision_tools/measurement/measure_it_articles/2003_101303/ray_01.jsp).

Gartner, *Successful IT Outsourcing*, August 2003.

M. Lacity and L. Willcocks, *Global Information Technology Outsourcing: Search for Business Advantage*, Wiley, Chichester (2001)

S. Cullen and L. Willcocks, *Intelligent IT Outsourcing: Eight Building Blocks to Success*, Elsevier, Oxford (2003).

12
Systems Development Outsourcing: Lessons from Litigation
Mike Chiasson, Al Dexter and David Wotherspoon

1   Introduction

Organisations outsource their information technology (IT) for multiple reasons: to increase service and product flexibility; reduce costs of production; restructure internal IT staff; realise cost savings through lower-priced contracts for maintenance of in-house information systems; and to gain knowledge about new trends in IT (McFarlan & Nolan, 1995). In this paper, we focus on system development outsourcing (Lacity & Hirschheim, 1993; Sabherwal, 2003), which we define as the purchase and development of IT in order to develop organisationally specific information systems.

Despite many possible benefits from outsourcing, there are substantial risks as well (Bahli & Rivard, 2002; Willcocks, Lacity & Kern, 1999). For example, there may be increased financial or strategic risk from delays, or a poor system product. Naturally, these outcomes can create serious conflicts between the parties to an outsourcing project.

Drawing upon our experiences as expert witnesses or legal counsel during system development outsourcing conflicts, we examine the processes that inhibit or promote vendor-client agreement on the system changes, which inevitably occur. These processes include the system requirements, timing and payments. We identify important issues and controversies in system development outsourcing during various systems development lifecycle phases of a significant conflict between a vendor and customer. We argue that common processes across these stages prevent the awareness and possibility for negotiated changes, resulting from both changes in customer expectations and directions, and from development barriers and issues identified by the vendor during development. We then examine alternative approaches to resolving outsourcing conflict that we believe will facilitate the negotiated changes in these contracts.

2 Issues and controversies

Despite the strategic opportunities, system development outsourcing encounters significant challenges. The Standish Group report of 2001 (Standish, 2001) illustrates the problems with unmet expectations and failure in both in-house and outsourced software development projects. Of the approximately 283,000 software development projects surveyed, 23 per cent were technical failures that never worked, and 49 per cent were late, over budget, or functionally incomplete.

Contractual and relational processes are two broad approaches to system development outsourcing. Contractual processes focus on the development of contracts that specify and clarify the various roles of the partners, and the outcomes to be developed and delivered in the partnership. Relational processes focus on behaviours and activities that build trust between the partners, which help to ensure clear communication and desired outcomes between parties throughout the relationship. Components within these two broad approaches include: the contract and its tight or loose enforcement or interpretation (Malhotra & Murnighan, 2002); the customer-vendor relationship and the level of trust (Poppo and Zenger, 2002); the business and technical uncertainty (Marcolin, 2002); client and supplier expertise and the nature of the system assets produced and shared (Bahli & Rivard, 2002).

In cases where there is high business and technical uncertainty, expertise is low, and the system assets which are to be developed are highly specific with little use outside of the relationship, relational strategies are appropriate and probably essential to success. Relational strategies allow the parties to adjust and adapt over time as the Information Systems (IS) requirements are developed and often renegotiated, and as business and technical uncertainty changes. Tight contracts bind the parties to fixed system requirements that will need to be changed because of technical and business uncertainty. Tight contracts may also prevent the development of relational processes and trust between the two sides which are required for dealing with uncertainty.

In contrast, low technical uncertainty, high expertise, and the development of non-specific assets that have uses outside of the relationship dictate the use of tight and detailed contracts. In this context, tight contracts can be written in order to specify the exact system requirements, the timeline to develop the various components, and payment. In this case, relational strategies are less important because the project can be clearly defined at the outset – the required system, the price, the timing and the costs.

From our collective experiences working with one or both sides on troubled system development projects, these broad arguments are informative. However, in system development outsourcing, most projects have some considerable uncertainty at the outset. The important issue is how the parties work together to resolve the uncertainty, how contracts are used to specify requirements or the processes for determining and resolving system requirements, and how system and financial rewards are allocated to the participants over time and project fulfillment. Studies of outsourcing relationships across time are important to address how the two broad strategies and the components shape successful and unsuccessful outcomes.

It is our view that while tight system requirement details in the contract appear to favour the customer, our experiences suggest that they often favour neither side during system development conflict. The reason is that when conflict arises, both sides point to the over-developed certainty of contractual requirements in claiming that the requirements either fall inside (for the customer) or outside (for the vendor) requirements. We also find that the insertion of unconditional but often unenforceable promises by the vendor in many contracts force legal counsel and IT experts to take considerable time distinguishing vague marketing promises from contractually binding obligations. In the end, a productive customer-vendor relationship comes down to give-and-take, which when acknowledged in the contract through various dispute resolution processes helps keep the partnership and the project on track. The final step is a well-defined termination process that will allow the customer to find other partners if fundamentally dissatisfied with the project's direction (thus allowing them to re-enter the market), and the vendor to find other customers.

We address these issues by examining the processes that increased conflict, failed to facilitate negotiated changes, and led to litigation between a customer and vendor. We focus on problems and solutions to various stages of outsourcing; the development of a request-for-proposal (RFP), the response to the RFP, contracting and project management, and litigation.

3   Problems and solutions

We highlight process problems and solutions to negotiated changes, using as an illustrative example, a representative case study that we constructed from various conflicts. Problems and solutions reflect issues that restrict both the recognition of and a need for negotiated change.

3.1   Developing RFPs

The case involves serious conflict between a system software developer (hereafter SSD) and a large financial institution (hereafter LFI). LFI wished to acquire an integrated system for customer relationship management (CRM). A national consulting firm acted for LFI in creating a detailed RFP, which included the process, timetable, submission requirements as well as the contract terms and conditions. The RFP required the vendor to provide a complete 'turn-key' system that could be immediately used by the customer, for a fixed price. The RFP included numerous system requirements at various levels of functional and technical detail. The scope of the RFP was both broad and detailed. It required a vendor to set out all applications software, hardware, and telecommunications equipment, and an implementation plan for most of LFI's provincial and territorial offices throughout Canada. This Canada-wide project required a user interface in both English and French language versions. Furthermore, despite being a fixed priced contract, the RFP specified a need for flexibility and relative ease in modifying future requirements. Throughout this and other developmental stages, the customer's senior executives took a largely hands-off approach to the project, believing the RFP was the agreement with any potential vendor.

Problem: The RFP process by its very nature, locks in the system requirements. There is an implicit assumption that the customer knows what the system should do, and what features it should include. Thus, despite considerable uncertainty in practically any software development project, the process forces both the customer and the prospective vendor to write detailed system requirements prior to the commencement of the development. The apparent certainty in the RFP document masks the inherent uncertainty and shifting nature of system requirements, locking both the customer and the vendor into a set of specifications that often requires serious modification and adjustment as the project progresses. This prevents both sides from acknowledging the need for relational processes and adjustments to the agreement within and beyond the RFP and the contract.

Solution: The process solutions are both easy and difficult. Minor solutions include a focus on functional as opposed to technical requirements, and identifying uncertain areas in the RFP that will require additional investigation. The success of this strategy will depend on both sides acknowledging uncertainty, and agreeing to relational governance processes that allow adjustment to contractual terms in order to manage the technical and business uncertainty in the functional requirements.

However, current RFP logic assumes that the customer knows the detailed requirements, at the outset. Inconsistent with the popular consumer credo, the customers don't always know what they want. Brooks (1995) recommends the iterative approach to systems development, which engages the developers and customers in a process of give-and-take as they explore the emerging information system through successive cycles.

The hardest single part of building a software system is deciding precisely what to build. No other part of the conceptual work is so difficult as establishing the detailed technical requirements, including all the interfaces to people, to machines, and to other software systems. Therefore the most important function that software builders do for their clients is the iterative extraction and refinement of the product requirements. For the truth is, the clients do not know what they want. (1995, p. 199–200).

Rapid prototyping and extreme programming are software developer responses to the growing uncertainty about requirements at the start of projects. Schrage (2003) also argues that requirements analysis should be recast as expectations analysis, in order to avoid the cast-in-stone depiction of requirements. At issue here is how best to jointly serve customer and vendor interests within a project. The RFP paints the interests as separate and opposed. The customer is interested in a fixed-low price for a fixed or expandable set of requirements, and the vendor is interested in variable pricing for a fixed or reduced set of requirements. Recognising this tension, current solutions focus on using the RFP to define what the system should accomplish, i.e. its functional requirements, and less on how the system should do it, i.e. its technical details. This is especially important when technical and business uncertainty is high. In the more general sense, the RFP should move toward business and required functional components to achieve those objectives, and omit or describe uncertain areas that need further discovery. By doing so, both parties acknowledge the essential-certain and the essential-uncertain project components. To address these latter issues, more relational and procedural processes are necessary. Given that uncertainty is dependent on the actions of all parties, vendors should be allowed to respond to RFPs with revised specifications or requirements. Frequently, however, the vendor's ability to respond to an RFP is restricted.

3.2 Responding to RFPs

SSD's response to the RFP was extremely detailed. Its analysts claimed that they were able to develop a tailored customer relationship management system (CRMS), which would include: user controlled product and service definitions, flexible product and service pricing strategies, customer search capabilities, ad-hoc reporting, and other marketing analysis capabilities. SSD also contracted with a third party hardware supplier to provide the architecture. SSD had previously delivered a financial system to a smaller financial institution, and it claimed that it had the most advanced financial services support products in the world, both technically and functionally. However, whether SSD knew it or not, the scope of the work with LFI was much larger than any system it had previously handled. SSD took on the project because it wished to gain an increased foothold into this industry. It also was using a new development methodology that would allow system prototyping, while still guaranteeing a fixed price for the system.

Problem: There are numerous concerns with this typical response to an RFP which restricts future negotiated change. Specifically, vendors often restrict their response to the RFP with a low price and promises about unlimited time and talent in order to guarantee success. In doing so, they downplay any gaps in their expertise. It could be argued that these concerns are in-fact market processes that render the best deal for the customer. However, in uncertain and risky environments such as software development, market forces are weakened by the absence of perfect information, and the problem and nature of supplier-induced demand and emergent system requirements. Once the contract is signed, a temporary monopoly locks both the vendor and customer into a binding relationship that requires trust and flexibility. As a result, the project and system is largely shaped by the vendor and its relationship with the customer. At the time of the signing of the RFP, the business and technical uncertainty need to be acknowledged and shaped within this essentially locked-in relationship between the customer and vendor.

Solution: Again the solutions are easy and hard because each requires trust and honesty in portraying capabilities and strengths, and in producing healthy relational governance processes around contractual details. Vendors must have incentives to honestly portray their capabilities and inabilities. An incentive could be that customers acknowledge this accurate portrayal as a strength, and not a weakness. In the same vein, the customer should be honest about uncertain system requirements and business strategies. These uncertain areas should be released from fixed price and system requirements, paying the vendor based on time and materials in order to jointly explore system and business requirements. Alternatively, the current RFP can omit these areas until requirements and costs are more accurately determined. At that stage, parties can write amendments to the RFP. This leads to our discussion of contracts and project management which are closely tied to the development of and response to RFPs.

3.3   Contracts and project management

Since both sides felt the system could be clearly specified in the RFP, they chose a single fixed price contract, with tight requirements, timelines and costs. In order to develop this type of RFP, the business and technical uncertainty was considered to be low and manageable, and client and supplier expertise was considered to be high. However, because of the perceived certainty of the project, the contract included limited dispute resolution processes and termination clauses. There appeared to be little concern about conflict between the parties. With assumed certainty in the contract, top management in both companies stepped away from the day-to-day management of the project that prevented continued relational exchanges and the development of relational governance processes.

As the project unfolded, the system turned out to be on the cutting edge of CRMS applications. At the same time, LFI's revised business strategy was still emerging. These factors created serious negotiation problems for both parties within the tight RFP and contract, after it was signed. In terms of technical uncertainty, much effort was required to examine various networking, switching and telecommunications configurations. This examination would determine ease of use, maintenance, growth, security and recovery risks, and expected costs. The customer also had little experience with system development projects using PC-based computing technology. As a result, shortly after the contract signing, the vendor decided that the hardware was to be outsourced to a third party. In addition, the new software was to be written in a fourth generation language and on a more modern PC-based client-server network environment. Because of tight contractual details and the RFP's inclusion of a pre-specified management solution and architectural strategy, project time, system and cost uncertainty increased dramatically.

Added to this complexity were LFI's existing systems, which were written in a third generation language for a 1970s mainframe computing technology platform. It was later discovered that the architecture specified in the RFP for the new system was mismatched with these legacy systems. Thus, system development was stalled by the mismatched architectural platforms. At the same time, technical and business uncertainty in LFI produced an explosion in requests for system changes, despite a fixed price and time to completion. LFI wanted the system to be delivered on a tight time schedule in order to implement its strategic acquisition of other financial institutions. LFI also wanted the improved systems to easily integrate its IT with the IT of its various acquisitions.

In addition to modifying the system requirements, LFI also began modifying several of its financial products and services in anticipation of the new functionality. The number of modifications appeared reasonable to LFI because the mushrooming detailed requirements appeared to be within the functional scope of the RFP. The list soon included: new insurance product offerings; new pricing structures; new administrative activities to link external organisations coupled with attendant electronic fund transfer mechanisms, and new user interfaces.

SSD was also expected to develop an understanding of both the architecture and the personnel training requirements, and to identify opportunities for system and business improvement from an in-depth review of LFI's financial products or business processes. Only one week of meetings were scheduled to accomplish these tasks. SSD also absorbed a second company that would assist in the completion of this project, and it also hired new management and several new development personnel for the project. While the second company and the new management were well-educated in information systems, they lacked the detailed knowledge of the client and the financial services industry. Within months of the contract signing and with only one year to complete the entire project, it fell substantially behind schedule.

As a software engineering organisation, SSD had also developed a detailed approach to system development change, documenting and costing each change to LFI. On the other hand, LFI felt the project was a strategic partnership. As a result, LFI believed that system changes should be easy and quick, while SSD felt system changes required detailed system and cost justification.

Problem: The signing of a contract demands technical and business certainty at that point in time. Because it is a legal document, it also points both sides towards contents that will be defensible in a court of law. A contract can produce a broad range of outcomes between two extremes: a foundation for agreement or a foundation for conflict. The outcome depends on the business and technical uncertainty, what is included or excluded from the contract, and whether the partners view the contract in similar ways. Problems emerge when the business and technical uncertainty is ignored, when the contract includes uncertain requirements specified in terms of certainty, and when one side perceives the contract as a fixed agreement, while the other perceives it as a partnership, with substantial flexibility for change.

In our case, all three issues were present. Business and technical uncertainty were high but ignored; the RFP and the contract detailed uncertain functionality; and the customer perceived the contract as both a partnership and a deal with an arms-length supplier, while the vendor perceived it as a fixed agreement. As a result, the customer continued to add requirements to the project, perceived by the vendor to be beyond the contractual terms. The contract omitted detailed relational processes for handling and resolving the increasing conflict, and the separate and competing views of the deal produced antagonism and suspicion.

Solution: One possible solution is to avoid writing detailed contracts until greater certainty is achieved. However, contracts do have a role in negotiating both the spirit and details of a business arrangement. Instead, we suggest that partners need to consider a series of contracts or stages within a contract in laying the groundwork for a productive partnership that manages business and technical uncertainty, and ensures both sides understand the nature of the relationship. This may require that initial contracts are necessarily vague on some of the system details, but focus on common interests and relational processes. During this early stage, various intangible assets such as learning and knowledge exchange may be the basis for compensation. As project certainty is resolved, however, more detailed contracts can be written from the broader agreements, which focus on specific systems and payment timings.

Without the broader agreements and negotiation, fixed price and system contracts can be the source of much conflict over inevitable system changes. Many of the assumptions behind these contracts, especially at the outset of a system development project, are ill-suited to system development outsourcing. These include: a belief that requirements can be written down once and early; that customers understand their technical and functional needs in advance of talking with vendors; and that a single contract initiates a project and ends the negotiation. Instead, both customers and software developers need to assume that system requirements will frequently change, that some form of prototyping and user involvement is required to elicit requirements, and that customers need to work with a vendor in order to determine the functional and technical requirements. Contracting, system development and communication are continuous activities. Related to fixed price contracting and the exasperation between the two sides is the most common and damaging form of conflict resolution: litigation.

3.4 Litigation

The changing requirements and the scheduling delays produced antagonism between the SSD and LFI. The customer felt the vendor was dragging its feet on system changes and the vendor felt the customer was taking advantage of general clauses in the contract. The customer threatened legal action, pointing to general promises in the contract as proof of the vendor's breach of the contract. The vendor responded with a revised schedule, highlighting the re-organisation of its management and adding additional development team members in order to improve system development and get the project back on schedule. The customer's lack of response was perceived by the vendor as tacit approval of the revised schedule on the part of the customer. The contract did specify a dispute resolution process that required both parties to 'operate in good faith and use their best efforts to work continuously and actively together to resolve a dispute'. It further specified that either party, if dissatisfied with the progress of the contract, could submit 'any dispute to arbitration'. Despite this seemingly clear conflict resolution process, the interpretation of the process itself became disputed, requiring lawyers from both sides to interpret whether actions fell inside or outside the dispute resolution boundaries. In the end, each party initiated arbitration and the customer initiated a law-suit, claiming misrepresentation, negligence and breach of contract.

   Problem: Very often, one or both sides quickly invokes adversarial solutions when project problems emerge. This often results in adversarial views of the deal and lack of trust in the other party, which restricts and prevents good-faith and negotiated system changes. Both sides perceive the other side's position as essentially wrong and mean-spirited, and with all communication now channeled through the lawyers, trust disappears. In supporting their version of events, both sides appeal to the certainty of the contract. The vendor points to specific system requirements in the contract in order to limit the amount of additional work being requested by the customer. The customer points to promises in the contract in arguing for the system changes. It is apparent during legal proceedings that both sides have produced two very different interpretations of even relatively clear contract details. These views result in a deep-seated suspicion of the other's actions as malicious opportunism. Because of the insertion of unconditional but often unenforceable promises by the vendor in many contracts, legal counsel and IT experts must take considerable time distinguishing vague marketing promises from contractually binding obligations.

By employing litigation immediately, partners abandon mutually beneficial business solutions. And despite pursuing litigation in order to seek redress, the process is used to seek advantage at the expense of the other partner, and in many cases to irreparably damage the partner. We believe that both sides invoke this process in order to yield a favourable result, without realising that law suits are time consuming and expensive, embarrassing, and often more costly to win or lose than the original contract price.

Solution: Important solutions require that both sides acknowledge that system requirements do change, and a process is required to handle the inevitable vendor-customer friction of system change. Instead of looking to the certainty of requirements in the contract, partners should take advantage of contractual certainty in clearly defining processes for managing negotiated system change. These processes should specify alternatives to resolving disputes through litigation for handling negotiated change and imposing healthy relational processes onto both sides. A major failing in all of our cases was an inability to anticipate the need for system change, and failing to write about how change should be handled and negotiated. Without a clear set of meta-rules, the only process for resolution was an adversarial process, either through the courts or arbitration. As a result, troubles are largely due to the absence of alternative frameworks and processes for resolving inevitable disputes that allow both sides to negotiate a change to the deal that considers both parties' interests. Also, neither party had acknowledged partnership breakup before the project was complete, and the contract contained few well-developed termination clauses.

When conflict arises, and it is inevitable that they will, partners often resort to the one certain process that leads to resolution but which is the most expensive and least effective method to resolve the dispute: the courts. The court process is adversarial with each side putting its own case as high as possible while attempting to destroy the case advanced by the other side. Most court systems are very busy and so having a case heard is fraught with delay. It is common for at least two years to pass between the time an action is started and the time it comes to trial. With a need to resolve and negotiate change, the delay associated with court trials does and should frustrate many litigants. Thus many professionals, including ourselves, are motivated to look for alternative means of resolving conflict. Other factors also motivate this desire, for example that court proceedings are open to the public, and thus may embarrass the litigants. It is these issues we examine in our *alternatives* discussion.

4 Alternatives

Key to our argument is a need to define a set of escalating and explicit processes that allow negotiated change to the information system throughout the project. We acknowledge that the extent of negotiated change will vary across projects, but given the inherent uncertainty of many system development projects, various processes need to be considered in system development outsourcing.

These processes will include both third party and private mechanisms that can be invoked to resolve issues when they arise. We argue that these processes are not alternatives to relational governance, but augment and steer these processes. They do so by using the certainty of the contract and formal dispute resolution, in order to highlight gradual third party processes that remind both sides that negotiated project and system change is inherent and hard-wired into the project terms.

The two most common conflict resolution processes outside of the court system are mediation and arbitration. Both are typically invoked after a conflict has become extant and both require the consent of all parties to use these alternate processes. A key difference between the two is that mediation is not binding but arbitration is. Formal mediation involves the use of a neutral individual whose goal is to assist the parties in finding a solution to the conflict in order to avoid the time and expense of litigation or arbitration. Many mediators have taken specialised training in the mediation process. Mediators typically meet with all the parties together, then separate them and perform 'shuttle diplomacy' as a means of resolving disputes. They are often looking for the best business solution available for both sides. The advantages of this approach are that both sides can explore various solutions without a binding and adversarial process. However, for this to work, both sides must be willing to honestly engage in the meditative process, without resorting to antagonistic and stonewalling tactics.

Arbitration on the other hand, is very much like litigation except that it is typically done in a boardroom setting rather than a court and with one or more arbitrators rather than a judge. Arbitrators are usually lawyers or former judges. They may be selected for subject matter expertise. The arbitrator is given the authority by all the parties to make a binding award. Like litigation, it is also an adversarial process, typically with witnesses giving evidence under oath, cross examination and oral argument. Each side is attempting to convince the arbitrator to award as much as possible to them through this adversarial process. However, there are many advantages to arbitration over litigation. These include the ability of the parties, assuming they can agree, to select an arbitrator. This joint selection process may be important where the issues are technical. Arbitration can often be conducted on a schedule that is significantly faster than the courts. It is also private which may be important when information is confidential or the issues may be embarrassing to the parties. The disadvantage of arbitration is that it is time-consuming, adversarial and the binding results can result in zero-sum outcomes for one or both sides.

Given the complexity of many outsourcing projects, and indeed many other IT related projects, with tight time lines, evolving requirements and specifications, even mediation and arbitration may not be sufficient to keep a project on track. We recommend a multi-tiered approach aimed at early identification of issues with relational intervention at the outset, escalating toward a process certain to achieve a result as the last step.

Everyone must recognise that issues will arise and that some will turn into disputes. The parties should understand that this is inevitable and does not necessarily imply fault. A common point of disagreement will be whether or not something is in or outside the scope of the project. Outsourcing agreements must have a change protocol and it should be slavishly followed. Where the parties cannot agree, that can be noted and resolved at a later date without impairing the schedule. There is no one solution that will work for all projects but important considerations include mechanisms for early detection and resolution of issues, a tiered mediated issue resolution process that begins with relational processes and escalates to those that are more adversarial if conflict remains unresolved with early negotiations and mediation. Ultimately, there must be a mechanism for reaching a binding solution where the parties cannot agree on a resolution. These should be structured so that when conflicts arise, the project schedule is not challenged and payment obligations are fulfilled. This can be achieved through various means such as having payments made into trust so that the customer remains financially committed to the project and the vendor knows it will be paid, subject to resolution of disputes.

Some alternative methods involve the parties in developing their own dispute resolution processes. For example, identifying disputes at the level of the programmer or other similar positions, i.e. at the lowest level possible for resolution is important. If a dispute cannot be resolved at this level, it could go to the project manager and the customer's equivalent person. If these managers are unable to resolve the dispute, it will then go forward to their respective supervisors. If they are unable to resolve the conflict, it will then go to a committee involving the most senior person from each organisation. For smaller companies, this will be the president or CEO. For others, it may be a vice-president. The members of this committee should not be closely involved in the project and they should be motivated by the overall company's business objectives. While these committees do not usually have binding authority, given the seniority of the committee members, they have great persuasive authority. Indeed, in our experience just the thought of having to defend a dispute before one's own superior can be an effective means of achieving compromise.

A related and proactive approach is to develop a dispute review board at the project's outset (http://www.drb.org/concept.htm). As described by the Dispute Review Board web-site, the board is created at the outset with three respected, impartial and experienced members who are selected by one partner, and approved by the other. These members are members of the project from the outset. They are provided with the contractual details, and have a day-to-day role in monitoring and evaluating the project's progress. They meet with both sides during the project and attempt to resolve problems at the job level.

Ultimately, there must be a binding mechanism for resolving conflict. The courts are always there. Arbitration has many attractions to it and is a beneficial alternative to the courts if the parties can agree on arbitration. But there are also alternatives within the arbitration format. One interesting one, that we have seen utilised in an outsourcing contract is 'baseball', or final offer arbitration (Marburger, 2004). In this process the parties put their final position to the arbitrator who has the authority to select only one of the two, and not some other hybrid resolution – although Marburger suggests hybrids appear to be emerging from the process. This is used in Major League Baseball to resolve all salary disputes. Since both parties know that the arbitrator will select the most reasonable position advanced, they are forced to make a reasonable offer. Although seldom used as yet in the outsourcing context, its facility to inspire reasonableness may see increasing the use of final offer arbitration in the future.

5 Conclusion

Many organisations are turning to IT outsourcing, including system development, in order to increase service and product flexibility, reduce production and maintenance costs of IT, and to gain access to the newest IT systems and skills. Despite the benefits of system development outsourcing, the risks are substantial for both the vendor and the customer.

In this chapter, we examined the processes and factors that contributed to severe conflict between IT vendors and customers. Particularly, we examined processes that inhibited and solutions that would promote the negotiated change of system requirements. What we found is that various problems in each stage of the project contributed significantly to outsourcing conflict. The stages included: the development of the request-for-proposals, the vendor response to an RFP, contract and project management, and litigation. The development of an RFP assumes technical and business uncertainty, and anticipates both requirements and price certainty. The solution is to find a middle-ground between detailed requirements and identifying uncertain and open areas within the RFP itself. The response to RFPs forces the vendor to provide the lowest price, and for both sides to market themselves by ignoring technical and business risk. Therefore, an honest assessment of business and technological risk, and how vendor and customer expertise will manage this risk, is prevented. Solutions involve clear discussion about partner strengths and weaknesses. The identification of uncertain areas in the RFP by both the customer and the vendor allow for future negotiated change of requirements, payment, and timing.

Tight contracts focus on requirements and differing project management expectations exacerbate negotiated change. Tight contracts lock-in very detailed and often unrealistic expectations about the system, and the nature of the customer-vendor relationship. As a result, two different responses emerge during the project – customers demanding additional features, and vendors resisting such changes. The solution is to focus on portfolios of initially loose and later tight contracts in order to set expectations, and to ensure requirements can change while vendors are properly compensated for such change. It is also important that both sides avoid the one big and detailed contract in order to effectively manage a development project. Finally, many of the previous assumptions lead to litigation when problems emerge. By this point, each side is engaged in producing two diametrically opposed versions of events and pursuing unilateral advantage. The solution is to use contractual certainty to develop escalating and alternative resolution processes that manage business and technical uncertainty, and direct partner attention and relational processes to the inherent need and expectation of negotiated system change. It is the ability to negotiate system, time and payment changes that will increase the success of system development outsourcing.

References

B. Bahli and S. Rivard, 'A Validation of Measures Associated with the Risk Factors in Information Technology Outsourcing', *HEC Working Papers (02–05)*, November (2002).

F. Brooks, *The Mythical Man Month: Essays on Software Engineering* (Reading MA: Addison-Wesley, 1995).

R.S. Fortgang, D.A. Lax, and J.K. Sebenius, 'Negotiating the Spirit of the Deal', *Harvard Business Review* (February 2003) 66–75.

M.C. Lacity and R. Hirschheim, 'The Information Systems Outsourcing Bandwagon', *Sloan Management Review*, 35:1 (1993) 73–86.

M.C. Lacity and L.P. Willcocks, 'An Empirical Investigation of Information Technology Sourcing Practices: Lessons from Experience', *MIS Quarterly*, 22:3 (1998) 363–408.

D. Malhotra and K. Murnighan, 'The Effects of Contracts on Interpersonal Trust', *Administrative Sciences Quarterly*, 47:3 (2002) 534–559.

D.R. Marburger, 'Arbitrator Compromise in Final Offer Arbitration: Evidence from Major League Baseball', *Economic Inquiry*, 42:1 (2004), 60–68.

B.L. Marcolin, 'The Spiraling Effect of IS Outsourcing Contract Interpretations', in R. Hirschheim, A. Heinzl, and J. Dibbern (eds), *Information Systems Outsourcing:*

Enduring Themes, Emergent Patterns and Future Directions (Springer-Verlag: Germany, 2002).

F.W. McFarlan and R.L. Nolan, 'How to Manage an IT Outsourcing Alliance', *Sloan Management Review*, 36:2 (1995) 9–23.

L. Poppo and T. Zenger, 'Do Formal Contracts and Relational Governance Function as Substitutes or Complements?', *Strategic Management Journal*, 23 (2001) 707–725.

R. Sabherwal, 'The Evolution of Coordination in Outsourced Software Development Projects: A Comparison of Client and Vendor Perspectives', *Information & Organization*, 13 (2003) 153–202.

M. Schrage, 'Lies, Damned Lies and Requirements; The Road to Applications Development Hell is Paved with Rigid Code Requirements', *CIO*, 17:2 (2003) 60–62.

Standish Group. *Extreme Chaos*. www.standishgroup.com (2001).

L. Willcocks, M. Lacity and T. Kern, 'Risk Mitigation in IT Outsourcing Strategy Revisited: Longitudinal Case Research at LISA', *Journal of Strategic Information Systems*, 8 (1999) 285–314.

Part VII
Looking Ahead – Issues for the Future

13
The Future of Offshore Outsourcing as a Strategic Management Tool
Mark Kobayashi-Hillary

1 Introduction

In 1942, the economist Joseph Schumpeter first used the phrase 'Creative Destruction' to describe the constant evolution of a free-market economy.

Schumpeter described how new and better ways of doing business will be created and old methods will be discarded (Schumpeter, 1942). During the 1990s dot.com bonanza years the term bordered on cliché as Internet evangelists and dot.com Chief Executives insisted the only good business was an e-business.

Creative destruction is now being applied more frequently to descriptions of the very structure of organisations in the twenty-first century. Academics have long debated the potential for outsourcing as a business tool and for several decades outsourcing has been used by manufacturers seeking particular expertise and service companies sub-contracting non-core tasks to trusted partners.

The change in focus over the millennium period has been the opportunity to outsource skilled service-sector tasks to offshore locations such as India and the Philippines, all made possible by the tumbling costs of international communication and the Internet.

While many companies have rushed to utilise skilled services in lower-cost environments, some have resisted for reasons of patriotism or just an inability to manage the offshore process. Much of the negative media coverage on this topic fails to acknowledge that it is not simple to transfer knowledge across the globe and continue to deliver services smoothly.

This chapter explores the drivers that have created the present situation leading on to examine the future drivers and inhibitors of offshore outsourcing or offshoring as it is often termed. Based on these observations, it is possible to make some elementary predictions for offshoring.

2 Force field methodology

Perhaps the best way to examine where we are today and how offshore outsourcing may develop in future is through the use of force field analysis

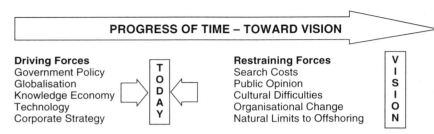

Figure 13.1   Driving and Restraining Forces

(Lewin, 1951). This tool allows change to be described as a state of imbalance between driving and restraining forces.

Although force field analysis is usually used where there is a definite vision of the future, rather than future-gazing, it is possible to make some important observations about the influences on offshore outsourcing even if the future remains unclear. For the sake of this analysis I shall assume that a desirable vision is for companies to be able to determine their own global strategy, allowing the use of offshoring when and where appropriate for their business.

There are a number of driving forces that have taken offshore outsourcing to its present state and restraining forces that are shaping and controlling future development and some of these are set out in Figure 13.1.

3   Driving forces

3.1   Government policy

Government policy influences the countries seeking to perform work offshore and can make the recipient nations more or less attractive. This may be through supporting and facilitating companies who are considering work with an offshore partner or providing foreign direct investors with attractive tax breaks and local benefits. A good example is India, which has prospered from offshoring by establishing a strong industry body (NASSCOM) to lobby on behalf of all local technology and technology-enabled service companies.

Some offshoring issues need the control of national legislation. Tony Khindria is the founding partner of Lexindia, an Indian law firm with offices in London, Delhi and Paris. Khindria explains the problems related to storing and utilising personal customer data: 'The range of obligations that must be met are wide ranging and are very relevant to businesses that seek to invest in India. Using the current trend of outsourcing as an example, there are data protection requirements which relate to the security service levels which by law must be imposed upon a service provider; and the steps which must be taken by a European business before data which includes information about individuals is sent outside the European Economic Area to countries such as India.'[1] Governments across the world are considering these dual-issues of how to promote offshoring to their countries and growing their own industry by allowing these companies to provide remote services and also to utilise them. National attitudes vary because many choose to focus on the perceived loss of local jobs caused by offshoring, though most politicians remain pragmatic. Stephen Timms is a good example. Timms is the UK Minister of State for Energy, E-Commerce and Postal Services. When questioned about the jobs issue he said: 'Clearly, where there are people who lose their jobs as a result of outsourcing then that is a very serious problem and we have a responsibility as a government to ensure help is provided to get those people back to work as quickly as possible. We are not taking a completely hands-off approach to this issue at all. The government has an obligation to be supportive, but we do not want to undermine the potential contribution to UK competitiveness.'[2]

Ian Prisk is the CEO of Black Coffee Software in Wellington, New Zealand. Prisk is supportive of the approach taken by the New Zealand government. He said: 'The New Zealand government is quite determined to build one hundred, one hundred million dollar companies over the next few years. This is simply not possible without an offshore focus.'[3]

In contrast, the US federal government announced in early 2004 that it would no longer allow subcontracted work to be performed offshore. Though federal contracts make up less than two per cent of the work being outsourced to India, there is a clear warning message to the advocates of free trade. Government actions can be both drivers and restraining forces in this world of global operations.[4]

3.2 Globalisation

The discussion on globalisation is often confused. I want to focus on the fact that increased national interdependence has encouraged offshore outsourcing. Not only are skilled people finding it easier to move around the globe seeking better opportunities but companies are finding it easier to source particular skills in the best location. There is no longer a requirement to source skilled employees in your own backyard and whether you bring those skills to your home nation or set up an operation where the expertise is located is your call.

The social scientist Manuel Castells believes that people with the right knowledge skills are already above the laws of immigration policy (Castells, 1996): 'There is, increasingly, a process of globalisation of speciality labour. That is, not only highly skilled labour, but labour which becomes in exceptionally high demand around the world and, therefore, will not follow the usual rules in terms of immigration law, wages, or working conditions. This is the case for high-level professional labour: top business managers, financial analysts, advanced services consultants, scientists and engineers, computer programmers, biotechnologists, and the like. But it is also the case for artists, designers, performers, sports stars, spiritual gurus, political consultants, and professional criminals.'

Offshore outsourcing has been driven by globalisation because there are some key benefits for consumers from the global organisational model (Kobayashi-Hillary, 2004):

- Business services and products are subjected to greater transparency when used across many nations.
- Choice of suppliers becomes more attractive when any global supplier can be chosen, rather than just local service providers.
- Competition is created by this choice, ensuring an improved service and better pricing.

In general, offshoring does benefit from the globalisation of labour markets and competition. Most consumers care more for service and quality than whether their call is answered in Manila or whether their children's toy is manufactured in China. In *Funky Business*, Kjell Nordström and Jonas Ridderstråle comment on this attitude (Nordström & Ridderstråle, 2001): 'It is the older generation that remains loyal to nationally produced goods. The British buy British. The French buy French and the Americans buy American out of long-held habit. It is an expression of patriotism. The young couldn't care less. Today, it's made by BMW, made by Nokia, made by Alessi, made by Sony. What matters is who – not where. It's made by – not made in.'

Marco Mukherjee, Sourcing Strategy Director of Customer Operations for UK bank Abbey, believes that large organisations need to go global just to meet the changing requirements and shifting focus of their customers. He explains: 'Organisations will have an evolving portfolio of onshore and offshore locations which best meets their requirements for cost, quality and risk – the differentiation will however become less as offshore centres become part of the organisation's virtual network.'[5]

In some developed nations with a small population, globalisation has driven the adoption of offshore outsourcing as a way of attracting business. Ian Prisk of Black Coffee Software believes that any New Zealand company that wants to achieve success must embrace a global business model: 'Offshore outsourcing is most definitely strategic for Black Coffee Software. The NZ market is quite limited in scope for any company to develop to any reasonable size; therefore many NZ companies have the export market firmly in their sights from day one.'

Globalisation is creating an unprecedented market for skills and services across the world, allowing companies to source manufacturing and services from the location that best combines quality and price.

3.3 Knowledge economy

The term itself is somewhat tarred by the dot.com crash in 2000. However, the birth of the Internet and its use by the public for the past decade has created a genuine environment where information is a highly valued commodity. Combine the connectivity of the Internet with the tumbling prices of international telecommunications and there is an environment that is more conducive to offshore work than at any other time in history.

In his book *Does IT Matter?* Nicholas G. Carr explains that he sees a commoditisation of products and services in a knowledge economy environment allowing formerly creative skills such as computer programming to easily be transferred offshore (Carr, 2004). In the book Carr comments: 'The increasing use of lower-paid overseas workers to write code echoes, of course, the earlier shift of manufacturing capacity offshore. And the parallels go even deeper. As the software requirements of companies become more modular, the development of code is coming to look less like a creative service and more like a manufacturing routine'.

Black Coffee Software is an example of this. Their concept was to be the best in a niche area. Software is a product that can be delivered remotely. Though some onshore sales and support does need to be close to the customer, most of the design and development work can all be performed back in Wellington. To make the idea work, Black Coffee had to embrace the knowledge economy practice of delivering the best possible product from a remote location using a combination of information and communications technology.

Ian Prisk explains their approach: 'For a New Zealand based company, operating in the UK (for example) is expensive. It is also essential. Relationships – in our view – simply cannot be developed and maintained without an onshore presence. The NZ way is not one of flashy or high-pressure sales people. We are a pragmatic bunch, well suited to getting on with the task at hand and completing it efficiently and effectively.'

The New Zealand government has in fact launched a marketing venture based on their website www.outsource2newzealand.com. This uses both public and private money to highlight their local knowledge companies and is a good demonstration of a government promoting their nation as an attractive destination for offshore outsourcing.

3.4 Technology

Seven out of ten employees in the UK believe that a computer is important or essential for their job and this ubiquity of technology is also driving the offshoring revolution.[6] Black Coffee software can focus on their Java programming in Wellington just as Infosys can in Bangalore. The code produced by these remote computer programmers can be delivered across the Internet almost instantaneously.

Science writer James Gleick published his book *Faster* in 1999 about the acceleration of everything and how it would affect modern society (Gleick, 1999). As he predicted, the book itself has dated since publication, just like modern technology. The PC I am typing this chapter on was a high-specification machine in 2000 yet it is now eclipsed by far cheaper computers with six times the processing speed. James Gleick believes that our mind-set is changing as society adapts to a new acceptance of, followed by the requirement for, speed. Earlier years show how previous technological advances were quickly assimilated into our lifestyle: 'By 1915, in the fourth decade of commercial telephone service, the American transcontinental system had developed the capacity to handle 3 simultaneous voice calls. A generation later, AT&T developed a coaxial cable that could handle 480 calls at once. By the 1980s, individual Telstar satellites had enough capacity for nearly 100,000 telephone links, though they were more likely to use the bandwidth for television transmission. Now terabit transmission is coming online – one trillion bits per second, or enough for three centuries of a fat daily newspaper.'

Marco Mukherjee of Abbey believes that technology is one of the key factors enabling organisations to even consider an offshore model. He explains: 'There is an increase in offshore providers and potential offshore locations because technology continues to act as an enabler to remove barriers to entry for non-voice processes. However, it is recognised that the lead time to mobilise "customer touch points", where brand values and customer experience are key, is significant – hence selecting and investing in the right partner is critical.'

Management guru and former McKinsey consultant Kenichi Ohmae has identified three broad themes about how technology is changing the landscape for globally operating organisations (Ohmae, 1995):

- Information can flow freely throughout the world instantaneously.
- It is possible to track information about people, products and services in real time.
- The customer can compare and contrast your service with other firms throughout the world.

Twenty, or even 10 years ago these were difficult issues for any senior executive to contend with. The technology was not good enough to allow a global market in information, yet today there is a considerable infrastructure available in the Internet and this is improving at an accelerating rate. Technology has driven offshore outsourcing to where it is now and innovations such as Voice over Internet Protocol (VoIP) will ensure that it continues to be one of the key drivers.

3.5 Corporate strategy

Outsourcing has been with organisations for centuries. One only has to read the political musings of Machiavelli to realise that mercenary forces used to prowl Europe in search of 'business' – outsourced armies. More recently, EDS was providing IT management services to other companies in the 1960s. The recent wave of interest in offshoring of services has developed as the communications technology has matured. The world experienced a similar wave of offshoring in the 1970s as Asia developed its manufacturing expertise, so the concept of domestic and offshore outsourcing has been with us for some time. However, the strategic use of contracted services has entered into boardroom vogue over the last decade and is now a management mantra that is unlikely to change for some time.

Charles Handy, a management writer and professor emeritus of the London Business School, offers one of the best explanations of the new management credo in his shamrock theory, published in *The Age of Unreason* (Handy, 1989). As any Guinness drinker knows, the shamrock is the Irish national emblem. It was used by Saint Patrick to symbolise the holy Trinity. Handy uses it to describe the three groups of people within an organisation:

- Core workers for essential and managerial tasks.
- Contract employees for non-essential work.
- Flexible workers, temporary, part-time and occasional labour.

Handy described how companies would employ an essential core team, around which they would hire contracted expertise for specific time-bound projects. In addition, there would be the flexible labour needed for maintenance, sorting the mail and cleaning the office. This structure became the dominant management ideology of the 1990s, further emphasised by the concept of *core competence* as described by CK Prahalad and Gary Hamel (Prahalad & Hamel, 1994). This focuses on the first section of Handy's trinity and describes how the core competence of an organisation is what it does well or better than others. For example, Ford can design and build motor vehicles that sell across the world but they do not need to be leading experts in tyre design or seat trimmings – these competences can be more effectively managed by experts in those fields and so it makes sense for Ford to outsource those functions.

Marco Mukherjee of Abbey is a leading advocate of this corporate model and he believes that this is driving the future of offshoring. He said: 'The future for offshoring will be linked to the overall outsourcing trend which will continue over the next few years as organisations look to focus on strategic or core competencies and seek to access new capabilities and pursue improving service, quality and productivity more cost-effectively. The offshore market will increase as organisations seek to gain competitive advantage by entering the globally outsourced market to manage costs and increase the flexibility of their operations.'

Atul Vashistha is Chairman and CEO of neoIT, a consulting firm based in the US that advises clients on offshoring of IT and business processes.

Vashistha believes that corporate strategy is maturing with regard to offshoring as more organisations start globalising their entire chain of processes – the value-chain – rather than just limiting offshore work to specific projects. He explains: 'When we see what our clients are doing, what we see is that the focus is shifting from projects to process. As that starts happening, what is also happening is we are moving from low-end processes to critical and more core processes. Companies are looking at this and recognising that these areas are not where they are just going to reduce cost, but they are part of a global delivery model. This is where there is an intersection between the required expertise and cost.'[7]

This is a shift in management mindset to the concept of a strategic delivery model and is a concept very familiar to Richard Finn, Managing Director of Penna Change. Finn is a leading advisor on corporate change and a veteran of many change programmes that often involve offshoring. Finn believes the concept of core competence remains the most important strategic tool: 'Organisations have to manage their overheads with great care and with a strategic eye on what are their core competencies. I would argue that anything that is not a core competence is a candidate for outsourcing, rather than the other way around. So what is core to your business?

- Something which gives competitive advantage.
- Something that would give competitive advantage to a competitor.
- Something which is difficult to replicate.

Successful organisations in the future will be the ones that minimise their overhead, and outsource anything that isn't core. This makes almost all back-office functions candidates, as well as anything that has heavy capital costs that are not core. BP has now outsourced more than 70 per cent of its costs, not a bad benchmark.'[8]

This great leap forward in corporate strategy has some dangers; however I will examine those in the section on public opinion.

4   Restraining forces

4.1   Search costs

Search costs are the often forgotten issues related to offshoring. Whilst the focus may be initially on cost, the search costs affect the entire process and can be a significant slice of the entire offshoring budget. The search issue is that offshore outsourcing is not a simple procurement exercise. It involves a complex series of decisions based on a selection process where internal procedures and external vendors all need to be assessed. Search costs can be summarised as:

- Which country should I use? In the first few years of the twenty-first century India has emerged as the dominant offshore destination for technology and technology-enabled services. However, a shock election victory for the left-of-centre Congress Party, the 10 new members of the European Union and Chinese catch-up could all influence where an organisation may want to locate offshore expertise.

- How should I arrange the contract? Some organisations choose to 'go captive' by creating their own offshore subsidiary firms. Some outsource to a service company. Some create a joint venture with a local partner and some outsource their process using a Build Operate Transfer (BOT) deal where they work with a local partner, but retain an option to go captive – if it all works out.

- What should I move offshore? The process of determining what can move, what should move and what cannot move will often be a complex mapping exercise where the organisation learns more about its own internal processes than it has ever known – even before moving anything offshore. Once processes are described then priorities and phasing need to be planned so the organisation can continue to deliver internal services as a transition takes place.

- How can I exit or change the contract? This is often forgotten in the haste to prioritise services that should move, yet discussions over the contract length and renegotiation process should be completed before the first contract is signed and this will require negotiation itself.

4.2 Public opinion

On the whole, public opinion of offshore outsourcing is negative. Macroeconomic reports from analysts such as McKinsey, Gartner and Evalueserve have failed to shift the public perception that a job created in one nation must mean a job is lost elsewhere, though all these economic reports demonstrate a positive net effect to countries that utilise offshore outsourcing. The cover story of *BusinessWeek* magazine on 3 February 2003 summed up the general mood amongst employees throughout the developed world: 'Is your job next?'

Though it often seems government policy – in any nation – rarely reflects popular opinion, in March 2004 the United States Senate voted by 70 to 26 on a measure that would forbid the outsourcing offshore of any work on contracts that are paid for with federal funds. The policy will not enter into US federal law until the Commerce Department can prove that a ban would not harm the economy or lead to more job losses.

This US Senate vote may reflect public opinion; however it is out of step with government policy in other leading economies, such as the UK, where offshoring is seen as a business enabler. Richard Finn, Managing Director of Penna Change believes that the US attitude is influenced by the Patriot Act, introduced after the 9/11 terrorist attacks: 'Offshoring is not patriotic.'

Marco Mukherjee of Abbey believes that there is a division between the US and Europe on offshoring and that regulatory bodies such as the Financial Services Authority (FSA) or Securities Exchange Commission

(SEC) will also be influential: 'There is increasing pressure in the US to stem the flow of jobs offshore. This has become a major issue in the 2004 US presidential election. We are likely to see some legislation controlling offshore activity in the US due to this offshore backlash.'

The UK research firm ContactBabel published a report in 2004 that suggests only a small number of customers need to defect to a competitor for there to be a cost in financial and brand image terms.[9] ContactBabel found:

- Of those customers who had actually experienced offshore customer contact themselves, 14.2 per cent defected to another supplier. Only 3.2 per cent of customers who have not had experience of offshore service defected to another supplier.
- Telephone and insurance providers were the most likely to have experienced the greatest levels of customer defection, with respectively 2.2 per cent and 2.3 per cent of customers changing supplier based on offshoring.

It is worth stressing that this research is focused on the offshoring of customer contact roles, such as call centre agents, and not technical or back-office processes. However, the summary of their research is ominous for those who may be considering an offshore customer service programme:

'Although the proportion of customers who have actually defected can seem low (e.g. only an additional 1.7 per cent of utilities customers changed supplier based on their dislike of offshore customer contact last year), the sheer weight of numbers that this actually represents is extremely significant and can actually wipe out all of the cost savings which offshoring can bring. Worryingly for UK businesses with offshore contact centre operations, customers who have actually experienced offshore interactions are four-and-a-half times more likely to have defected compared to those customers who have not yet experienced it.'

There is clearly a public backlash against the concept of offshoring, but the situation is opaque and remains unexplained to most people. In macro-economic terms, there is a true benefit to offshoring and economists across the world are busy producing reports that explain the effect of free trade and how offshoring can benefit its supporters. However, the very nature of changing global labour markets and regional losses mean that the short-term ride may be rough for some nations or individuals even though the long-term benefits are clear.

4.3 Cultural difficulties

Working away from home can expose the organisation and individual line managers to an entire raft of new problems related to the work culture of the new country where work is being performed. This can be an issue when working with a new partner through an outsourced arrangement, though it is most acute where the organisation has opted to create a captive subsidiary. Often it will be managers from headquarters who are flown in to set up the new organisation, without any form of cultural acclimatisation. Group dynamics can be very different in some regions, when compared to the US or Western Europe. This can make meetings an arduous process for reasons such as lack of participation or fear of contradicting the manager. Though women have rightly achieved equality in the West and religion is usually left at the office entrance, this position is not universal and it can sometimes be detrimental to start imposing your own standards on a team of people with very different values.

The Asian concept of face is important when managing teams in Asian countries. It is important to understand that losing face is a blow for any team member and they will usually avoid it, so the manager needs to understand how to arrange the hierarchy so he or she can lead and allow the team to make occasional mistakes without feeling they need to be swept under the carpet.

Jokes are often hard to carry across cultures and languages, especially the English use of sarcasm and irony. This can cause no end of confusion when used on a team that has no experience of people who say the opposite of what they really mean.

All these basic cultural issues can cause teething problems for an offshore programme. It can be hard to manage across cultures and languages and for this reason there are several cross-cultural consultants and training programmes vying for your business. However, while the training programmes can be a useful primer for managers who need to spend time in a far-flung foreign culture, there is really no way to succeed other than through experience. For this reason, most offshore programmes need a manager or management team who are either locals or who have been through the experience before.

4.4 Organisational change

Most offshoring programmes could actually be termed change programmes or Business Process Reengineering to apply a more formal title to the process. When a process is moved offshore it is almost always changed to improve the way it works, either by the company that plans to offshore the process or by the outsourcing partner seeking efficiencies in the work they have just taken on.

Atul Vashistha of NeoIT has found that some companies are using offshoring as a lever to achieving change. He said: 'We see companies using the offshore process to transform their own processes. When they start looking at the financial accounts or transaction processing they are not just looking at "where I can do my data entry?", but they are thinking "in the long run who can completely transform my ability to do these processes?" It requires the ability to leverage new technology. Sometimes it means finding the ability to focus on a set of new customers.'

In addition to the change surrounding the actual process that moves, the remaining parts of the organisation need to learn how to interact with the outsourced operation. It is quite different to have a business function that is outsourced to a subsidiary or third party compared to having a team of people in the hall at the end of the office. Reporting lines and inter-action between business units has to change and vendor management becomes a critical part of the arrangement – a new function as vendors did not need to be managed when the function was internal.

Aaron Clarke is Director of Financial Services and Banking for Sonata Software, an Indian technology company. He believes that a company should ensure its partner company is of similar size: 'If you go too small then you don't have the right expertise or domain knowledge, but you can interact with the person who created the business. Too large and you don't have the attention to detail. This can be a two-edged sword. Many of the larger companies are fairly mature in their approach to vendors, so they can engage with the larger vendors. It always pays to have a mid-level vendor involved because of the better attention to detail and execution.'[10]

Clarke goes on to stress the issues around the organisation of differing process quality benchmarks: 'Some smaller organisations have very flawed processes. Outsourcing these flawed processes will only lead to disaster. A vendor using the Capability Maturity Model (CMM) at level 5 [highest possible quality] wants transparency and good processes, but a client without any process or understanding will create immense frustration.'

The difficulty in trying to weld together differing organisations into seamless partners is one that Richard Finn of Penna Change believes can cause offshoring projects to fail. He said: 'Outsourcing creates a new organ-isation architecture which, by definition, needs to be managed in new ways. We know that a practitioner can rarely manage processes that they used to work on. It takes new skills and competencies to manage vendors. Once more than a few processes are outsourced, then the organisation needs to strategically manage the network of which they are the hub. This is a very different challenge to managing a single organisation.'

It is not only the fact that the organisation moves from being the centre of all activity to being the hub of activity, where all the work is taking place at the end of the spokes. There is also the question of intellectual property – the knowledge and ideas your company possesses. If someone else is doing all the operational work then they need to understand everything your company is doing, not just a few key elements. Richard Finn com-ments: 'A key strategic risk for any organisation outsourcing is losing knowledge to the outsourcer and the capability to exploit knowledge for R&D and process improvement.'

In fact, Gartner has estimated that 10 per cent of IT jobs in IT companies in the UK have already moved offshore and the percentage is increasing. However, they also note that about 10 per cent of any offshore contract value needs to be spent on relationship management, meaning that there is hope for those technical teams yet. Brian Sutton is chief educator at training specialist QA. On the changing skill profile requirements Sutton said: 'The key to individual and corporate success is flexibility. And the route to increasing individual flexibility lies in increasing the breadth of core competencies. Reliable trends point towards non-technical skills being a key competence area for IT personnel in tomorrow's organisation.' Sutton summaries the issue by adding: 'The time is ripe to be bold and develop yourself for the challenges of tomorrow.'[11]

In addition, there is the process of keeping an eye on the entire change programme and managing the ongoing relationship between the client and vendor organisations. Rob Aalders is author of *The IT Outsourcing Guide*. He explained to me the importance of programme governance: 'Programme governance addresses the question "are we doing the right things?" This requires the company to have defined criteria to select from the universe of possible projects and select those that provide the greatest value – in whatever manner the company chooses to measure value. The value criteria should include risk/reward ratios, strategic alignment, fixing corporate haemorrhages and the like. If the organisation does not have sound corporate programme governance they may undertake an even greater number of worthless projects because "it's cheap to do so".'[12]

It may be a requirement that an entirely new department or team is created just to manage the vendor or subsidiary relationship. How this team is structured and managed is just one more issue to be resolved during the offshoring process.

4.5 Natural limits to offshoring

Although public opinion is generally against offshoring, there is a natural limit to what can be moved. This is a key issue to remember and does restrain some projects that have reached the feasibility stage.

Marco Mukherjee of Abbey reiterates the legislative and regulatory pressures that are particularly strong in the financial services industry: 'There is a natural limit to offshoring as not all processes will be suitable based on an assessment of areas such as labour intensity, interdependency, continuity, risk, availability of required skills and regulatory constraints. My UK view is that as price becomes less of a differentiator, and the import of skills to the UK boosts capability, there may be an appetite for companies to relocate operations within the UK.'

Mukherjee has an interesting perspective. Not only does he feel that there is a genuine natural limit to offshoring, but a combination of this natural limit and service price increases in countries such as India may make it more attractive to relocate services at home. A company in London or New York could save money by locating essential services in Newcastle or Omaha, yet not run the risks involved in moving offshore. Atul Vashistha of NeoIT echoes the view that there is a natural limit for some specific processes. He said: 'There are limits associated with offshore outsourcing for many reasons. One is because of the risk perception of offshoring some companies have. Some are more related to the capabilities that exist. In addition, when a process requires complex decision making and the process requires complex communications, the ability to offshore reduces dramatically. However, over a period of time, processes tend to get less complex.'

Vashistha believes that the complexity of integration between a client and vendor is a further limiting factor, but he is not too concerned about the US legislators. He explains: 'In highly regulated industries the compliance checks will become more complex. For example, [in the US] because of the Sarbanes-Oxley act, the compliance required from service providers will be significantly higher than what is required today. An example is the focus on healthcare that Hillary Clinton brought to the issue. It did not really end up in legislation but it did change how healthcare is provided in the US. I think the same thing will happen to offshoring. Regulators will pay much more attention to offshore outsourcing now, not because of the law, but because of increased corporate responsibility. Because of that, companies will have to jump through more hoops to satisfy the regulators that they are doing things right.'

Although the detractors and supporters of offshoring rarely mention it, there does appear to be a natural limit to the work that can be performed remotely.

5 Conclusion

In this chapter I have tried to steer clear of future-gazing. It is all very well attempting to make outlandish future predictions for offshore outsourcing, but those predictions are often hard to justify based on evidence of the present market and often tainted by self-interest. I hope that by examining what has driven offshoring to its present position and what is restraining future growth, it should be possible to make some educated guesses at what the key issues will be over the next few years.

I have found it very interesting to conclude that there are natural limits to offshoring and this has even been verified by other industry practitioners and observers. The issues of risk, perception and corporate integration all play a part in limiting the extent to which offshoring can operate. However there is clearly strategic value in using offshoring to focus on the core competences of an organisation and to let the experts get on with what they do best. In fact, analysts Gartner are now calling offshoring a 'mega-trend'.[13]

During my research, Aaron Clarke of Sonata Software discussed an idea with me where consulting firms or other impartial experts might provide a buffer-zone between a client and vendor with differing quality capabilities, thus reducing the integration impact. If this arrangement becomes more common then it could change the natural limit, making the offshoring process less risky for more clients.

Rob Aalders stressed that any manager who is offshoring should not burn his bridges when going offshore as the international factor means change is inevitable. Economies change and the country or supplier you have chosen may not be the best of breed within a few years. This flexibility should see contract times being reduced and flexible exit plans being a pre-requisite.

Other key conclusions are:

- Consulting firms will focus on eliminating the risks involved with offshoring.
- Buying organisations and consultants will mature and be able to refine the search process – choosing better partners or more effectively creating their own operation.
- Technology such as VoIP will make the offshore option increasingly attractive due to consistently tumbling infrastructure costs.
- Emerging destinations and vendor companies will ensure that offshoring continues to grow even if some of the original pioneers, such as India, suffer as business is lost to other nations.
- Eastern Europe will become a far more attractive destination through EU membership and government grants that aim to attract foreign direct investment.
- Smaller enterprises (Small to Medium-size Enterprises) will be able to participate in offshoring, especially through the use of auctions for particular skills and collaborative ventures to pool their buying power.
- New services will be created and offered. High-value Business Process Outsourcing such as legal, accounting and research work will grow to be worth $50 billion a year by 2008 according to Indian research firm EvalueServe.
- Large internal IT departments will become a thing of the past. However, this will not necessarily impact employment prospects; technical staff will be employed by service companies – not all offshore.
- Government and education providers need to consider the long-term prospects for business education and life-long learning programmes.
- The organisational change process is potentially more important than the consideration of offshoring as a business strategy. Any strategy needs to be delivered at operational level so the change process at home must be taken as seriously as the transition to an offshore location.

What can be concluded from this analysis is that offshoring is an important strategic tool that is being adopted by most large organisations. It is not something we can change or avoid and we cannot revert to an age before cheap communication and the Internet. However, offshore outsourcing is not a benign process; it does affect some individuals along the way even though the net effect to an economy should be positive. This changing world of work is actually the most pervasive effect of offshoring and will remain far beyond the time when most individuals accept that for a company to use global resources is a normal practice for the twenty-first century.

Notes

1. Tony Khindria, Personal email to the author, 31 May, 2004
2. Mark Kobayashi-Hillary, Stephen Timms in India, http://www.bpoindia.org/news/timms-feb-2004.shtml, Feb 2004
3. Ian Prisk, Personal email to the author, 1 June 2004
4. Senate votes to stop outsourcing, BBC News (http://news.bbc.co.uk/1/hi/business/3535893.stm), March 5, 2004
5. Marco Mukherjee, Personal email to the author, 2 June 2004
6. Nathan M., Carpenter G., Roberts S., 'Getting by, not getting on – Technology in UK workplaces', The Work Foundation (iSociety), London, November 2003
7. Atul Vashistha, Telephone Interview with the author, 25 May, 2004
8. Richard Finn, Personal email to the author, 27 May, 2004
9. ContactBabel, 'Finding the Balance: The Effect of Offshore Customer Contact on Profit and Brand', June 8, 2004
10. Aaron Clarke, Telephone interview with the author, 4 June, 2004
11. Brian Sutton, Update your skills if you want to prosper, Computing (www.computing.co.uk) June 24, 2004
12. Rob Aalders, Personal email to the author, 29 May, 2004
13. Mega trend means mega backlash for India, Offshore Outsourcing World (http://www.enterblog.com/200406220849.html), June 22, 2004

References

A. Schumpeter Joseph, 'Capitalism, Socialism and Democracy' (New York: Harper, 1975) [orig. pub. 1942], pp. 82–85.
C. Handy, 'The Age of Unreason', Arrow, London, 1989.
C.K. Prahalad and Hamel G., 'Competing for the Future', Harvard Business School Press, Boston, 1994.
J. Gleick, 'Faster', Abacus, New York, 1999.
K. Lewin 'Field Theory in Social Science'. Harper and Row, New York, 1951. My thanks go to Professor George Bell, the MBA Course Director of London South Bank University, for suggesting the general force field structure of this paper.
K. Nordström and J. Ridderstra[o]le, Funky Business, FT Prentice Hall, London, 2000.
K. Ohmae, 'The end of the nation state', The Free Press, New York, 1995.
M. Castells, 'The Rise of the Network Society', Blackwell, London, 1996.
M. Kobayashi-Hillary, 'Outsourcing to India: The Offshoring Advantage', Springer-Verlag, Berlin, 2004.
N.G. Carr, 'Does IT Matter?', Harvard Business School Press, Boston, 2004.

14
Utility Computing: A Better Model for Outsourcing Success?
Jeff Kaplan

1 Introduction

Utility computing is a new approach to architecting and delivering computing power and business applications on an automated, 'on-demand' basis. Utility computing is being enabled by a new generation of technologies that are more flexible and responsive to fluctuating business requirements. Interest in utility computing is being driven by the same budgetary demands for a greater return on investment (ROI) from technology that is driving outsourcing.

The movement towards utility computing is also in response to a growing belief among IT users that the fundamental functionality and value of IT are becoming commoditised, and should be structured like other established utilities to meet the common computing requirements of end-users.

This is a view of IT that has been advocated by Nicholas Carr in his landmark Harvard Business Review article entitled, *'IT Doesn't Matter'*, and book entitled, *'Does IT Matter? Information Technology and the Corrosion of Competitive Advantage.'*

While many associate utility computing with a myriad of emerging technologies ranging from autonomous systems to web services, it is also an outgrowth of application and managed services that emerged during the dot.com era. Utility computing has also become synonymous with broader IT and business process outsourcing arrangements.

This chapter will examine how utility computing differs from the xSPs of the past, why many enterprises are pursuing utility computing via outsourcing arrangements, and how enterprises can leverage application and managed services as 'out-tasking' alternatives to minimise the risks of adopting utility computing while satisfying their corporate objectives.

2 Why many enterprises view utility computing as an outsourcing, not a technology solution

Everyone seems to have their own idea of what utility computing means. No matter how utility computing is defined, the key drivers for this new model are:

- The escalating complexity and the ongoing challenges of making IT work.
- The sluggish economy and escalating pressure to reduce operating costs.
- The growing demand for greater IT reliability and business value.

In addition to legacy systems being too inflexible and costly to maintain, enterprise applications, ranging from customer relationship management (CRM) to supply-chain management (SCM), have taken too long for organisations – large and small – to implement, integrate and maintain.

As the features and functions of today's hardware systems and enterprise applications become less differentiated, and the hassles of implementing and administering these applications continue to aggravate enterprises, there is a growing interest among enterprises to acquire this functionality in a more cost-effective and reliable way. This desire is driving the demand for utility computing and rekindling the fortunes of a nearly extinct species of suppliers, known as 'application service providers' (ASPs) and 'managed service providers' (MSPs).

Some equate utility computing with established utility models that permit a 'plug and play' environment in which users can obtain computing power and business applications on a pay-as-you-go basis wherever and whenever they want. Others see utility computing simply as a more rapid means of assuring the availability of computing power and business applications.

The potential benefits of utility computing can be summarised as:

- Higher system utilisation/optimisation
- Better application management/ maintenance
- More predictable operating costs
- Greater return on IT investment
- Renewed focus on core competencies

There are a number of new technologies that are enabling utility computing to become a reality. These include:

- Grid computing
- Blade technology
- Virtualisation

- Web services and Service-Oriented Architecture (SOA)
- Service provisioning

There are also more established technologies that are essential components of utility computing, including:

- *IP networking* is a critical component in the utility computing model because the rapid and reliable electronic delivery of on-demand computing power and business applications is dependent on high-speed networks.
- *Security* is also pivotal to ensure the privacy of individual users and partitioning of multiple enterprises sharing the same utility computing resource.
- *Service level management* (SLM) software systems is necessary to effectively monitor and measure utility computing performance. SLM software enables enterprises and service providers to establish service level objectives (SLOs) and measure the actual performance of an IT operation in meeting an organisation's quality-of-service (QoS) expectations. Figure 14.1 summarises these technologies.

But utility computing is more than a new set of technologies. It also requires new service-oriented software applications, operational processes and staff skills.

This is a tall order for most enterprises. They lack the independent perspective to objectively evaluate their existing IT systems and staff in order to determine the right utility computing plan to meet their corporate needs. They also often lack the in-house technical skills and experience to select, integrate and manage the relatively embryonic enabling technologies necessary to achieve their utility computing objectives.

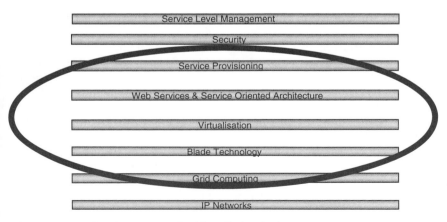

Figure 14.1 Utility Computing: Enabling Technologies
Source: © 2004, Thinkstrategies [wwwthinkstrategies.com]

Rather than make the extraordinary investment in technology and staff necessary to build their own utility computing solutions, most enterprises pursuing this new IT operations model are leveraging outside service providers.

Ultimately, enterprises are hoping utility computing will permit them to refocus their corporate energies on their primary business rather than managing IT. They believe that creating a stable, reliable, and cost-effective computing platform brings them one step closer to eliminating this function as a critical internal business element.

Therefore, many enterprises equate the migration to utility computing with outsourcing all or out-tasking part of their IT operations.

3   The history of shared services models

Whether these enterprises are seeking to transfer all of their IT operations to a single outsourcer, or looking for a set of specialised 'out-tasking' solutions to meet specific business requirements, utility computing has become the latest example of the 'shared services' model which has been a part of the IT industry since the 1960s.

At that time, companies such as EDS and a variety of aerospace corporations leased or resold a portion of their massive computing operations to corporate customers in 'facilities management' arrangements.

The dot.com era produced the web-hosting business and created a new breed of application, security, storage and management service providers, or xSPs. These services provided enterprises with a new assortment of selective outsourcing or out-tasking, pay-as-you-go alternatives to the wholesale outsourcing arrangements.

Rather than hand over their entire IT operations to an outsourcer, enterprises could now acquire on a 'subscription' basis specific IT management functions or business applications that augmented their ongoing operations.

Driven by the inflated expectations of the period, many web hosting companies, application service providers (ASP) and managed service providers (MSP) solutions were encouraged by Venture Capitalists (VCs) and investors to aggressively build massive hosting facilities and management centres before real demand for their services materialised.

As a result, most of the first generation of hosting companies and ASP/MSPs died under the financial weight of their over-built and under-subscribed capital investments as the hype of the Internet economy subsided. Their demise threatened to discredit the fundamental value proposition of web hosting and xSPs.

However, in today's conservative economic climate a growing number of enterprises are returning to web hosting and xSP services, as a method of offloading or out-tasking part of their current IT management

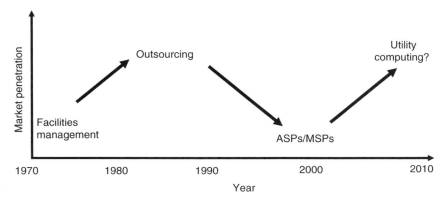

Figure 14.2 The Origin of Utility Computing Services
Source: © 2004, Thinkstrategies [wwwthinkstrategies.com]

operations, and a first step towards adopting utility computing strategies and plans.

This evolution is illustrated in Figure 14.2.

4 Enterprises equate today's services with tomorrow's utility computing solutions

While there are many skeptics who doubt vendors can fulfill their utility computing promises, a growing number of enterprises believe they are already generating real benefits from this new IT architecture by leveraging a variety of existing services.

For instance, many enterprises have abandoned traditional customer relationship management (CRM) and salesforce automation applications from Siebel, SAP, PeopleSoft and Oracle in favour of Salesforce.com's hosted application services, and view this type of 'on-demand' software service as a form of utility computing.

USA Today considers its web hosting arrangement originally signed with LoudCloud before it was acquired by EDS a utility computing solution because it enables the company to market new advertising alternatives on an on-demand basis.

These enterprises are not concerned about the exact name or definition for utility computing, and aren't interested in debating whether web hosting, software or managed services, or another specific technical capability or service is a true example of utility computing. Instead, they view these services and the technologies that enable them as clear examples of the potential cost-savings and strategic advantages of utility computing.

This open-minded view has created multiple paths to developing a utility computing environment as shown in Figure 14.3.

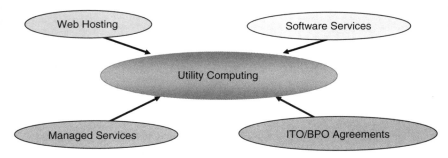

Figure 14.3 Utility Computing Multiple Points of Entry
Source: © 2004, Thinkstrategies [wwwthinkstrategies.com]

It has also heightened the competitive climate by permitting a wide array of players to fight for a share of the utility computing market.

4.1 Competitive landscape

Competition is creating a 'buyer's market' for enterprises seeking utility computing solutions. A widening array of hardware and software vendors, systems integrators and outsourcers, telecom carriers, specialised service providers and even regional VARs are offering a variety of outsourced utility computing alternatives.

4.2 System vendors

Utility computing has escalated the age-old hardware, software and services battle between IBM and Hewlett-Packard (HP). These major systems vendors are re-architecting their products to make them more effective in web environments and more responsive to corporate requirements. They are also pushing their consulting and outsourcing capabilities as the best means for enterprises to achieve their utility computing objectives.

However, the systems vendors are doing more than just pushing their mega-outsourcing capabilities as a path to migrating utility computing. They are also offering application and management services to enterprises that want to take an incremental approach to utility computing. IBM and HP are working with the established software companies to provide hosted application services. They are also offering packaged security, storage and content management services on a subscription basis.

4.2.1 IBM

IBM claims to be making a $10 billion investment in new utility computing technology and solutions. This investment has manifested itself in a new generation of Web Services oriented, middleware solutions that make it easier for organisations to develop and deploy utility computing architectures. IBM has also made a series of acquisitions to accelerate its Web Services, middleware development. The company has made over 15 acquisitions in the past three years, including:

- Rational Software Corporation, which provides open, industry standard tools, best practices and services for developing business applications and building software products and systems, including embedded software for devices such as cell phones and medical systems.
- Trigo Technologies, Inc., a leading provider of product information management middleware.
- Think Dynamics, a privately held provider of resource automation software that permits on-demand orchestrated provisioning.

IBM has also embraced open systems and the Linux operating system as its primary platform for delivering utility computing solutions.

IBM has gained the greatest mindshare and marketshare in the utility computing market on the strength of its 'On-Demand' branding campaigns.

The company has also developed potent business consulting and outsourcing capabilities, spearheaded by its PriceWaterhouseCoopers Consulting unit acquisition and its overall Global Services outsourcing experience. The Global Services and Business Solutions group are now primarily responsible for selling and delivering IBM's On-Demand solutions.

IBM's first major utility computing deal was signed in 2002 with American Express to help the credit card and financial services company fundamentally change its computing environment and improve its IT Return on Investment (ROI).

4.2.2 Hewlett-Packard

Hewlett-Packard is promoting an 'adaptive' computing model as its competitive alternative to IBM. This model is based on HP's Darwin Architecture that creates more flexible and automated organisational processes, business applications and IT infrastructure.

While the technical design of HP's model may differ from IBM's approach, the fundamental component parts of blade technology, grid computing architecture, business consulting and outsourcing services are relatively similar. Its acquisition of Compaq Computer was also aimed at adding both technology and service capabilities to HP's portfolio to keep pace with IBM.

In 2003, Hewlett-Packard made its presence known in the utility computing market with similar wins at Proctor & Gamble, and GATX where HP is supplying SAP solutions as part of their utility computing solution.

4.3 Other system vendors

EMC, Sun Microsystems and Unisys have also established utility computing strategies. Neither EMC nor Sun has adopted an outsourcing services initiative to support their utility computing strategies. Instead, they are emphasising their new utility computing products and traditional service capabilities.

Unisys is using utility computing as the latest catalyst of its shift from a product-centric orientation toward a services-lead business model. Unisys' transformation was initiated in the early 1990s when it found it increasingly difficult to compete on the strength of its products. As a consequence, Unisys has placed a tremendous emphasis on its outsourcing and systems integration skills for the past decade. It is using its track record of success in the services sector rather than its product leadership as a key selling point in the utility computing market.

4.4   Software vendors

Many of the independent software vendors (ISVs) are developing their own hosted software services to tighten their hold on existing customers and win additional ones.

Oracle claims more than half of its new customer deployments include a hosting arrangement. Siebel has paired with IBM to market an on-demand CRM solution. PeopleSoft and SAP are also teaming up with a variety of vendors, outsourcers and independent ASPs to offer hosted application services.

But, the 'net-native' ASPs, such as Salesforce.com and NetLedger, are still selling lower cost, easier to implement and administer CRM and financial applications specifically built to be delivered via the web.

For the ISVs to be successful long-term, they must re-architect their software so it can be easily provisioned in an on-demand environment, and restructure their licensing agreements so they can accommodate pay-as-you-go pricing schemes.

Today's quickly evolving ASP offerings are giving the ISVs practical experience to address both these utility computing challenges.

5   Transfer or transform

Unlike simple xSP services and traditional outsourcing arrangements which simply transfer existing IT responsibilities from an enterprise to a service provider, utility computing aims to transform the way IT functions are designed and delivered.

Utility computing solutions generally replace inflexible legacy systems with more responsive computing capabilities on an 'on-demand' basis. They also permit users to pay as they go for the volume of service they need rather than pay a fixed amount for a static computing capability.

Utility computing differs from individual application or managed services by combining both the hardware and software an enterprise needs into a multi-dimensional set of system and application solutions. So, rather than acquiring applications, storage, security and hosting services from a variety of service providers, utility computing services are provided by a single, strategic source.

For instance, if an enterprise is interested in a CRM solution it might go to Salesforce.com. Or, if it needs high-speed networking capabilities it could go to a variety of telecommunications carriers. But, if an enterprise wants all of its IT functions and key applications to be provided in an integrated, on-demand fashion, then it would choose a single source for an integrated, utility computing solution from companies such as IBM, Hewlett-Packard, EDS and an assortment of other providers targeting the small and mid-size business (SMB) sector.

Enterprises are attracted to the utility computing outsourcing model because it enables them to gain economic benefits by reducing the number of suppliers they rely on, which can produce lower service fees and management costs.

An increasing number of enterprises are not only outsourcing their IT operations but also contracting to have third-parties perform various business functions, such as billing and call centre services. This has led to the rapid growth in business process outsourcing (BPO) that has become closely associated with IT outsourcing (ITO) and utility computing solutions. All three are being adopted to transform the way enterprises leverage technology and perform business tasks.

Figure 14.4 shows where utility computing fits in the hierarchy of IT service alternatives.

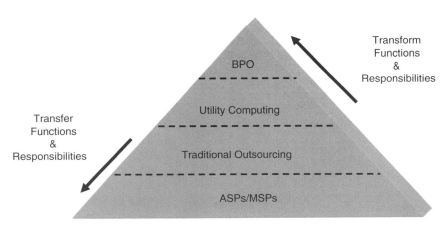

Figure 14.4   Where Utility Computing Fits
Source: © 2004, Thinkstrategies [wwwthinkstrategies.com]

6 Market adoption patterns for utility computing

Given the various points of entry for utility computing solutions, enterprise interest and adoption of utility computing services is growing more dramatically than many industry observers realise at both the high-end of the market among major corporations and the low-end by small- and mid-size businesses (SMBs).

The financial services industry has been an early adopter of utility computing technologies, often leveraging outsourcers and various managed services. In 2001, J.P. Morgan Chase Investment Bank initiated a project to combine seven separate financial risk management systems on a single grid computing platform to lower IT operating costs while increasing IT flexibility and service to the company's internal customers.

One of the first companies outside the financial services industry to pursue the utility computing approach and report measurable results was Fluor Corporation in 2003. The $10 billion global construction and engineering firm signed a seven-year, $351 million outsourcing agreement with IBM that included 32 separate projects aimed at converting its legacy systems to a utility computing model. As part of this agreement, 350 Fluor employees worldwide moved to IBM.

The goal of the Fluor project was to convert 80–90 per cent to its IT operations to a utility computing model. All of Fluor's desktop, server and data centre systems are being consolidated and standardised. About 60 per

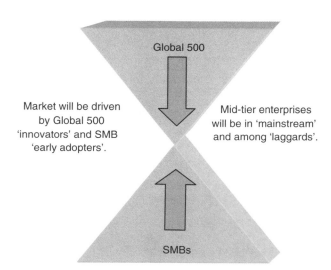

Figure 14.5 Bifurcated Utility Computing Market Adoption
Source: © 2004, Thinkstrategies [wwwthinkstrategies.com]

cent of its IT department now operates on the utility computing model, and Fluor's fixed IT costs have dropped to 25 per cent from 95 per cent three years ago, producing $60 million in cost savings per year.

Many large and small enterprises are migrating to utility computing models via ASP, MSP and web hosting services. Figure 14.5 shows the multi-directional or bifurcated adoption pattern among major corporations and SMBs that are simultaneously implementing utility computing solutions.

Another key element in the broad-based adoption of utility computing solutions will be further market segmentation of these IT offerings. This segmentation process is likely to occur in four dimensions:

1. Lifecycle services
   a. These services help enterprises plan, design, implement, maintain and manage their utility computing solutions.
2. Technology solutions
   a. These solutions focus on specific technology functionalities ranging from network infrastructure to business applications.
3. Vertical market applications
   a. These applications address specific industry requirements and might be paired with a business process outsourcing arrangement.
4. Size of business solutions
   a. These horizontal solutions satisfy the business requirements of enterprises based on their size.

This market segmentation pattern is illustrated in Figure 14.6

These highly segmented utility computing service alternatives enables enterprises to incrementally and selectively out-task their IT requirements that

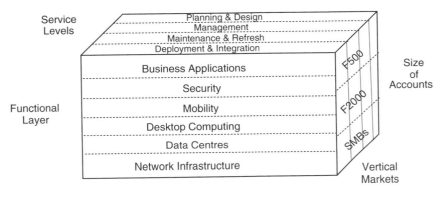

Figure 14.6 Utility Computing: Market Segmentation
Source: © 2004, Thinkstrategies [wwwthinkstrategies.com]

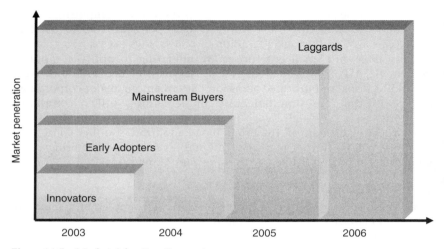

Figure 14.7   Market Adoption Forecast
Source: © 2004, Thinkstrategies [wwwthinkstrategies.com]

mitigate the risks of a major outsourcing agreement aimed at converting to a utility computing model too quickly.

Given the various utility computing service alternatives, only the innovation laggards will be climbing onboard the utility computing services bandwagon by 2006, as illustrated in Figure 14.7.

7   Utility computing: potential problems

While market acceptance of utility computing is growing, there are still many pitfalls that stand in the way of successfully adopting this new IT model. These issues include:

- Technology standards
  - Industry standards are essential to ensure the integration and inter-operability of a vast array of proprietary hardware and software products across a heterogeneous, multivendor environment.
  - There are no comprehensive standards for utility computing. Instead, there are numerous industry standards organisations and 'working groups' that are debating various technical issues. These include the DCML, or Data Centre Mark-up Language Organisation that is proposing standards that allow developers to build software tools that manage technical resources such as servers, storage devices and business applications.
  - Until these industry groups establish meaningful standards, the utility computing market will be driven by the de facto standards promoted by the leading vendors.

- Vendor dependencies
  - Because of the lack of industry standards, the leading vendors cannot ensure the inter-operability of their products across multi-vendor operating environments.
  - In order to achieve the full potential of today's utility computing solutions, enterprises must commit themselves to a primary supplier that can deliver a cohesive solution. This requires enterprises to establish strategic sourcing relationships that could intensify their dependency on a primary supplier.
  - Outsourcers offering utility computing solutions are seeking to establish favourable pricing schedules and specific SLAs to encourage enterprises to establish strategic sourcing relationships.
- System failures
  - Today's utility computing technologies are still relatively new and generally untested across a variety of operating environments. This means that enterprises must be careful not to rely too heavily on this technology without thoroughly testing its compatibility in their operations.
  - This has led many enterprises to develop detailed service level agreements (SLAs) and adopt a phased deployment strategy that permits them to test their utility computing implementation on a step-by-step basis.
- Application inadequacies
  - Application partitioning, integration and metering are a significant challenge for traditional ISVs because many major legacy applications are not designed to permit real-time, on-demand computing capabilities. Therefore, the 'net-native' ASPs and established hosting companies will continue to have an advantage.
  - The established ISVs are attempting to re-architect their legacy software programmes to fit within utility computing environments.
- Packaging & pricing issues
  - All the utility computing solution suppliers are struggling to package and price their products and services in an attractive and profitable fashion. Part of the challenge is to calculate their internal solution delivery costs. The other challenge is to determine the true business value of their solutions. Suppliers are also attempting to differentiate their offerings based on packaging and pricing methods.
  - Effectively measuring and charging for utility computing consumption will be a challenge until the applications and systems include proper provisioning capabilities, and the internal or outsourcer staff is trained to administer the billing process.
- Organisational barriers
  - The fragmented nature of many enterprise IT departments makes it a challenge to develop and deploy a comprehensive utility computing

solution that could dramatically change their IT operations. Even if an enterprise chooses to resolve these issues via an outsourcing arrangement, it could still face resistance from the business units accustomed to legacy systems and custom applications.

- This fragmented organisational environment also poses a challenge for deploying a unified utility computing solution across an enterprise. This challenge has lead many organisations to outsource their utility computing initiatives, or to leverage a vendor's change management consulting capabilities.
- Demonstrating service quality and business benefits
  - The xSPs, systems vendors, ISVs and outsourcers must prove that their service solutions are reliable and produce measurable business benefits to convince enterprises that utility computing can be effective.
  - Quantifying the return on investment requires a clear understanding of an enterprise's current costs, and the time and ability to accumulate financial data regarding operational changes as a result of utility computing. Many enterprises do not have data regarding their current IT operations, making it difficult to measure the change in performance levels due to a migration to utility computing.

8　Making the in-sourcing vs. outsourcing decision

Given the complexities of implementing utility computing, it is very likely an enterprise will have to outsource all or part of the migration process. The key to success will be determining where, when and how to outsource, and how to measure the success of the outsourcing arrangement.

As we have seen, outsourcing doesn't have to entail handing the entire utility computing initiative over to an outside company. Instead, enterprises can out-task a variety of planning, design, implementation and ongoing management responsibilities.

In order to determine which phase of the utility computing migration process can or should be outsourced, enterprises should ask the following questions:

- Can we objectively assess our utility computing requirements?
- Which applications or infrastructure components will cause the greatest challenges when it comes to implementation, maintenance and management issues?
- Are there any business reasons that would preclude using an outside service provider to deliver and manage a utility computing solution?
- What metrics can we use to evaluate the effectiveness of our outsourcing arrangement?

9 Steps to success for leveraging XSP services to achieve utility computing objectives

Adopting a utility computing outsourcing strategy can create a significant challenge for many enterprises. With as many as half of the major outsourcing engagements of the past failing to meet their original business objectives, managing a successful outsourcing relationship is tough enough. Adding the goal of transforming the IT environment by moving to a utility computing model compounds the outsourcing challenge.

In order to employ an outsourcing strategy to achieve utility computing objectives, it is essential that enterprises avoid the outsourcing mistakes of the past. Specifically, enterprises shouldn't view outsourcing as a simple way to offload their IT problems to another company to deal with. Instead, it must be seen as a collaborative effort to transform a legacy environment into a new computing architecture to meet their long-term business objectives.

Whether an enterprise chooses a wholesale outsourcing agreement or packaged out-tasking service approach to migrate to a utility computing model, they should follow the same steps to achieve their corporate objectives. The goals and objectives of a utility computing outsourcing agreement must be clear. But, even more important is the ongoing monitoring, measurement and reporting process that permits the enterprise to assess and modify the migration and ongoing management policies and procedures.

Here are specific steps to set and achieve these objectives.

9.1 Form a coordinating committee

A multidisciplinary coordinating committee consisting of every major business function and IT department unit should be established to lead the utility computing planning, design, implementation and ongoing management process. It should also play a pivotal role in working with outside solution providers to resolve issues, modify operating procedures and reset objectives where necessary during the migration and ongoing management processes.

9.2 Assess your technical capabilities

It is essential for enterprises to conduct a thorough assessment of existing systems, applications, performance and utilisation levels, as well as technical skills and business requirements. This assessment enables enterprises to collect baseline data on the current utilisation levels of their existing infrastructure, and determine where to consolidate and standardise hardware and software platforms. It also permits enterprises to determine where to focus their in-house staff and where to leverage outside services.

9.3   Set realistic business goals and objectives

Given the embryonic nature of today's utility computing technologies and the limited utility computing benchmark metrics, it is important to establish modest operating and financial goals, and a reasonable timetable for achieving cost-savings and incremental new revenues. Enterprises should also proceed with caution and begin with proof-of-concept pilots that don't seriously disrupt their ongoing operations during the migration process.

9.4   Establish ongoing monitoring and reporting procedures

Enterprises should implement application and system performance measurement tools and reporting procedures to monitor the impact of initial utility computing deployments and the ongoing operation closely. This will ensure the utility computing initiative is meeting business and technical expectations, and providing the objective data necessary to demonstrate business value. It also permits enterprises to identify any problems and make appropriate modifications. It is also important for the performance results to be transmitted in business terms to the enterprises' executives, end-users, partners and customers.

10   Summary and conclusions

The migration to utility computing is happening. Rather than adopting embryonic utility computing technologies themselves, many enterprises are leveraging a growing assortment of outsourcing and out-tasking alternatives to fulfill their utility computing objectives.

Comprehensive outsourcing arrangements can make sense for some companies, like Fluor Corporation, seeking to thoroughly transform their IT operations and willing to rely on a primary vendor such as IBM to migrate to a utility computing architecture completely.

Many other enterprises will prefer an incremental approach to adopting utility computing that employs a variety of ASPs and MSPs to assume responsibility for specific IT and business functions.

In either case, enterprises should follow a stringent set of IT and business best practices to be successful. They must set realistic goals, know their internal capabilities and corporate priorities, evaluate the delivery capabilities and cultural fit of their solution provider, and establish measurable service level objectives and reporting mechanisms to monitor success.

Following these steps and leveraging outside resources can make utility computing a reality for many enterprises.

References

Carr, N. 'Does IT Matter: Information Technology and the Corrosion of Competitive Advantage', Harvard Business School Press; April 2004.
Carr, N. 'IT Doesn't Matter', Harvard Business Review; May 2003.

Index

.